Juvenile Delinquency
in a Free Society

Juvenile Delinquency in a Free Society

Selections from the President's Commission
on Law Enforcement and Administration
of Justice

Robert W. Winslow

San Diego State College

Dickenson Publishing Company, Inc., Belmont, California

Library of Congress Catalog Card No.: 68–21052
Printed in the United States of America

Preface

The readings in this book are drawn from the seventeen-volume report of the President's Commission on Law Enforcement and Administration of Justice, a nineteen-man commission appointed by President Lyndon B. Johnson. This report, the most comprehensive study of crime and juvenile delinquency undertaken in the nation's history, is based upon eighteen months' work with one hundred and seventy-five consultants and hundreds of advisers representing a broad range of opinions and professions; countless visits to courts, prisons, and police stations; three national conferences; five national surveys; hundreds of meetings; and interviews with tens of thousands of people.

In the choice of materials for this volume, selections have been drawn from the various task force reports of the Commission; the general report, *The Challenge of Crime in a Free Society;* and the field surveys.

Juvenile Delinquency in a Free Society is more practical than the Commission series itself for actual classroom use, since it condenses essential readings from many volumes into a single volume and reorganizes the Commission materials into traditional textbook format.

Chapters 3–5, 7, and part of Chapter 12 are compiled and condensed from *Task Force Report: Juvenile Delinquency and Youth Crime.* Chapter 1 is drawn from the Commission's general report *The Challenge of Crime in a Free Society.* Chapter 2 is taken from *Task Force Report: Crime and Its Impact—An Assessment.* Chapter 6 is based on the two-volume series *Field Surveys IV: The Police and the Community.* Chapters 8–11 are drawn from the report "Corrections in the United States" by the National Council on Crime and Delinquency, in Appendix A of the Commission's *Task Force Report: Corrections,* and part of Chapter 12 is taken from that same volume.

The readings in this volume coincide with the order of chapters in most texts on juvenile delinquency. Chapter 1 deals with the concept of delinquency. Chapter 2 describes the ecological or spatial patterning of delinquency. Chapters 3–5 are concerned with the various etiological factors in delinquency—socioeconomic factors, family, and schools. Chapters 6–11 deal specifically with the juvenile justice system—including the police, the juvenile court, juvenile detention, probation, institutions, treatment programs, and aftercare. Chapter 12 concludes with a national strategy for prevention and control of juvenile delinquency.

The result, we believe, is a volume of selections unequaled in scope, comprehensiveness, and timeliness of results by any text or reader on juvenile delinquency today.

Robert W. Winslow

Contents

✓

*Juvenile Delinquency
in a Free Society*

1 *Introduction*

America's best hope for reducing crime is to reduce juvenile delinquency and youth crime. In 1965 a majority of all arrests for major crimes against property were of people under 21, as were a substantial minority of arrests for major crimes against the person. The recidivism rates for young offenders are higher than those for any other age group. A substantial change in any of these figures would make a substantial change in the total crime figures for the Nation.

One of the difficulties of discussing the misconduct, criminal or not, of young people is that "juvenile" and "youth" are not precise definitions of categories of people. People are legally juveniles in most States until they pass their 18th birthdays, but in some States they stop being juveniles after they turn 16 or remain juveniles until they turn 21. The problems and behavior patterns of juveniles and youths often are similar.

· · · · ·

To prevent and control delinquency, we must first know something about the nature of delinquency and the dimensions of the problem. We need to know how serious delinquency is. How much of it is there? How many of our youth are involved? What sorts of illegal acts do they commit? What have the trends in delinquency been in the past, and what can we expect in the future? We also need knowledge about the people who became delinquent—information such as where most delinquents live and under what economic conditions.

But we are severely limited in what we can learn today. The only juvenile statistics regularly gathered over the years on a national scale are the FBI's Uniform Crime Reports, based on arrest statistics, and the juvenile court statistics of the Children's Bureau of the U.S. Department of Health, Education, and Welfare, based on referrals of juveniles from a variety of agencies to a sample of juvenile courts. These reports can tell us nothing about the vast number of unsolved offenses, or about the many cases in which delinquents are dealt with informally instead of being arrested or referred to court. Supplementing this official picture of delinquency are self-report studies, which rely on asking selected individuals about their delinquent acts. While efforts are made to insure the validity of the results by such means as guaranteeing anonymity, and verifying results with official records and unofficial checks, such studies have been conducted only on a local and sporadic basis, and they vary greatly in quality.

Clearly, there is urgent need for more and better information. Nonetheless, enough is available to give some of the rough outlines of juvenile delinquency in the United States.

Seriousness of the Delinquency Problem

Volume

Enormous numbers of young people appear to be involved in delinquent acts. Indeed, self-report studies reveal that perhaps 90 percent of all young people have committed at least one act for which they could have been brought to juvenile court. Many of these offenses are relatively trivial—fighting, truancy, running away from home. Statutes often define juvenile delinquency so broadly as to make virtually all youngsters delinquent.

Even though most of these offenders are never arrested or referred to juvenile court, alarming numbers of young people are. Rough estimates by the Children's Bureau, supported by independent studies, indicate that one in every nine youths—one in every six male youths—will be referred to juvenile court in connection with a delinquent act (excluding traffic offenses) before his 18th birthday.

Youth is apparently responsible for a substantial and disproportionate part of the national crime problem. Arrest statistics can give us only a rough picture—probably somewhat exaggerated since it is likely that juveniles are more easily apprehended than adults. In addition, it may be that juveniles act in groups more often than adults when committing crimes, thus producing numbers of juvenile arrests out of proportion with numbers of crimes committed. But even with these qualifications, the figures are striking. FBI figures reveal that of all persons arrested in 1965 (not counting traffic offenders) about 30 percent were under 21 years of age, and about 20 percent were under 18 years of age. Arrest rates are highest for persons aged 15 through 17, next highest for those aged 18 through 20, dropping off quite directly with increases in age, as table 1 . . . indicates.

The picture looks even worse if attention is directed to certain relatively serious property crimes—burglary, larceny, and motor vehicle theft. The 11- to 17-year-old age group, representing 13.2 percent of the population, was responsible for half of the arrests for these offenses in 1965 (table 2). Table 1 shows that the arrest rates for these offenses are much higher for the 15- to 17-year-olds than for any other age group in the population. But not all of the acts included within these categories are equally serious. Larceny includes thefts of less than $50, and most motor vehicle thefts are for the purpose of securing temporary transportation and do not involve permanent loss of the vehicle. Moreover, although juveniles account for more than their share of arrests for many serious crimes, these arrests are a small part of all juvenile arrests. Juveniles are most frequently arrested or

Table 1—Arrest Rates for Different Age Groups—1965

[Rates per 100,000 population]

Age groups	Arrest rates for all offenses (excluding traffic)	Arrest rates for willful homicide, forcible rape, robbery, aggravated assault	Arrest rates for larceny, burglary, motor vehicle theft
11 to 14	3,064.4	71.0	1,292.3
15 to 17	8,050.0	222.8	2,467.0
18 to 20	7,539.6	299.8	1,452.0
21 to 24	6,547.2	296.6	833.7
25 to 29	5,366.9	233.6	506.7
30 to 34	5,085.8	177.5	354.4
35 to 39	4,987.4	132.5	260.4
40 to 44	4,675.3	94.0	185.4
45 to 49	4,102.0	65.3	131.9
50 and over	1,987.4	24.2	55.2
Overall rate	3,349.9	99.9	461.5

SOURCE: FBI, Uniform Crime Reports Section, unpublished data. Estimates for total U.S. population.

referred to court for petty larceny, fighting, disorderly conduct, liquor-related offenses, and conduct not in violation of the criminal law such as curfew violation, truancy, incorrigibility, or running away from home.

It is an older age group—beyond the jurisdiction of almost all juvenile courts—that has the highest arrest rate for crimes of violence. The 18- to

Table 2—Percent of Arrests Accounted for by Different Age Groups—1965

[Percent of total]

	Persons 11–17	Persons 18–24	Persons 25 and over
Population	13.2	10.2	53.5
Willful homicide	8.4	26.4	65.1
Forcible rape	19.8	44.6	35.6
Robbery	28.0	39.5	31.4
Aggravated assault	14.2	26.5	58.7
Burglary	47.7	29.0	19.7
Larceny (includes larceny under $50)	49.2	21.9	24.3
Motor vehicle theft	61.4	26.4	11.9
Willful homicide, rape, robbery, aggravated assault	18.3	31.7	49.3
Larceny, burglary, motor vehicle theft	50.5	24.7	21.2

SOURCE: FBI, Uniform Crime Reports Section, unpublished data. Estimates for total U.S. population.

24-year-old group, which represents only 10.2 percent of the population, accounts for 26.4 percent of the arrests for willful homicide, 44.6 percent of the arrests for rape, 39.5 percent of the arrests for robbery, and 26.5 percent of the arrests for aggravated assault (table 2).

Trends

In recent years the number of delinquency arrests has increased sharply in the United States, as it has in several Western European countries studied by the Commission. Between 1960 and 1965, arrests of persons under 18 years of age jumped 52 percent for willful homicide, rape, robbery, aggravated assault, larceny, burglary and motor vehicle theft. During the same period, arrests of persons 18 and over for these offenses rose only 20 percent. This is explained in large part by the disproportionate increase in the population under 18 and, in particular, the crime-prone part of that population—the 11- to 17-year-old age group.

Official figures may give a somewhat misleading picture of crime trends. Over the years there has been a tendency toward more formal records and actions, particularly in the treatment of juveniles. In addition, police efficiency may well have increased. But, considering other factors together with the official statistics, the Commission is of the opinion that juvenile delinquency has increased significantly in recent years.

The juvenile population has been rising, and at a faster rate than the adult population. And an increasing proportion of our society is living in the cities where delinquency rates have always been highest. These trends and the increase in the total volume of crime that they appear to foretell are testimony enough that programs for the prevention and control of delinquency deserve our full attention.

Who the Delinquents Are

Almost all youths commit acts for which they could be arrested and taken to court. But it is a much smaller group that ends up being defined officially as delinquent.

Official delinquents are predominantly male. In 1965 boys under 18 were arrested five times as often as girls. Four times as many boys as girls were referred to juvenile court.

Boys and girls commit quite different kinds of offenses. Children's Bureau statistics based on large-city court reports reveal that more than half of the girls referred to juvenile court in 1965 were referred for conduct that would not be criminal if committed by adults; only one-fifth of the boys were referred for such conduct. Boys were referred to court primarily for larceny, burglary, and motor vehicle theft, in order of frequency; girls for running away, ungovernable behavior, larceny, and sex offenses.

Delinquents are concentrated disproportionately in the cities, and particularly in the larger cities. Arrest rates are next highest in the suburbs, and lowest in rural areas.

Delinquency rates are high among children from broken homes. They are similarly high among children who have numerous siblings.

Delinquents tend to do badly in school. Their grades are below average. Large numbers have dropped one or more classes behind their classmates or dropped out of school entirely.

Delinquents tend to come from backgrounds of social and economic deprivation. Their families tend to have lower than average incomes and social status. But perhaps more important than the individual family's situation is the area in which a youth lives. One study has shown that a lower class youth has little chance of being classified as delinquent if he lives in an upper class neighborhood. Numerous studies have revealed the relationship between certain deprived areas—particularly the slums of large cities—and delinquency.

> *It is inescapable that juvenile delinquency is directly related to conditions bred by poverty. If the Fulton County census tracts were divided into five groups on the basis of the economic and educational status of their residents, we would find that 57% of Fulton County's juvenile delinquents during 1964 were residents of the lowest group which consists of the principal poverty areas of the City of Atlanta. Only 24% of the residents of the county lived within these tracts.* Report of the Atlanta Commission on Crime and Juvenile Delinquency, *Opportunity for Urban Excellence* (1966), p. 24.

Thus Negroes, who live in disproportionate numbers in slum neighborhoods, account for a disproportionate number of arrests. Numerous studies indicate that what matters is where in the city one is growing up, not religion or nationality or race. The studies by Shaw and McKay . . . followed a number of different national groups—Germans, Irish, Poles, Italians—as they moved from the grim center of the city out to better neighborhoods. They found that for all groups the delinquency rates were highest in the center and lowest on the outskirts of the city.

There is no reason to expect a different story for Negroes. Indeed, McKay found Negro delinquency rates decreasing from the center of the city outward, just as they did for earlier migrant groups. And when delinquency rates of whites and Negroes are compared in areas of similar economic status, the differences between them are markedly reduced. But for Negroes, movement out of the inner city and absorption into America's middle class have been much slower and more difficult than for any other ethnic or racial group. Their attempts to move spatially, socially, economically have met much stiffer resistance. Rigid barriers of residential segregation have prevented them from moving to better neighborhoods as their desire and capacity to do so have developed, leading to great population density and to stifling overcrowding of housing, schools, recreation areas. Restricted access to jobs and limited upward mobility in those jobs that are available have slowed economic advance.

It is likely that the official picture exaggerates the role played by social and economic conditions, since slum offenders are more likely than suburban offenders to be arrested and referred to juvenile court. In fact, recent self-report studies reveal suburban and middle-class delinquency to be a more significant problem than was once assumed. But there is still no reason to doubt that delinquency, and especially the most serious delinquency, is committed disproportionately by slum and lower-class youth.

A balanced judgment would seem to be that, while there is indeed unreported delinquency and slower resort to official police and court sanctions in middle-class areas than in the central sectors of our cities, there is also an absolute difference in the amount and types of crimes committed in each area. In short, the vast differences represented in official statistics cannot be explained by differential police or court action toward children of varying backgrounds. There are, in fact, real differences leading to more frequent assaults, thefts, and breaking and entering offenses in lower socioeconomic areas of our urban centers. Wheeler and Cottrell, *Juvenile Delinquency—Its Prevention and Control* (Russell Sage Foundation 1966), pp. 12–13.

[*President's Commission on Law Enforcement and Administration of Justice,* The Challenge of Crime in a Free Society (*Washington: U.S. Government Printing Office, 1967*), *pp. 55–57.*]

Self-Reported Delinquency

.   .   .   .   .

There is a common belief that the general population consists of a large group of law-abiding people and a small body of criminals. However, studies have shown that most people, when they are asked, remember having committed offenses for which they might have been sentenced if they had been apprehended.[1] These studies of "self-reported" crime have generally been of juveniles or young adults, mostly college and high school students. They uniformly show that delinquent or criminal acts are commit-

---

[1] The following studies are representative of the different populations surveyed in these "self-report" studies and of the different types of methods used to get the information: Austin L. Porterfield and Stanley C. Clifton, *Youth in Trouble* (Fort Worth: Leo Potishman Foundation, 1946); Fred J. Murphy, Mary M. Shirley, and Helen L. Witmer, "The Incidence of Hidden Delinquency," *American Journal of Orthopsychiatry,* 16:686–696, October 1916; James F. Short, Jr., "A Report on Incidence of Criminal Behavior, Arrests and Convictions in Selected Groups," *Research Studies of State College of Washington,* 22:110–118, June 1954; F. Ivan Nye, James F. Short, Jr., and Virgil J. Olson, "Socioeconomic Status and Delinquent Behavior," *American Journal of Sociology,* 63:381–389, January 1958; Robert Dentler and Lawrence J. Monroe, "Early Adolescent Theft," *American Sociological Review,* 26:733–743, October 1961; John P. Clark and Eugene P. Wenninger, "Socioeconomic Class and Area as Correlates of Illegal Behavior Among Juveniles," *American Sociological Review,* 27:826–834, December 1962; Maynard L. Erickson and LaMar T. Empey, "Class Position, Peers, and Delinquency," *Sociology and Social Research,* 268–282, April 1965; Martin Gold, "Undetected Delinquent Behavior," *The Journal of Research on Crime and Delinquency,* 3:27–46, January 1966. Similar results have also been discovered in extensive studies with the "self-report" technique in Norway and Sweden. See Nils Christie, Johs. Andenaes, and Sigurd Skirbekk, "A Study of Self-Reported Crime," and also Kerstin Elmhorn, "Study in Self-Reported Delinquency Among School Children in Stockholm," in Karl O. Christiansen, ed., *Scandinavian Studies in Criminology* (London: Tavistock Publications, 1965), vol. 1, 86–146.

ted by people at all levels of society.[2] Most people admit to relatively petty delinquent acts, but many report larcenies, auto thefts, burglaries, and assaults of a more serious nature.

One of the few studies of this type dealing with criminal behavior by adults was of a sample of almost 1,700 persons, most of them from the State of New York.[3] In this study, 1,020 males and 678 females were asked which of 49 offenses they had committed. The list included felonies and misdemeanors, other than traffic offenses, for which they might have been sentenced under the adult criminal code.

Ninety-nine percent of the respondents admitted they had committed one or more offenses for which they might have received jail or prison sentences. Thirteen percent of the males admitted to grand larceny, 26 percent to auto theft, and 17 percent to burglary. Sixty-four percent of the males and 29 percent of the females committed at least one felony for which they had not been apprehended. Although some of these offenses may have been reported to the police by the victims and would thus appear in official statistics as "crimes known to the police," these offenders would not show up in official arrest statistics.

Such persons are part of the "hidden" offender group. They evidently at one time or another found themselves in situations that led them to violate the criminal law. However, most people do not persist in committing offenses. For many the risk of arrest and prosecution is deterrence enough, while others develop a stake in a law-abiding way of life in which their youthful "indiscretions" no longer have a place.

What is known today about offenders is confined almost wholly to those who have been arrested, tried, and sentenced. The criminal justice process may be viewed as a large-scale screening system. At each stage it tries to sort out the better risks to return to the general population. The further along in the process that a sample of offenders is selected, the more likely they are to show major social and personal problems.[4]

[2] In reviewing the results of his own and earlier studies, Martin Gold ("Undetected Delinquent Behavior," *The Journal of Research on Crime and Delinquency*, 3:27–46, January 1966) notes that more frequent and serious delinquencies are reported by lower class youngsters; but this result, which accords with official police records, is found primarily in those studies which have used interviews rather than anonymous questionnaires to secure the self-reports. The questionnaire studies have shown only slight or insignificant relationships between social class and educational level and crime. Gold tried a new technique for validating the interview method. He checked the responses of his subjects against the independently obtained reports of the subject's friends about his delinquencies. He then classified his subjects as follows: truthtellers (72 percent); questionables (11 percent); and concealers (17 percent). The interview method seems to offer the best chance to correct for overreporting, but may possibly induce greater concealment.

[3] James S. Wallerstein and Clement J. Wyle, "Our Law-Abiding Law Breakers," *Probation*, 25:107–112, March-April 1947.

[4] For a discussion of the selection process as it occurs in juvenile court, see Robert D. Vinter, "The Juvenile Court as an Institution," in *Task Force Report: Juvenile Delinquency and Crime*, President's Commission on Law Enforcement and Administration of Justice (Washington: U.S. Government Printing Office, 1967), appendix C; Nathan

From arrest records, probation reports, and prison statistics a "portrait" of the offender emerges that progressively highlights the disadvantaged character of his life. The offender at the end of the road in prison is likely to be a member of the lowest social and economic groups in the country, poorly educated and unemployed, unmarried, reared in a broken home, and to have a prior criminal record. This is a formidable list of personal and social problems that must be overcome in order to restore offenders to law-abiding existence. Not all offenders, of course, fit this composite profile, as a more detailed examination of the arrest, probation, and prison data reveals.

.   .   .   .   .

Studies made of the careers of adult offenders regularly show the importance of juvenile delinquency as a forerunner of adult crime. They support the conclusions that the earlier a juvenile is arrested or brought to court for an offense, the more likely he is to carry on criminal activity into adult life; that the more serious the first offense for which a juvenile is arrested, the more likely he is to continue to commit serious crimes, especially in the case of major crimes against property; and that the more frequently and extensively a juvenile is processed by the police, court, and correctional system the more likely he is to be arrested, charged, convicted, and imprisoned as an adult. These studies also show that the most frequent pattern among adult offenders is one that starts with petty stealing and progresses to much more serious property offenses.[5]

[*President's Commission on Law Enforcement and Administration of Justice*, Task Force Report: The Challenge of Crime in a Free Society (*Washington: U.S. Government Printing Office, 1967*), *pp. 77–78.*]

Goldman, *The Differential Selection of Juvenile Offenders for Court Appearance* (New York: National Council on Crime and Delinquency, 1963); Martin Gold, *Status Forces in Delinquent Boys* (Ann Arbor: University of Michigan, Institute for Social Research, 1963). For a discussion of the sorting-out process among adult criminals, see Edwin H. Sutherland and Donald R. Cressy, *Principles of Criminology* (7th ed., Philadelphia: Lippincott Co., 1966), pp. 411–416, 429–441, 484–487.

[5] Clifford R. Shaw, *The Jack Roller* (Chicago: University of Chicago Press, 1930), republished with a new Introduction by Howard S. Becker as a Phoenix Book, University of Chicago Press, 1966; Clifford R. Shaw, *The Natural History of a Delinquent Career* (Chicago: University of Chicago Press, 1931); Harold S. Frum, "Adult Criminal Offense Trends Following Juvenile Delinquency," *Journal of Criminal Law, Criminology and Police Science*, 49:29–49, May-June 1958; Henry D. McKay, "Subsequent Arrests, Convictions and Commitments Among Former Juvenile Delinquents," President's Commission on Law Enforcement and Administration of Justice, *Selected Consultants' Papers* (Washington: U.S. Government Printing Office, 1967). A summary version of McKay's paper appears in Henry D. McKay, "Report on the Criminal Careers of Male Delinquents in Chicago," in *Task Force Report: Juvenile Delinquency and Youth Crime, supra* note 4, appendix E. For further data and discussion on this process of escalation to more serious criminal careers, see the Commission's General Report, pp. 265–266.

2 *The ecology of juvenile delinquency*

The National Commission on Law Observance and Enforcement published the second major ecological study of the Institute of Juvenile Research in Chicago in 1931.[1] This study was of particular significance since it demonstrated that the characteristic patterns for delinquency rates in Chicago could also be found in Philadelphia, Richmond, Cleveland, Birmingham, Denver, and Seattle. Three of their major findings about the distribution of delinquency rates have been repeatedly borne out in subsequent studies, subject only to local and usually accountable variations:

1. *Juvenile delinquents are not distributed uniformly over the City of Chicago but tend to be concentrated in areas adjacent to the central business district and to heavy industrial areas.*

2. *There are wide variations in the rates of delinquents between areas in Chicago.*

. . . . .

3. *The rates of delinquents tend to vary inversely with distance from the center of the City.*[2]

. . . . .

These patterns in the distribution of delinquency rates have stood up remarkably well under tests in many cities throughout the country and have also been found in Mexico City and Honolulu.[3]

. . . . .

Distribution of Juvenile Offenses

Most of the studies dealing with juvenile delinquents show spatial distributions in the city only according to the total delinquency rate or occasionally the rate of truancy. A recent study

[1] Clifford R. Shaw and Henry D. McKay, "Social Factors in Juvenile Delinquency," *Report on the Causes of Crime* (Washington: National Commission on Law Observance and Enforcement, 1931), pp. 2, 13.

[2] *Id.* at pp. 383–385.

[3] Andrew W. Lind, "Some Ecological Patterns of Community Disorganization in Honolulu," *American Journal of Sociology*, 36:206–220, September 1930; Norman S. Hayner, "Criminogenic Zones in Mexico City," *American Sociological Review*, 91:428–438, August 1946.

in Madison, Wis., however, divides the city into three relatively distinct areas and provides information on the types of acts by juveniles which resulted in a contact with the police.[4] A police contact in this study meant any interaction between a Madison police officer and a juvenile which resulted in a report being filed with the Crime Prevention Bureau of the police department.

The distribution of different types of acts by juveniles resulting in a' police contact are shown distributed among the three districts of Madison in table 1 according to the place of residence of the offenders. The rates are

Table 1—Delinquent Acts Resulting in Police-Juvenile Contacts, by Zone of City: Madison, Wis. 1950–55[1]

Acts	Average acts per 1,000 juveniles per year			
	Central	West	East	Total city
Incorrigible, runaway	34.10	13.55	29.97	26.65
Disorderly conduct	31.82	14.05	22.40	23.65
Contact—Suspicion, investigation, information	25.92	6.47	17.80	17.61
Theft	23.35	4.37	13.30	14.61
Traffic (operation)	16.45	11.45	12.37	13.73
Vagrancy	19.77	4.27	12.90	13.03
Liquor	9.17	1.65	7.77	6.49
Burglary	4.77	.67	4.17	3.36
Auto theft	4.15	1.77	2.85	3.06
Sex offenses	2.13	.20	1.23	1.27
Traffic (parking)	1.27	.87	.90	1.06
Truancy	1.12	.47	1.00	.91
Assault	.75	.00	.40	.42
Other delinquent acts	10.08	3.04	6.02	6.76
Total delinquent acts	185.05	63.13	133.08	132.65

[1] Sample of City of Madison juveniles from files of Crime Prevention Bureau, 1950–55.

Source: Lyle W. Shannon, "Types and Patterns of Delinquency in a Middle-sized City," The Journal of Research in Crime and Delinquency, v. 1, January 1964, p. 60–62.

for the period 1950–55 and are based on school estimates of the juvenile population age 6 to 18. They reflect the results of a sample of 1,876 juveniles whose records showed a total of 4,554 acts or police contacts, an average of 2.47 acts per person. The west district in table 1 is an area of high income, middle and upper class residents. The east district is composed of laboring and middle class residents of moderate income, and the central zone has residents of the working class and lower working class with generally low incomes.

The variation in police contact with juveniles in these districts is quite large. The rate is only 66 per 1,000 juveniles for those living in the west zone, but for those in the east zone it is more than twice as great (138) and for those in the central zone it is nearly three times as great (193). It is clear from table 1 that a considerable amount of police contact with juveniles is not for acts which would be criminal for an adult. Furthermore, these types of contact are experienced proportionately much more often by those resid-

[4] Lyle W. Shannon, "Types and Patterns of Delinquency in a Middle-sized City," The Journal of Research in Crime and Delinquency, 1:53–66, January 1964.

ing in the central and east districts. This is particularly true of contacts involving suspicion, investigation, or information. The west district juvenile rates come closest to the other districts in connection with acts involving vehicles. The relative likelihood that a juvenile will be involved in a serious criminal act shows quite sharp gradations from one district to another with the exception of burglary where the central rate (5) is very close to the east rate (4) but greatly different from the west rate (1).

The trustworthiness of such findings on the geographical distribution of delinquent acts depends, as do nearly all of the data presented in this chapter, on how well the agency statistics reflect the distribution of all serious acts of delinquency or crime that actually happen. This will clearly vary in relation to the seriousness of the offense, whether the act is reported to the police or not, whether it can be detected by the police or not, whether the record system is accurate or not, and a number of other factors. However, for the purpose of comparing different areas of a city, it is not necessary to know about every act that occurs. Official information would still be adequate for most crimes to show the *relative* variation in crime rates between different city areas, providing that the offenses and the offenders in these areas have roughly the same chance of coming to official notice and action. There is increasing evidence from studies of police handling of juvenile offenses that this assumption is probably true, especially for the more serious offenses which are not confined within the family context, as in the case of domestic assaults.[5] These studies show that relatively little discrimination based on race, social class, or income appears to operate for the more serious offenses. In both recording and disposing of juvenile offenses, the arrest history of the offender, the type of offense, and the age of the offender appear to have the most effect in deciding what action to take.[6]

In disposing of minor offenses, however, such criteria as race, family status, and income level may enter into the official decision sufficiently to bias the statistics against the lower income areas of residence. Recent studies also indicate that this type of bias in the delinquency statistics, produced by a greater likelihood that official action resulting in a record will take place in the poorer areas, varies from one city to another depending on the type of police department and the standards of the police officer. Two recent comparative studies of a "professional" police department and an old-time "fraternal" police department indicate important differences in

[5] Nathan Goldman, *The Differential Selection of Offenders for Court Appearance* (Washington: National Research and Information Center and National Council on Crime and Delinquency, 1963); A. W. McEachern and Riva Bauzer, "Factors Relating to Disposition in Juvenile Police Contacts," in Malcolm W. Klein, ed., *Juvenile Gangs in Context* (Englewood Cliffs, N.J.: Prentice-Hall, Inc., 1967), pp. 148–160. For additional references and a useful review see David J. Bordua, "Recent Trends: Deviant Behavior and Social Control," *The Annals of the American Academy of Political and Social Science*, 369:149–163, January 1967.

[6] Goldman, *id.* at pp. 125–132.

police recording and disposition of juvenile offenses.[7] The professional department arrested a larger proportion of the juveniles with whom they came in contact and released fewer of them. The fraternal department was more reluctant to arrest and refer to the court. However, the professional department was more likely to ignore such factors as race, family status, and economic status. The fraternal department was more likely to take these criteria into account in the recording and disposition of offenses, but even when these were taken into account, they affected primarily the way minor offenses were handled. Evidence on this point is also available from a study of communities in the area of Pittsburgh which found that the rate of referral of Negro juvenile offenders to court for serious offenses was 87.5 percent of those arrested and the rate for white children was 79.3 percent. However, for minor offenses the rate of referral for Negro children was 53.2 percent and the white rate 22.6 percent.[8] This type of bias would over-represent the Negro areas of residence as compared to white areas in juvenile statistics on court referrals by place of residence.

Apparently, the biasing effect of public attitudes, economic and social status, and police criteria for decisions do affect significantly the recording and disposition of offenses and offenders; and consequently the rates for different areas of the city. Several studies, for example, have now shown that police reactions to the attitude of the juvenile toward the authority of the police make a great deal of difference in the decision to arrest and record a contact, and it may be that persons of a racial minority group and low economic status in a slum area will be more likely to be defined as having a defiant and hostile attitude.[9] Nevertheless, the available studies and findings do encourage the belief that, if only the more serious offenses are counted, a reasonable amount of confidence may be placed in the picture they present of the relative variation in the delinquency rates between different city areas.

.   .   .   .   .

Trends in the Crime and Delinquency Rates of City Areas

As we have seen, the studies of different types of crime and delinquency rates have established that these rates follow a fairly consistent pattern in

[7] James Q. Wilson, "The Police and the Delinquent in Two Cities," in Stanton Wheeler, ed., *Controlling Delinquency* (New York: John Wiley & Sons, forthcoming publication); Aaron Cicourel, *The Social Organization of Juvenile Justice* (New York: John Wiley & Sons, forthcoming publication).

[8] Goldman, *supra* note 5, p. 127.

[9] Irving Piliavin and Scott Briar, "Police Encounters with Juveniles," *American Journal of Sociology*, 70:206–214, September 1964; Carl Werthman, "The Function of Social Definitions in the Development of Delinquent Careers," in *Task Force Report: Juvenile Delinquency*, President's Commission on Law Enforcement and Administration of Justice (Washington: U.S. Government Printing Office, 1967), appendix J; Carl Werthman and Irving Piliavin, "Gang Members and the Police," in David J. Bordua, ed., *The Police: Six Sociological Essays* (New York: John Wiley & Sons, in press).

their distribution throughout the geographical areas of the city, and that this pattern shows a considerable amount of similarity among American cities. A further question concerns the stability of this pattern of crime rates from one time period to another. Do these rates show any trends? Do changes in the area rates alter the relative standing of these areas in the total crime distribution pattern of the city? Do the higher crime rate areas remain the higher crime rate areas?

The pace of change is swift in American cities. Commerce and light industry invade the less intensively utilized land spaces. Old slums are torn down and replaced by high-rise apartment units. Older migrants to the city are displaced by more recent arrivals competing for low cost housing and unskilled laboring jobs. New highways cut through the territory of old ethnic enclaves of immigrants, creating new physical boundaries to movement and community identity. In all this incessant turmoil, growth, and change what happens to the geographic patterns of crime and delinquency rates which existed before?

The answer appears to be that the general pattern of distribution of crime and delinquency rates among the various areas of the city remains the same, even though some of these rates may change drastically in a few areas where major shifts in land use and population composition have occurred. This conclusion rests, however, on relatively few studies that have been carried out in the same fashion, for the same city, and at different time periods. In the recent study of Seattle, for example, a special effort was made to collect comparable data on the area crime rates in the years 1939–41 to compare with the 1949–51 series.[10] Though the *actual* or *absolute* rates for different crimes were not the same in the two time periods, due partly to changes in definition and classification of crimes, the same pattern of *relative* variation from the central to the outer zones of the city remained the same. The similarity of the patterns of distribution of crime rates among city areas for the two periods varied somewhat. For example, the patterns for highway robbery for these periods showed a correlation with each other of 0.94, nonresidential burglary 0.93, nonresidential robbery 0.81, and residential burglary 0.65.

The most fully developed time series of the geographic distribution of crime and delinquency rates in a city are those assembled for Chicago.[11] Table 2 shows the rates for different series of delinquents who were referred to the Juvenile Court of Cook County over a 40-year period from 1900 to 1940. The rates are shown for the city of Chicago, which is divided into five 2-mile concentric zones with the focal point of the zones located in the center of the central business district. Though the *absolute* sizes of the rates

[10] Calvin F. Schmid, "Urban Crime Areas Part II," *American Sociological Review*, 25:669–670, October 1960.

[11] For the most current statement on these studies see Henry D. McKay and Solomon Kobrin, *Nationality and Delinquency* (Chicago: Institute of Juvenile Research, Department of Mental Health, State of Illinois, 1966).

differ, the same *relative* tendency for the rates to be highest in zone 1 (the central district zone) and lowest in zone 5 (the outermost part of the city) holds for all series, except for the reversal of rank in zones 4 and 5 in the first series, 1900–1906. During this 40-year period Chicago experienced enormous growth in population and industrial and economic power. It also was confronted with the task of assimilating wave after wave of new immigrants with very different cultural values and expectations. In the light of this ceaseless turmoil of change and new development, the relative stability of the relationships between the zonal rates is impressive.

Though the comparison of rates by city zones is useful to demonstrate the stability of relationships between delinquency areas, it also obscures important changes in neighborhood rates of delinquency as the result of social

Table 2—Rates of Delinquents Per 100 Males, 10–17 Years of Age, in Chicago by 2-Mile Concentric Zones, for Selected Time Periods 1900–40

Years	Zone				
	I	II	III	IV	V
1900–1906	16	9	6	4	6
1917–23	10	7	4	3	3
1927–33	10	7	5	3	2
1934–40	9	9	6	4	2

Source: Henry D. McKay and Solomon Kobrin, "Nationality and Delinquency" (Chicago: Institute of Juvenile Research, Department of Mental Health, State of Illinois, 1966).

and economic change. We need much more detailed study of the way in which the changing character of life in the city affects the rates of delinquency and crime in the many different geographical areas of the city. It will require more intensive study of the trends in rates in the same areas in relation to the various physical, demographic, economic, and cultural changes which may have occurred. Such studies should also take account of the effects of changes in the organization, policies, and practices of the criminal justice system itself. From such studies we could obtain a much clearer idea than we now possess of the way delinquency rates reflect the existing structure of life within these areas and the way they are affected by changes both inside the area and in the city as a whole.

McKay has taken a beginning step in this direction by drawing trend lines of delinquency rates for 74 community areas of the city of Chicago.[12] These trend lines are based on five different series of delinquents appearing before the Juvenile Court of Cook County from 1927 to 1962. Selected for special study were the five community areas where the trend in rates

[12] Henry D. McKay, "A Note on Trends in Rates of Delinquents in Certain Areas of Chicago," in *Task Force Report: Juvenile Delinquency,* President's Commission on Law Enforcement and Administration of Justice (Washington: U.S. Government Printing Office, 1967), appendix F.

showed the greatest increase and the five areas showing the greatest decrease in rates. The areas showing the greatest increase were areas where "a largely middle class white population was replaced by a Negro population coming partly from other city areas and partly from outside of the city." Four of the areas showing the greatest decrease in rates extend directly southward from the central business district and are areas which have formed the heart of the Negro community for more than 30 years. The fifth area of greatest decrease is on the outskirts of the city where there has been a rapid increase of population, but where the population is 93 percent white. The increases in area rates were attributed to the breakdown of institutional controls and the disruption of roles and opportunities to participate in local political and economic institutions due to the fact that a new racial group moved in and displaced the former residents. Conversely, it was suggested that the areas showing decreasing delinquency rates are areas where new institutional controls and more stable role relationships have had time to become established.

> These areas of greatest decrease in rates of delinquents were the areas with the highest rates 30 or more years ago. At that time they resembled, in many ways, the characteristics of the areas of highest rates in the nineteen sixties. The evidence is not conclusive, but it seems that in the thirties the institutional and role disruption in these areas was very much the same as the disruption in communities (showing the greatest increases in rates), * * * during the past few years.
> * * * Surely the most suggestive finding of this study of trends in rates of delinquents is the finding that in the same period the areas of greatest increase and the areas of greatest decrease in rates of delinquents, were areas occupied primarily by Negro people. Note that these opposite changes took place over the same period of time in different parts of the same city.[13]

One cannot assume on the basis of these findings that order will gradually emerge from disorder by some "self healing" process. Much effort has been expended to develop more stable institutions and community relationships in these decreasing rate Negro areas, and the delinquency rates are still above the average for the city. These findings do indicate, however, the great importance of studying more closely what happens to the institutions in an area when a new group moves in. If it is true that the period of transition creates a chaotic situation which becomes resolved only when the new group develops its own network of institutionalized roles, then crime prevention programs might concentrate on how these roles, so essential for social control, might be developed more swiftly.

·   ·   ·   ·   ·

[13] *Id.*

The Relationships of Nationality and Race with Crime and Delinquency by City Areas

From the data presented thus far it appears that the application of ecological methods to the description and understanding of crime and delinquency has yielded only fragmentary insights and guidelines for action. However, a better realization of the potential and value of this type of analysis can be secured from the results relating nationality and race with crime and delinquency.

At the time of the Wickersham Commission in the late twenties and early thirties, the country was aroused about the state of lawlessness reflected in the operations of organized criminal syndicates in the illegal manufacture and distribution of alcoholic beverages.[14] Many of these organized criminal gangs were recruited from the immigrant populations in the big city slums, and these areas provided a base of operations.[15] In addition there was public concern about the excessive over-representation of foreign-born immigrants and their children among those arrested, convicted, and sentenced for crime or disposed of by the juvenile court for delinquent acts.[16] This public concern, which is evident again today in connection with the high crime and delinquency rates exhibited by the new minority groups inhabiting the slums of large cities, found reflection in detailed studies of the relation between ethnicity and crime.

The greatest contribution of data for public consideration of this problem was made through the series of studies in Chicago.[17] The use of ecological methods permitted them to go beyond the simple relationship between crime rates and nationality. It enabled them to demonstrate the operation of a relatively effective process of assimilation of these different nationality groups into the mainstream of American economic and social life. With this assimilation the high rates of crime and delinquency as well as a number of other social problems disappeared. It enabled them to focus public attention on the conditions of life, and on cultural and social change, rather than on inherent criminality as a function of national origin.

The problem of public stereotyping of certain nationality groups at that time as inherently criminal is not unlike the criminal stereotyping of the Negro and other minority groups today. These early studies did not attempt to refute the clearly demonstrable fact that the crime rates of certain nationality groups were disproportionately high. Instead, they amassed

---

[14] National Commission on Law Observance and Enforcement, *Enforcement of the Prohibition Law of the U.S.*, Vol. 1, No. 2 (Washington: U.S. Government Printing Office, 1931).

[15] *Ibid.*

[16] Shaw and McKay, "Social Factors in Juvenile Delinquency," *supra* note 1, p. 96.

[17] See Shaw and McKay, *Juvenile Delinquency in Urban Areas* (Chicago: University of Chicago Press, 1942), p. 5 et seq. Also see McKay and Kobrin, *id.* at p. 140.

evidence to show that while this fact was attributable, in some measure, to the social and cultural traditions of these groups, mainly it was a consequence of the socially disorganized nature of the conditions under which they were forced to live. The overwhelming thrust of the evidence was that the high rates of crime were not a consequence of being German, Irish, Scandinavian, Polish, Italian, or Slavic, but a consequence of their life situation.

Three types of data were assembled for studying the relation of race, nationality, and nativity with crime and delinquency rates. These data related to

(1) The succession of nationality groups in the high-rate areas over a period of years;

(2) Changes in the national and racial backgrounds of children appearing in the Juvenile Court; and

(3) Rates of delinquents for particular racial, nativity, or nationality groups in different types of areas at any given moment.[18]

Marked changes were noted in the composition of the population inhabiting the high delinquency and crime rate areas near the central district over a period of many years. The Germans, Irish, English-Scotch, and Scandinavians in Chicago were gradually replaced by the Italians, Polish, and persons from Slavic countries. Despite the change in population the rates remained high relative to other areas in the city. Nor were those families left behind by each nationality group the most delinquent. They actually produced fewer delinquents than their proportion in the population of the area would lead one to expect.[19]

As the older immigrant group moved out, their children appeared proportionately less often in the Juvenile Court, and the court intake reflected instead the disproportionate appearance of the new arrivals. Nor did the children of the disappearing nationality groups raise the court intake in their new areas either for foreign-born or native-born children.[20]

Comparison of the rates for whites and Negroes, native and foreign-born, and old and new immigrants, classified by the area rates for white delinquents, shows that all of these groups have rates that range from high to low. Each racial and nationality group shows a considerable range in rates. At the same time these different groups produce much the same rate when they live in the same areas.[21]

There is some difficulty in comparing the rates for different groups at any one time because of the concentration of the new groups in the high rate areas. Nevertheless, when tracts are compared that are closely comparable in living conditions, very similar rates are revealed. In more recent compari-

[18] Shaw and McKay, *id.* at p. 149.
[19] *Id.* at pp. 151–152.
[20] *Id.* at p. 152.
[21] *Id.* at pp. 152–153.

sons of the rates for Negro and white delinquents in Chicago, considerable difficulty was encountered in identifying comparable areas for the two groups. Even in the same tracts the whites were found to occupy the better quarters and were, of course, not subject to the same discrimination in access to employment and other opportunities.[22] In the last major sample in the Chicago studies, the 1934–40 Juvenile Court Series, application of a method of statistical standardization for partially equating the population distribution of white and Negro males yielded a standardized delinquency rate of 4.41 per 100 white youth age 10–17 and 14.55 per 100 Negro youth.[23] Despite this difference the study concludes,

> All of the materials in this study indicate that if situations could be found where Negro and white children had equal opportunities in all meaningful aspects of life, the widely observed differences in rates of delinquents would be greatly reduced and perhaps would disappear.[24]

This limitation in the ecological method, the difficulty of locating comparable living conditions for the comparison of the experience of different population groups, was explored in some detail in a study in Baltimore.[25] Two white and two Negro areas were selected so as to permit as full an equating as possible of the conditions of life and the demographic characteristics of the population between each pair of matched Negro and white areas. Because of the segregation each area was quite racially homogeneous. Furthermore, the paired areas had about the same size population, similar age and sex differences, predominantly lower occupational levels, the same low levels of education, comparable size households, generally low health status though somewhat lower in the Negro areas, and general comparability on such indices as condition of dwellings, homes with radios, refrigeration equipment, and presence of central heating unit. The chief differences were that the white populations, predominantly of foreign-born extraction, were a settled population of long residence in their areas, while the Negro populations had sizeable groups of new migrants. Home ownership was much greater among the whites, the Negroes being primarily renters. The Negroes also paid higher rents for comparable dwelling units. The whites were "one step up the occupation ladder above Negroes."[26]

The results showed considerably higher rates of felons convicted in 1940 in the Negro as compared to the matched white areas. The white rates for males were 2.36 and 2.21, while the rates for the respectively paired Negro areas were 15.11 and 12.47.[27] The juvenile delinquency rates, however, per

[22] McKay and Kobrin, *supra* note 11.
[23] *Id.* at table 57.
[24] *Id.* at p. 125.
[25] Earl R. Moses, "Differentials in Crime Rates Between Negroes and Whites," *American Sociological Review*, 12:411–420, August 1967.
[26] *Id.* at p. 417.
[27] *Id.* at table V, p. 418.

1000 population, age 6–17, for the years 1939–42 were much closer. The white rates were 14.4 and 22.0, while the Negro area rates were 26.7 and 28.4.[28]

The discrepancy in the crime rates might have been anticipated since, as we have already seen in other studies, the differences which did exist between the Negro and white areas are ones which show high associations with crime rates, such as the high percentage of home ownership in the white area, a stable white population and a mobile Negro population and somewhat higher occupational status in the white area, that is, more craftsmen, foremen, and kindred workers as contrasted with laborers and domestic service workers among the Negro population. What is surprising is the relatively close correspondence in delinquency rates despite these differences. Nevertheless, the study does indicate the grave difficulties in locating truly equated areas for such controlled comparisons.

The basic findings in the Chicago studies of the spatial distribution of nationally and racial delinquency rates have not gone unchallenged. The primary objection is that the concern with documenting the effects of the process of assimilation on the delinquency rates within each nationality group led to the neglect of significant differences in the crime and delinquency rates of nationality groups arising from different tolerances in their own cultural and historical tradition for various forms of deviance.[29] Reference has been made to the low rates of delinquency and crime in areas of Oriental settlement, to significant differences in the delinquency of children of Russian Jewish immigrants and Italian immigrants in New York City though they entered at much the same time, and to the high rates of arrest of Jewish boys for violating street peddling laws.[30] It seems to be generally conceded that these cultural differences can influence significantly the *actual* or *absolute* size of the delinquency rate.[31] However, the main propositions of the Chicago studies rest not so much on the actual size of the rates but the relationship between these rates. It is the *relative* difference between area rates for the same or different nationality groups depending on their length of residence in the city and the amount of movement toward the better integrated, more comfortable and settled areas toward the periphery of the city that supports the principal findings.[32]

The Cultural Enclave

One of the most significant findings of the ecological studies has been the identification of enclaves of culturally different insulated groups who have

[28] *Id.* at p. 418.
[29] Christen T. Jonassen, "A Re-evaluation and Critique of the Logic and Some Methods of Shaw and McKay," *American Sociological Review*, 14:608–614, October 1949. Also see rejoinder by Shaw and McKay, pp. 614–617.
[30] Sophia M. Robison, *Can Delinquency Be Measured?* (New York: Columbia University Press, 1936), pp. 187 and 122.
[31] Shaw and McKay, *supra* note 29, p. 615.
[32] *Ibid.*

maintained low rates of crime and delinquency despite exposure to poverty, discrimination, exploitation, and disadvantageous conditions. Perhaps the most striking capacity to do this has been observed in areas of Oriental settlement in large cities. In Seattle a school district comprised of 90 percent Japanese boys showed a low delinquency rate of 5.7 despite the fact that the rate for the rest of the area was 27.7.[33] This district was located in a very deteriorated section of town with "the highest concentration of homicides, houses of prostitution, unidentified suicides, and cheap lodging-houses in Seattle."[34] Of the 710 boys who were sent to the Parental School (a boy's reform school) from 1919 to 1930 from Seattle, only three were Japanese, and the cases of these three indicated that they had lost "vital contact with the racial colony."[35]

This same type of situation was observed and studied in Vancouver. In an 8-year period (1928–36) a total of 4,814 delinquents appeared in the Vancouver Juvenile Court.[36] Only 19 were Orientals. During this period the delinquency rate for the whites was 15.65 per 1,000 and for the Orientals 1.0 per 1,000.[37]

Further investigation revealed that the Oriental children in Vancouver resided in areas of high delinquency and they attended schools with bad delinquency records. Furthermore, the status of the Oriental was low. He experienced discrimination and was often the object of active hostility. The explanation seems to be that strenuous efforts were made to maintain family discipline and loyalty, to sustain a common concept and respect for their national origin, and to promote actively the pursuit and study of the Oriental religion, language, and culture.[38]

How long can this type of insularity maintain itself under the pressures for participation in modern life? There are historical examples to indicate that this is very difficult. A study of a Russian colony of immigrants in Los Angeles reported in 1930 that 5 percent of the children appeared before the juvenile court in the first 5 years of residence in a highly delinquent area. In the second 5 years of residence 46 percent were referred to the court, and in the next 10 years 83 percent were referred to the court.[39] Similarly, in Honolulu it was discovered that the Orientals who became involved in serious delinquency were most likely to be those who had previous associations with members of other groups.[40]

No one seriously suggests that it is easier to maintain control over the

[33] Norman S. Hayner, "Delinquency Areas in the Puget Sound Region," *American Journal of Sociology*, 39:319, November 1933.

[34] *Ibid.*

[35] *Ibid.*

[36] Helen G. MacGill, "The Oriental Delinquent in the Vancouver, B.C., Juvenile Court," *Sociology and Social Research*, 22:430, May-June 1938.

[37] *Ibid.*

[38] *Id.* at pp. 432–438.

[39] Pauline V. Young, "Urbanization as a Factor in Juvenile Delinquency," *Publications of the American Sociological Society*, 24:162–166, 1930.

[40] Lind, *supra* note 3, p. 217.

behavior of children in a high as compared to a low delinquency area, but the fact is that many succeed. A recent study in New Haven suggests that the proper kind of family and school climate can provide a certain amount of insulation from highly delinquent surroundings and secure commitment to conventional goals.[41] The study included a sample of all youth born in Greater New Haven in 1942–44 whose supervising relative was on the Aid to Dependent Children rolls in 1950. Records were examined for the years between the sixth birthday and the 19th. Data came primarily from welfare, school, and police records. By 1962, a total of 34 percent had become known to the police or the juvenile court, compared to a delinquency rate of 18 percent for a control group of youth of the same age, sex, type of neighborhood, school performance, and lowest class level. However, the ADC group did show twice as many living in public housing, twice the number moving three or more times over an 11-year period, three times as many Negroes, and over ten times more broken homes.[42]

The delinquency rates among the ADC group varied markedly by race, sex, and school performance, all the way from no delinquency cases among 75 white females who were successful in school to 71 percent arrested or referred to court among 38 Negro males who were failing in school.[43] Additional significant differences appear when family deviance and the nature of the neighborhood of residence are considered. A "deviant family" was defined as one in which "one or both parents are in prison or mental hospital, or the parent has had a series of marriages, separations, multiple illegitimacies, or 'cut and run' affairs."[44] Those from deviant families are more delinquent, 41 percent to 31 percent, but deviant families had twice as much effect on Negro as compared to white youth. School success seems to compensate to some extent for the effects of deviant families, since among the successful in school 33 percent from the deviant families were delinquent, and 27 percent of those from nondeviant families were delinquent. However, among those failing in school 71 percent from deviant families were delinquent as compared to 45 percent of those from nondeviant families.[45]

Consideration was also given to the effect of residing in a deviant neighborhood, which was defined as of the lowest class standing in social and economic characteristics and having a high delinquency rate.[46] Negro youth were more than twice as likely as white youth to live in deviant neighborhoods. The effect of the deviant neighborhood is much greater on boys than on girls, since 71 percent of the boys from deviant neighborhoods were delinquent compared to 47 percent of the boys from nondeviant neighbor-

[41] Erdman B. Palmore and Phillip F. Hammond, "Interacting Factors in Juvenile Delinquency," *American Sociological Review*, 29:848–854, December 1964.
[42] *Id.* at p. 849.
[43] *Id.* at table 1, p. 850.
[44] *Id.* at p. 850.
[45] *Id.* at table 3, p. 851.
[46] *Id.* at p. 851.

hoods, while the comparable percentages for girls were 14 and 16 percent.[47] Here again the effect of living in a deviant neighborhood is likely to be worst for those boys failing in school. Perhaps success in school insulates the boys to some extent from complete responsiveness to delinquent influences in the neighborhood or perhaps those least involved in neighborhood life are most likely to succeed in school. Among those boys failing in school who were from deviant neighborhoods, 82 percent were delinquent compared to 53 percent of the school failures from nondeviant neighborhoods, while the comparable percentages for the school successes were 44 and 37 percent.[48]

As this study points out, some factors are additive in their effects. If one is male, Negro, and a school failure, the chances of developing a delinquent record are greater than if any of these factors were different. Other factors seem to be interactive. They have a selective and sometimes a cushioning effect. School success may offset many of the effects of deviant neighborhoods or families. Also being from nondeviant neighborhoods or families is associated with lower delinquency rates despite failure in school.

Explanations and Implications of the Distribution of Crime Rates

Studies of the patterns in the geographical distribution of crime and delinquency rates in cities have persistently tried to establish the chief characteristics of the areas in which the rates of both offenses and offenders are highest. They have tried many types of indicators with varying degrees of success. Considering that these studies have been undertaken in different cities containing very different populations, in different regions of the country with diverse cultural traditions, and in different time periods ranging back to the beginning of the century, the results have shown a considerable degree of consistency concerning the location of serious crime problems.

These studies have not assumed that the factors found to be associated with these delinquency rates are causative. Instead they are regarded simply as indicators of characteristics of urban areas with spatial variations similar to those shown by the crime rates. There is also the underlying assumption that both the crime rates and other related social problems are being produced by certain common structural features of a social, economic, physical, and demographic character in the high rate areas that are not present or do not interact in the same way in the low rate areas. The interaction of these distinctive structural features of the area are regarded as setting the conditions and resources for living. To the extent that these conditions are so disadvantageous that it becomes difficult for the family to assert and maintain its authority in training children, or the schools to teach

[47] *Id.* at table 4, p. 851.
[48] *Id.* at table 5, p. 851.

effectively, or the employment system to recruit and sustain motivations toward successful conventional careers, higher rates of social problems, such as delinquency and crime, will occur.

The prevailing explanation of those conducting the ecological studies in Chicago of the high rates in certain areas of the city was in terms of social disorganization.[49] The high rates of transiency in these areas, the inability of the poor and unskilled new migrants to rely on old habits and customs as a guide to adjustment in the urban area, and the lack of stable institutions and relationships which the new migrant could trust contributed to a highly unstable set of social and cultural conditions in which to rear a family. These problems were compounded by the tendency for illegal practices and institutions to cluster in areas where the residents were not organized or equipped to defend their territory. The more fortunate groups brought customs and institutions from the old world which helped them to build cultural enclaves in which the process of assimilation could proceed more slowly, safely, and surely. As this assimilation progressed, they could begin to participate and accept responsible roles in the economic, social, and political life of the larger society. This increased security and economic well-being permitted them to move out and undertake commitments for themselves and their children to the accepted goals of the larger society.

From this perspective the Chicago ecologists identified the development of a stable and unified community as a major goal of action programs designed to prevent and control various social problems, including crime and delinquency. They saw a need to engage local participants in the task of developing indigenous institutions which they directed and which would reflect the critical needs of the residents themselves. This perspective resulted in the development of the Chicago Area Project in the 1930's and provided a body of action experience which has aided the development of many current delinquency area and poverty prevention programs.[50]

There are three other major explanations which have been advanced to account for the distribution of crime and delinquency rates and the characteristics of high rate areas. One of these points to the selective attraction of the poorer areas for many kinds of people, the poor, the emotionally disturbed, and the criminal, among others. This idea that many people who "drift" to unstable areas are already delinquent, or inclined to be so, has been frequently advanced but rarely studied. A very limited study was made in Decatur, Ill., of persons committed to the Illinois Prison System from Decatur.[51] The backgrounds of 73 residents were finally studied. Sixty-five of the 73 residents lived in delinquency areas of Decatur, but the

---

[49] Shaw and McKay, *Juvenile Delinquency in Urban Areas, supra* note 17, pp. 177–183.

[50] For a recent reevaluation of this project from the standpoint of a chief participant, see Solomon Kobrin, "The Chicago Area Project—A 25-Year Assessment," *The Annals of the American Academy of Political and Social Science,* 322:19–29, March 1959.

[51] Donald R. Taft, "Testing the Selective Influence of Areas of Delinquency," *American Journal of Sociology,* 38:699–712, March 1933.

study concluded that from 42 to 89 percent might be regarded as having been delinquent or criminal prior to coming to Decatur, or subject to the influence of other family members who had been criminal or delinquent elsewhere. The small numbers, inadequate records, and the inability to include delinquents and misdemeanants make this study rather inconclusive and leave the issue of the relative importance of "drift" unresolved.

A third explanation stresses the importance of conditions in the high delinquency areas and particularly the effect of a frustrating gap between the goals, aspirations, or expectations of residents in the area and the existence of either legitimate or illegitimate means to achieve them. The high rates of delinquency are thus a reflection of the limited legitimate opportunities. At the same time there are available more institutionalized illegitimate opportunities than are present in other less criminal and delinquent areas of the city.[52]

The fourth explanation calls attention to the social, economic, and political forces which come to bear on the city from the surrounding region and the country. The shape and distribution of the social areas of the city, the problems and opportunities, land use, and population composition are in a major way responsive to this larger network of constantly changing demands in the national process of technological, cultural, and economic growth. To understand the distribution of persons, institutions, and social problems, like crime, in the city, one must relate them to this larger social context.[53] However, just how these external forces might operate to affect the distribution of such social problems as crime in a city has not yet been clearly conceptualized.

It is not possible on the basis of current studies to determine which of these explanations will provide the most fruitful guidelines to action. They all, to some degree, have in common a focus on the operation of the social and economic system and the particular social processes which link people to it. Inherent in the operation of this system is to be found the source of the pressures which distribute people and crime rates among the various areas of the city. The path to understanding and successful action involves learning more about how it works, how it comes to bear on those who do or do not participate in it, and what types of changes in its structure or operation will enhance its utility and limit its costs.

Though these ecological studies of the distribution of crime and delinquency rates in cities have not been specifically addressed to a search for

---

[52] For an exposition of this explanation and related theories, see Richard A. Cloward and Lloyd E. Ohlin, *Delinquency and Opportunity* (Glencoe, Ill.: The Free Press, 1960).

[53] Eshref Shevky and Wendell Bell, *Social Area Analysis* (Stanford: Stanford University Press, 1955), pp. 3–19. Also see the paper by Judith Wilks in appendix A, President's Commission on Law Enforcement and Administration of Justice (Washington: U.S. Government Printing Office, 1967), pp. 138–156. The organization of this chapter was greatly aided by the interpretive comments in Wilks' paper pertaining to intracity variations in crime and delinquency rates.

causes of crime, they have produced many useful insights about the conditions of life with which crime and delinquency are most often associated. In calling attention to the close relation between the social and economic conditions of life and the adequacy of local institutions in meeting the needs of residents of high delinquency areas, such studies have pointed to the need for much more detailed investigation of these connections. This more intensive analysis would be greatly facilitated if police districts and the reporting of crime data coincided with the area boundaries used in reporting census data. It would also be extremely helpful if other types of social and economic data reported by public and private institutions, such as education, health, and welfare agencies, used comparable census area boundaries. This failure to use comparable area units has been one of the major restraints on the full exploitation of ecological methods for the analysis of crime problems. Nevertheless, the ecological studies have provided the beginnings of a theoretical explanation of the distribution of crime rates which justifies a broad attack on the underlying social and economic conditions which produce such heavy concentrations of both offenses and offenders in some areas of the city rather than others.

[*President's Commission on Law Enforcement and Administration of Justice,* Task Force Report: Crime and Its Impact—An Assessment (*Washington: U.S. Government Printing Office, 1967*), *pp. 60–61, 63–65, 67–68, 72–76.*]

3 Economic factors in delinquency

Our economy is an urban-industrial one; it reinforces, at the same time that it benefits from, the stratification system according to which social and economic rewards are distributed in such an economy. There is no need to belabor the point that there is poverty in America nor that there is social disorganization, particularly in urban centers. How much of this might have been avoided during the process of industrialization is by no means clear; nations attempting to plan their way into economic growth have not been notably successful in arranging a smooth transition to high levels of productivity, consumption, and social well-being.

After reviewing relevant data on delinquency in relation to social and economic conditions, Wilensky and Lebeaux assert that ". . . the physical and social aspects of urbanism and the stratification effects of industrialism [are] the master keys to delinquency."[1]

. . . . .

It is, of course, possible to be more than just slightly skeptical of the data and to argue that biases skew the results reported in most studies. Thus we know that many crimes are committed by members of the middle classes of all ages.

. . . . .

At the very least it is possible to assert with considerable confidence that while crime and delinquency are likely to occur in all income groups, the particular types that preoccupy us as a society are concentrated among males in lower income groups living in urban centers. Once again, values are operative and have the effect of coloring the priorities in our indignations. Homicides on city streets (or, more likely, as the result of payday arguments in the kitchens of low-income homes) thus concern us a good deal more in most discussions of crime than hazards of fatal shock from faulty domestic appliances sold to the

[1] H. L. Wilensky and C. N. Lebeaux, *Industrial Society and Social Welfare* (New York: The Free Press, 1965). Paperbound edition of volume originally published by the Russell Sage Foundation.

public by manufacturers, demonstrably harmful drugs that deform babies, pesticides that poison consumers, or steering mechanisms that cripple or kill motorists. Similarly we give relatively less attention to the $300 million of which customers (including school systems and low-income housing agencies) were defrauded by 29 heavy electrical equipment manufacturers than we do to the number of cars stolen by urban young people. And this is not simply a cynical assertion. Our tolerance for "big deviance" is reflected in the ruling by the Internal Revenue Service permitting damages paid to victims of the electrical conspiracy, in the 1960's, to be deducted from corporate income for tax purposes, as ". . . ordinary and necessary business expenses."

The serious bias is not that published data overstate the criminality occurring in low-income population groups, but that the categories used in reporting delinquency, reflecting our collective sense of concern and outrage, have the effect of understating the delinquency of other social groups. The delinquent and criminal acts that count, that do concern us, meanwhile, are more prevalent among low-income persons. This fact cannot be gainsaid by reference to the legal advantages enjoyed by upper income groups. We need simply recognize that the schema used for ordering criminal data give a different kind of emphasis to the deviance of more prosperous Americans. The latter group simply does not, to any statistically significant degree, pimp, pick pockets, run numbers, break and enter, or have family rows in which long bread knives may figure; they sell themselves less often into prostitution (whatever patronage they may provide), and they do not as often form gangs for purposes of despoiling school buildings or cemeteries. There have, of course, been instances in which Long Island mansions have been redecorated by what their parents, lawyers, and some journalists described as "high-spirited college youths."[2]

Thus one need only allow for the ideological character and dimensions of social outrage in order to accept the conclusion that low-income, urban people living in rented, crowded homes and neighborhoods commit a disproportionate number of crimes and delinquent acts. Here we may call attention to studies by Cohen, Lander, and Kvaraceus,[3] and to sections of the Crime Commission's report that deal with the demographic and other characteristics of criminals and delinquents.

. . . . .

These studies support the generalization that the types of criminal deviance that concern most Americans are prevalent ". . . among lower socio-economic strata much more than among middle and upper strata. The

[2] An expanded version of this discussion, together with relevant citations, is available from the author at Columbia University.

[3] Albert K. Cohen, *Delinquent Boys: The Culture of the Gang* (Glencoe, Ill.: The Free Press, 1955); B. Lander, *Toward an Understanding of Juvenile Delinquency* (New York: Columbia University Press, 1954); W. C. Kvaraceus, *The Community and the Delinquent* (New York: World Book Co., 1954).

statistics . . . are by no means conclusive . . . but the evidence points to their accuracy."[4]

The most compelling data may be found in two recent studies of the statistical covariations among data on unemployment, income and juvenile delinquency. These studies are more persuasive because they examine, through the use of multiple regression techniques,[5] the magnitude of changes in crime rates, within low-income populations, that are associated with variations in unemployment and income. One may, in short, not only locate delinquency, in gross terms, among lower income groups but measure the sensitivity of a number of delinquency data to changes in the earnings and labor market experiences of lower socioeconomic groups.

In the first of these studies—which really is a collection of smaller studies—Belton Fleisher of the University of Chicago examined delinquency data from 74 Chicago communities, 45 suburban Chicago communities, and the 101 cities upon which the FBI's "Uniform Crime Reports" are based, together with relevant data on income and unemployment. This analysis, cross-sectional in design, is supported by a longitudinal analysis of unemployment and delinquency rates in Boston, Cincinnati, and Chicago as well as by corresponding national data for the period 1932–61. (The second study, by Singell, is treated below.)

Fleisher's analysis is a sophisticated one indeed, for he has controlled, in the multiple regression equations he has employed in both sets of studies, for the impact of family dissolution, race, home ownership (as a measure of social stability and class), residential overcrowding, geographic mobility, regional differences in delinquency rates, immigration, and income distribution (i.e., dispersion of income). All of these are considered as factors potentially influencing the delinquency rates he sought to explain.[6]

He has also distinguished in his analysis between the "supply effect" and the "demand effect" of income on delinquency rates. Thus he compares the effects on the regressions of raising income of all families ("demand effect") and of raising the income of the lowest income quartile, thereby altering the magnitudes in the dispersion of income in the samples in the study. In changing the income of only the lowest quartile, he studies "supply effect" (i.e., influencing the effect of income via the number and value of crimes "available").

Without reproducing Fleisher's analysis here, it is useful to cite the conclusions he reached:

1. "The estimated effect of unemployment on delinquency is uniformly positive." Thus a 1-percent increase in unemployment is associated on the

---

[4] H. L. Wilensky and C. N. Lebeaux, *op. cit.*, p. 189.

[5] Multiple regression techniques permit one to move from a design in which one observes the association between two sets of characteristics to one in which the associations of many relevant factors are considered simultaneously.

[6] In a multiple regresson analysis the statistical contribution of each of these factors to delinquency rates is calculated in order to determine how much of the variance in these rates may be attributable to each of the factors.

average with an approximated 0.15-percent increase in rate of delinquency.[7]

2. There is also evidence suggesting that—

> . . . unemployment upon entering the labor market (especially for persons who enter before completing high school) can help explain the age distribution of juvenile delinquency. . . . Thus the age (16) at which delinquency rates appear to be highest is also the age at which the modal number of decisions to drop out of school are made by young persons who probably have low commitments to legitimate activity.

.   .   .   .   .

3. Data for Great Britain support conclusions on the relationships between unemployment and delinquency for youths over 17. The data for youths under 17 in the United States are unreliable, however, "due to an apparent bias-unwillingness to fingerprint younger offenders after World War II."[8]

Fleisher then turns his attention to income in the cross-sectional analysis mentioned above. Again his conclusions deserve extensive citation:

1. The "demand effect" of income may be interpreted to mean that an increase in family income of 1 percent results on the average in a 1.2-percent decline in the delinquency rate.[9]

2. The statistical "supply effect" of income is not as great as the "demand effect." Thus an increase of 1 percent in the dispersion of incomes would raise delinquency by 0.23 percent.[10]

3. The statistical effect of race is extremely small and insignificant.[11]

4. But the effect of population mobility "appears to be as expected; the estimated coefficient is large and highly significant statistically."[12]

5. The results vary only slightly as one moves from data on 101 cities to those on the 74 Chicago communities and the 45 suburban communities. Similarly, income effects do not vary much depending on whether one or another of the other independent variables is used in a number of compli-

---

[7] Belton Fleisher, *The Economics of Delinquency* (Chicago: Quadrangle Books, 1966), p. 68.

[8] *Ibid.*, p. 84.

[9] *Ibid.*, pp. 88–89.

[10] *Ibid.*, p. 89. This conclusion is arrived at by calculating the elasticity figure from the coefficient of the difference between the upper and lower income quartiles. The finding is interpreted to mean that income inequality is a factor in delinquency; if the gap between classes widens, delinquency goes up regardless of increases in the income of low-income units.

[11] *Ibid.*, p. 89.

[12] *Ibid.*, chapter 4. This conclusion is consistent with the job-seeking mobility patterns of low-income groups. See R. L. Stein, *Work History, Attitudes, and Income of the Unemployed* (Washington: U.S. Department of Labor Statistics, December 1963), Special Labor Force Report No. 37, PM13; and "Mobility of the Population of the United States," March 1964 to March 1965, "Population Characteristics of the United States, *Current Population Reports,* Series P20, No. 150, Apr. 14, 1966.

cated stratified analyses that control for race, regional differences, home ownership, education, and other likely factors.[13]

Double checking his results by considering data originally collected by others, Fleisher is able to confirm the existence of the general patterns he observed in his own data.[14]

. . . . .

Fleisher's results are consistent and corroborative of each other even when he altered the type of income data employed and when he considered data on property crimes of youths 17 years of age and under. The (small) differences observed in this part of his analysis are probably attributable to some underreporting in the delinquency rates of the very youngest group. Crimes of violence, meanwhile, do not stem, statistically speaking, from economic factors except for offenders below 17 years of age.[15] "One may speculate," says Fleisher, "that older delinquents have a more materialistic orientation toward crime than do the younger,"[16] a speculation that may or may not be valid. . . .

He summarizes the conclusions he has drawn from his empirical investigation in some numerical examples based upon the statistical interrelationships observed in the data he employed. . . . It should be clearly understood that he neither proves nor disproves anything about the causal relationships that may exist between delinquency and factors other than those that were specified and manipulated in his own analysis. As we shall see later, however, there is little inconsistency between his model and those developed by students who have focused on factors, like personal pathology, that are ostensibly noneconomic in nature. In his example he allows, for instance, for factors, like family stability, that are commonly supposed to be empirically linked to the psychological well-being of persons.

. . . . .

Fleisher's findings, meanwhile, are corroborated by Singell who used monthly data for Detroit to the same ends and utilized the same statistical techniques as Fleisher.[17] Before we remark upon Fleisher's challenge . . . and upon the policy implications that might be inferred from his analysis, it is well to consider even more data than has already been reviewed. One does not lay aside lightly the gnawing suspicions of some that the delinquency and the economic circumstances of some Americans both are attributable to the inadequacies and psychopathologies of these persons. The evidence is, to be sure, impressive even as it stands. Thus Fleisher has

[13] Ibid., chapter 14.

[14] D. J. Bordua, "Juvenile Delinquency and 'Anomie': An Attempt at Replication," Social Problems, III, No. 3, pp. 230–238; and R. J. Chilton, "Continuity in Delinquency Area Research: A Comparison of Studies for Baltimore, Detroit, and Indianapolis," American Sociology Review, XXIX, No. 1, pp. 71–83.

[15] Ibid., pp. 101–104.

[16] Ibid., p. 104.

[17] "Some Private and Social Aspects of the Labor Mobility of Young Workers," Quarterly Journal of Economics and Business, vol. 6, No. 1 (Spring 1966), pp. 26–27.

conducted eight separate studies; Singell's makes nine, and their findings (with a few reversals) square well with those in earlier studies by Ogburn and Thomas,[18] Henry and Short,[19] and Glazer and Rice.[20]

Additional evidence is better considered, however, in the context of a more analytical discussion, permitting us to see the statistical associations against the backdrop of institutional realities. It goes almost without saying that any of the policy alternatives this and the analysis in the next section may seem to imply must also be judged against institutional realities. The most persuasive evidence concerning delinquency would be evidence that permits us to identify the meaning of statistical linkages between economic marginality and deviance. At the same time policy alternatives are more promising to the extent they take into account other social objectives in addition to the reduction of deviance. The two following sections will consider these issues in order.

Economic Circumstance, Life Chances, and Delinquency

While it may be acceptable to most Americans to slight antitrust violations, offenses against the food and drug laws, unfair (i.e., illegal) labor practices, and a veritable host of "white-collar crimes" in their understanding of criminal deviance, it is not so easy to ignore the fact—implicit in the statistical discussion in the previous section—that delinquency appears with some frequency among well-situated population groups. Assuming even that crime rates understate middle-class delinquency, the sons and daughters of America's affluent families are present in sufficient numbers among the depressing figures on juvenile delinquency to disallow perfect correlations in analyses, like those by Fleisher, that focus exclusively on economic factors as these factors are traditionally understood.

A persuasive explanation for the observed delinquency rates of low-income youths should not be inconsistent with efforts to account for middle-class delinquency; in the best of worlds the explanations should be coextensive. Thus an explanation employing economic factors would be most compelling if it were constructed in such a way that it would fit all, or most, of the facts.

Such an explanation requires a broadened conception of economic factors to make room for experiences among "haves" in America that overlap in significant ways with those that occur among delinquent "have nots." These experiences—in school, in preparation for employment and in the labor market—help illuminate the otherwise anomalous empirical facts that not all low-income youngsters become delinquent and that not all upper income

[18] "The Influence of the Business Cycle on Certain Social Conditions," *Journal of the American Statistical Association,* XVIII, September 1922, pp. 305–340.

[19] *Suicide and Homicide* (Glencoe, Ill.: The Free Press, 1954).

[20] "Crime, Age, and Employment," *American Sociological Review,* XXIV, October 1959, pp. 679–686.

children are free of delinquency. Clear exposition is best served by dealing with life circumstances of low-income groups and then by dealing with other groups as we come upon overlaps reported in relevant studies.[21]

Consider the prospects of preschool children in poor American families. Family life is often unstable and households often headed by women; income is low, unpredictable and sometimes awarded only at the sufferance of righteous taxpayers. The adults in these families are likely to have been, themselves, born into poverty and to have achieved little education in a society in which education is a crucial factor in success. Indeed, "More than three-fifths of all spending unit heads whose fathers had less than nine grades of school went beyond that level themselves. Among the heads of poor families, fewer than two-fifths did so."[22] At the same time it is clear that one cannot account for poverty by focusing largely upon the alleged inadequacies of the poor themselves, for the overwhelming majority of poor people are chronically poor with many poverty-linked characteristics that are anchored in social structure. . . .[23]

While it is not clear, from these particular figures, whether the educational deficiences of poor adults in Morgan's study were the results of their parents' deficiencies, it is reasonable to argue that the modest nature of the educational achievements of the parents of the adult poor had a significant bearing upon these parents' poverty and thus upon the adults' own opportunities for (and dispositions toward) education. . . . [T]he relationship, meanwhile, between educational achievement and income is by now well known.[24]

Thus the poor preschool child, to a notable degree, inherits poverty and is immersed in it. The occupations of neighbors and friends are likely to be at the bottom of the hierarchy of skill and prestige that distinguishes vocations, callings, professions and occupations, on the one hand, from "jobs" on the other. It is also well known, by now, that these children are somewhat more likely to be nonwhite than white, to live in crowded dwellings, to have exceedingly mobile fathers,[25] and to experience great population changes in their neighborhoods. A sufficient literature has appeared in recent years to obviate the need to detail further facts descriptive of "the other America" in

---

[21] For purposes of this section the discussion is organized around juvenile delinquency and not crime; while not all juvenile delinquents become criminals, it is reasonably safe to assert that most adult criminals have committed delinquency or prior criminal acts.

[22] Morgan and others, *Income and Welfare in the United States* (New York: McGraw-Hill Co., 1962), chapter 16.

[23] *Ibid.*, p. 208.

[24] It is, of course, not absolutely clear what this positive relationship means. It could be that a substantial number of educated high-income people would have achieved high income for reasons that also explain their educational achievements: intelligence, personal access, and contacts, high motivations and aspirations. For a convenient discussion, see "Investment in Human Beings," *Special Supplement, The Journal of Political Economy*, vol. LXX, No. 5, pt. 2, October 1962.

[25] For a remarkably lucid discussion of the costs and benefits to the economy and to individuals of geographic mobility, see L. A. Sjanstad, "The Costs and Returns of Human Migration," in "Investment in Human Beings," *Special Supplement, The Journal of Political Economy, op. cit.*, pp. 80–90.

this paper; the academic experiences these children encounter after their preschool years, experiences that are critical for the futures they will be obliged to endure, are less well known.

The schools many of the poor, especially the nonwhite poor, attend, for example, are typically "separate" but most decidedly not "equal." In the higher grades they compare with custodial disciplinary barracks; according to one observer, they are staffed by frightened (and sometimes frightening) teachers; not infrequently they are headed by apathetic, frustrated, bureaucratic and sometimes even bigoted principals in systems governed by boards of education that are largely unresponsive to the realities of present-day cities.[26] Low-income children regularly suffer more specific discriminations in school as well, as a consequence of their families' economic circumstances. In New York City, according to one recent study, children in an eighth-grade class were asked to bring $26.50 in "extra money" to school in a 3-month period. In this class, 70 percent of the children came from families on welfare who received 25 cents a month for a junior high school child's extra expenses.[27] Their academic achievements are likely to be substantially lower than those of higher income children; reading skills are particularly undeveloped among poor children, a function of their backgrounds, their schools, and their peer group experience.[28] School failure under these circumstances is hardly surprising.

School failure, meanwhile, is highly correlated with leaving school.[29] The correlation between income and leaving school has also been well documented. Almost half of high school dropouts in 1964 were in families with less than $3,000 income—a proportion that is more than three times higher than that for graduates.[30] We may note also that the correlation between leaving school and juvenile delinquency is very high indeed. Finally it should be noted that school failure is systematically correlated with reading disability.[31]

The most consistent findings in research on poverty, meanwhile, empha-

[26] See, e.g., D. Rogers, "Politics, School, and Integration" (New York: Center for Urban Education, 1967), mimeographed for a well documented analysis of the workings of New York City's educational establishment.

[27] V. F. Haubrich, "Teachers for Big City Schools," in A. H. Passow, ed., *Education in Depressed Areas* (New York: Teachers College Bureau of Publications, 1963), p. 245.

[28] See *Equality of Educational Opportunity* (National Center for Educational Statistics, U.S. Office of Education, 1966). Convenient summaries of this lengthy document may be found in R. A. Zeckhauser, "An Analysis of 'Equality of Educational Opportunity'" (Office of Economic Opportunity, mimeo, 1966; and J. S. Coleman, "Equal Schools or Equal Children," *The Public Interest*, vol. 1, No. 4, Summer 1966, pp. 70–75.

[29] Cf. W. E. Schafer and K. Polk, *Delinquency and the Schools*, a report for the President's Commission on Law Enforcement and Administration of Justice (Washington: U.S. Government Printing Office, August 1966).

[30] See E. Ginzberg, M. Freedman, and I. Berg, "The Hidden Costs of Unemployment," in *Manpower Report of the President and a Report on Manpower Requirements, Resources, Utilization and Training* (Washington: U.S. Government Printing Office, March 1966), p. 59.

[31] Schafer and Polk, *op. cit.* The finding on the implications of reading ability is, of course, both predictable and understandable.

size the significance of opportunities for work, the significance of opportunities for education, and finally the significance of favorable attitudes toward work and the education necessary for their development. These findings obviously reflect the commitments and values of a society in which work is assigned a central place.

But while work—especially in well paid and prestigious occupations—is a cultural ideal and a condition for full-fledged participation in the social system, it is not an objective to which the children of the poor may aspire with much confidence. The facts of their poverty leave them disadvantaged; the perceived irrelevance of education to their parents'[32] occupational aspirations logically raises the question of the meaning of education, especially in slum schools, in relation to work.

It is at this point that the facts of upper class delinquency become relevant, for they clearly indicate that when nonpoor youngsters live in high-delinquency areas,[33] experience substantial neighborhood change, fail in school[34] and fail to see the relevance of education to work,[35] they have delinquency rates that are only slightly lower than those of low-income offspring. The studies from which these conclusions are taken were based on sufficiently large samples to make them more than simply suggestive. Indeed the Reiss-Rhodes study was based on a sample of 9,238 white boys, nearly 10 percent of whom were adjudicated delinquents.

That young people who are failing in school, in upper as well as lower income groups, might see their educations to be irrelevant, even in the face of the oft reported relationship between social reward and educational achievement, is after all not so hard to understand.[36]

.   .   .   .   .

If upper income children with reading problems, related academic underachievement and failure, and pessimistic attitudes concerning work turn to delinquency, we might reasonably expect to find the parallels in data on low-income youths that we have reported. It is worth noting in this context

[32] In this connection we need merely mention, as an illustration, that there are substantial differences between the wages and salaries of whites and nonwhites even when education is held constant.

[33] E. B. Palmore and P. E. Hammond, "Factors in Juvenile Delinquency," *American Sociological Review*, vol. 29, No. 6, December 1964, pp. 848–854; and A. J. Reiss, Jr., and A. L. Rhodes, "The Distribution of Juvenile Delinquency in the Social Class Structure," *American Sociological Review*, vol. 26, No. 5, pp. 720–732. These studies also suggest that low-income youngsters in "good" neighborhoods have low rates of delinquency.

[34] E. B. Palmore and P. E. Hammond, *op. cit.;* Schafer and Polk, *op. cit.*, chapter V.

[35] Schafer and Polk, *op. cit.* See also R. Dreeben, "Big City Dropouts and Illiterates" [a review of R. Dentler and M. E. Warschauer, *Big City Dropouts and Illiterates* (New York: Center for Urban Education, 1966)] in *Harvard Educational Review*, Spring 1967.

[36] Schafer and Polk, *op. cit.* Stinchcombe studied rebellion, not delinquency as such. His study is especially interesting for this reason. While delinquency rates overstate the role of low-income groups, popular discussion undoubtedly overstates the "rebelliousness" of upper-income young people by the omission of data on the "rebelliousness" of low-income youths.

that these parallels exist despite the alleged underreporting of delinquency among upper-income youths. That youngsters with bad academic experiences should contribute so massively to delinquency rates is, of course, to be deplored. There is growing evidence, however, that their attitudes about work and education reflect actual peculiarities of present-day trends in employment rather than an entirely faulty view of American reality. The fact is that educational requirements have been going up faster for most jobs than can be easily justified by the actual requirements for successful performance in these jobs; as long as this is the case it will be difficult to persuade youngsters to stay in schools in which they are failing in order to get jobs for which requirements are constantly increasing. . . . [L]abor market conditions, not job requirements, shape the changing requirements in one not atypical labor market.

It has been argued that changes in the educational achievements required of the labor force are justified (1) by the flexibility that accrues to managers as a consequence of having many people from among whom to select promotable candidates, and (2) by the increases in productivity attributable to education. Since educational requirements have gone up for all jobs, however, including those to which a person with more education than is required for his present job might aspire, the first argument is less than compelling. The second argument, meanwhile, finds no support at all. . . . It is, of course, possible that a small number of very highly educated personnel—scientists, managers, and engineers—may contribute to productivity increases, a possibility that is not considered. . . . [The data do] support the authors' conclusion that there is little, if any, relationship between changes in educational level since 1950 and changes in output per worker.[37]

. . . . .

. . . [T]he character of the supply of labor has been changing dramatically in the two decades 1940–60.[38] The implications of these changes are currently being explored in an extensive study by the writer, in which it is already clear that the costs to employers of work dissatisfaction, absenteeism and turnover among the better educated employees in a given job category are not, by any means, insignificant.[39] The industrial recruiting policies by which dropouts in particular, and the poor in general, suffer are not the blessing they appear to be even to employers.

Delinquents may, indeed, be personally inadequate—even the most con-

---

[37] A. Jaffe and W. Adams, "Educational Attainment and Modern Technology," *The Statistical News*, New York. Chapter of American Statistical Association, vol. 16, No. IV, December 1964, p. 2.

[38] It need not be emphasized that the demand for labor becomes a crucial variable. As the labor market loosens (i.e., supply exceeds demand) educational requirements become a screening device that excludes low-income, lesser educated youths from jobs.

[39] I. Berg, *Educational Requirements for Employment* (New York: Columbia University Graduate School of Business and Columbia Conservation of Human Resources Project, 1967).

strained psychologist can surely find grist for his mill in the "tangled pathology"[40] characteristic of the environment of the bulk of America's poor—but it is obviously not necessary to ignore economic factors in order to allow for such a possibility. The overlap in the experiences, in school and in the labor market, of delinquents from all income and class backgrounds, meanwhile, points to the inevitable conclusion that the economic circumstances of low income groups multiply many times the probabilities that they will contribute disproportionately to delinquency and to crime. The question that remains, then, is whether the policymaker wishes to pursue policies directed at alleviating conditions that account, statistically as well as analytically, for so large a portion of the variance in studies of delinquency.

Delinquents in high-delinquency populations may indeed be the inadequate children of indolent parents, as their critics would have us believe. Their inadequacies are, however, themselves reflections of economic and related social circumstances that determine opportunities, influence motives, help shape attitudes and fix the daily prospects for health and well-being. In America his work is, and has historically been, the activity by which we measure a man and his commitment to his society. Economic circumstances shape the prospects for opening up the way to that commitment as surely as they represent the returns that come from fulfilling it. As inadequate and antisocial as a hubcap thief may be, he can hardly be held responsible for the intergenerational nature of his poverty, his father's geographic mobility, the discrimination he may meet from employers who raise educational requirements or the pitiful condition of many schools in many urban neighborhoods. Neither can he be responsible for the systematic wage inequality between Negroes and whites, in virtually all occupations, if he is a Negro, or for technological changes that make his father's skills obsolete even in a "lily white" factory in New England. The difficulty with even proven cases of "inadequacy" among unemployed and delinquent youths, as explanations of both poverty and crime, is that they are of the order of circumstantial evidence. Here one is tempted to hold with Thoreau, who once said, suspiciously, "Some circumstantial evidence is very strong, as when you find a trout in the milk." The fact that upper-class children meet difficulties to the degree they experience failure in or do not see the relevance of their schooling is not to be carelessly dismissed as evidence of psychological maladjustment.

The conclusion from all the data on the sensitivity of delinquency rates to economic factors must then, inescapably, be that the problem of delinquency is at least theoretically amenable to the interventions of the policy maker. While low-income youngsters do not account for all delinquency, they do account for the majority of the acts that trouble us. The fact that

---

[40] A phrase used in a somewhat misleading (and much debated) analysis of the condition of the American Negro by former Assistant Secretary of State Daniel Moynihan, U.S. Department of Labor, 1965.

youngsters from other income groups who have shared in specific life experiences commonly endured by many poor Americans also become delinquent supports the contention that the analysis in this section holds true despite troublesome biases in data on delinquents. Where middle- and upper-class delinquents do appear in the data, it is possible to account for the fact within the framework of the analysis applied to other income groups.

[*From Ivar Berg, "Economic Factors in Delinquency," in* Task Force Report: Juvenile Delinquency and Youth Crime, *President's Commission on Law Enforcement and Administration of Justice (Washington: U.S. Government Printing Office, 1967), appendix O, pp. 305–315.*]

Affluence and Delinquency

In 1960 a United Nations Congress on "The Prevention of Crime and the Treatment of Offenders" met in London. Delegates from countries on every continent compared notes. The verdict was pessimistic: crime rates were increasing in nearly all countries, especially among adolescents, and rich countries were having as serious problems as poor countries.[41] In 1964 another United Nations Congress met in Stockholm and came to similar conclusions about adolescent crime. Economic growth, though it raised living standards, did not seem to reduce crime rates. Some criminological experts went further: affluence was itself a causal factor in the worsening crime problems of contemporary society.

What did these crime problems consist of? Rape? Murder? Assault? From crime reports in the daily newspapers of the large cities of the world—New York, London, Tokyo—one might think that crimes of violence were rising rapidly and constituted a major component of "the crime problem." In some places this was happening, but it was not a consistent trend. For example, in Scotland and in England and Wales, there was a steep rise in the crime rate between 1927 and 1962 . . . , but in neither country were crimes against the person an important factor. In Great Britain, crimes against the person consisted of less than 5 percent of crime in general. Furthermore, crimes against the person were not increasing faster than all crimes together. In Scotland, crimes against the person rose more slowly. Criminologists who disregarded the selective horror stories of daily newspapers and looked at crime statistics coldly have observed that the crime problem revolved mainly around theft. Insofar as crimes of violence increased, they were

[41] Second United Nations Congress on the Prevention of Crime and the Treatment of Offenders, *Report Prepared by the Secretariat* (New York: Department of Economic and Social Affairs, 1960), pp. 8–18.

mainly crimes like armed robbery rather than rape and murder. This thought may not console the gas station attendant shot during a holdup attempt, but it helps to explain the motivations of people who behave in ways summarized in the unrevealing category, "crime."

.   .   .   .   .

Affluence and Parental Control Over Children

One of the effects of affluence is to increase the life expectancy of everybody in the society, including, of course, parents. This means that a child in a rich industrial society has a far better chance of having both his parents alive and well during his adolescence. Another effect of affluence is to increase the divorce and separation rate. Why? Because industrialization enables women to support themselves—and their children, if need be.[42] Hence marital unhappiness is more likely to result in divorce or separation in rich industrial societies than in poor underdeveloped societies. But the most important effect of affluence on the family is to strip it down to jet-age size (mother, father, and their dependent children) and to isolate it physically and emotionally from other relatives. This is not true of all families even in the United States. And some industrial societies—Japan is a good example—have gone less far in de-emphasizing generational ties than have Sweden, Israel, and the United States. Still, families in industrial societies are characteristically small; they move from community to community as employment opportunities arise; they lack the bulwark of kinship and communal support that poorer societies had.

These effects of affluence on the family help to explain why delinquents come from broken or inadequate families in industrial societies. Broken and inadequate families cause delinquency in rich societies because these societies assign major responsibility to parents for the control of their children. In poorer rural societies, where in addition to their biological parents, neighbors, grandparents, uncles, aunts, and other assorted relatives supervise children, the death or divorce of parents does not lead to juvenile delinquency. In short, a truism of criminologists, that delinquents come from less stable families than nondelinquents, is a truism only for affluent industrial societies. And even for us it is not clear *why* it is true. Two quite different mechanisms have been suggested by experts to explain this relationship between parental inadequacy and juvenile delinquency:

Mechanism 1. Parental rejection and neglect damage the personality of

---

[42] In 1890, women constituted 15.8 percent of the white civilian labor force; in 1957 they constituted 34.1 percent. In 1890, divorced, separated, and widowed women constituted 28.6 percent of working women; in 1957 these categories constituted 40.4 percent of working women. U.S. Bureau of the Census, *Historical Statistics of the United States, Colonial Times to 1957* (Washington: U.S. Government Printing Office, 1960), p. 72.

the developing child. Lack of impulse control results from pathological socialization. The psychopathic or neurotic boy reacts with violence to trivial provocations, sets fires, and steals purposelessly.

Mechanism 2. Parental inadequacy and neglect, by reducing family control, thereby orient the boy toward his agemates in the neighborhood. The family and the peer group are in a sense competing for the allegiance of boys in high-delinquency neighborhoods. If the peer group is delinquent, a boy's desire for acceptance by his peers tempts him to participate in delinquent activities.

Some evidence supports both mechanisms; research is needed to distinguish the more important one. Such clarification would be useful because, if mechanism 1 predominates, juvenile delinquency will probably continue to rise in all urban industrial countries. It is unlikely that most family catastrophes can be prevented. Assuming that the emotional scars resulting from death, divorce, or the mental illness of a parent cause delinquency, then delinquency may be part of the price of living in a rich society. On the other hand, if mechanism 2 predominates, more effective programs of delinquency control can be designed than are available at present. Assuming that the main problem is a breakdown of family control over the child, thereby exposing him to the corrupting influences of the street corner gang, then supportive institutions can be developed to backstop parents.[43]

Supportive institutions may be needed anyway. After all, although "problem" families have less effective control over adolescents than "normal" families in affluent societies, under contemporary conditions all families have weak control over adolescents, especially over boys. This weakness of adult control is most obvious under pathological circumstances such as slum neighborhoods or broken homes. Its ultimate source, however, is not pathology but the increasing social fluidity resulting from the allocation of education, recreation, work, and family life to separate institutional contexts. These changes in social organization affect everyone in contemporary societies, but their impact is especially great on adolescents because adolescence is a period of transition. Youngsters must disengage themselves from the family into which they were born and raised and establish themselves in a new family unit. They must eventually withdraw from the system of formal education and assume an occupational role. While preparing to make these transitions and learning preparatory skills, many adolescents are socially adrift—except for such solidarities as they form with youngsters in the same situation as they. This is one reason for the development of "teenage culture." It is not the whole explanation. The affluence of industrial societies

---

[43] In Sweden, unmarried mothers not only receive allowances for their children. They are visited regularly by social workers who attempt to give some of the guidance that a husband-father might provide. Nevertheless, children from broken families have a higher delinquency rate than children from intact families. The supportive institution is not fully successful.

creates the material basis for an adolescent market. That is to say, adults in the United States, Sweden, Great Britain, the Soviet Union, Israel, and other industrial societies give adolescents substantial discretionary purchasing power, which enables adolescents to demand (and obtain) distinctive clothing, motion pictures, phonograph records, recreational facilities, and eating and drinking places.[44]

Teenage culture helps to ease the transition between the family into which the child was born and the family the young adult will create by marriage. Peers give the adolescent an emotional anchorage, but they constitute an unpredictable influence. Unless adolescents are organized under adult sponsorship, as boy's clubs, Scouts, and church youth groups are, they may mutually encourage one another to engage in a wide variety of unconventional or rebellious behavior. Delinquent gangs represent an antisocial development of adolescent autonomy; they are of course less pleasing to adults than scouting or 4-H clubs. Gang formation is possible in contemporary societies because the institutional structure, in adjusting to the requirements of urban industrial life, has (unintentionally) undermined effective adult supervision of adolescents. Of course, some families maintain better control over adolescents than others; and adolescent girls are generally better supervised than adolescent boys. The very technology of industrial societies emphasizes the independence of the adolescent from parental observation. In the age of the automobile, an adolescent's home may be the place where he sleeps and little else. The car is not the only means of avoiding adult surveillance, but the car symbolizes the looseness of the ties between adults and adolescents because it is such an effective instrument for escaping the eyes of adults.

The increased freedom of adolescents from adult control cannot be revoked. Not only technology but ideology is on the side of youthful independence. Contemporary societies are organized with the unit of participation the individual rather than the family. The child is not a representative of his family in the classroom or in the play group; as an adult he will participate in the economic and political systems as an individual also. This principle of individualism, implicitly embodied in social organization, is explicitly defined (outside of Iron Curtain countries) in the concept of "freedom." Adolescents are jealous of this prerogative. The freedom offered to adolescents is not always used wisely; the freedom to choose is the freedom to make mistakes. Delinquency is one mistake. On the other hand, many adolescents use their period of unsupervised freedom creatively: to establish commitments to educational and occupational goals, to learn how to relate to the opposite sex and, ultimately, to marry and have children. It would be throwing out the baby with the bath water to attempt to establish preindustrial control over adolescents to prevent some of them from using their freedom destructively.

[44] Mark Abrams, *The Teenage Consumer* (London: London Press Exchange, 1960).

Affluence and Education: Countervailing Forces on Delinquency

The new affluence has an important impact on the material aspirations of young people: on the desire for cars, transistor radios, cameras, and clothes. But affluence has also an impact on education. . . . [S]ubstantial proportions of adolescents in industrial countries now remain in school instead of going to work, which was the usual pattern up to a generation ago. Even for the United States, the first country to embark on mass secondary education, the change is recent. . . .

Why does affluence have this effect on educational aspirations? One reason is the increased public support of education made possible by large national incomes. Another is the greater resources of individual families, making it possible for them to forego the financial contributions of working adolescents. Both of these factors make for an increased supply of educational opportunities. Education is a substantial investment, both for society and for the individual family; rich countries can make this investment more easily. The demand for education—as opposed to the supply—depends on the motivation of young people themselves. This has been negatively demonstrated in recent crash programs in slum schools (e.g., the Higher Horizon program in New York) where substantial new resources did not make dramatic improvements in student accomplishments. Research is needed to clarify the conditions under which students are motivated to seek as much education as they can master. It is known that parental encouragement is important. And what if parents are not encouraging? Can teachers and other school personnel make up for this deficit? To some as yet unknown extent, they can.

The potentialities of fostering educational aspirations can perhaps be gauged by an unplanned experiment in the consequences of high aspirations. American children of Japanese, Chinese, and Jewish backgrounds do extraordinarily well in school and go to colleges and universities in disproportionate numbers. They also have extremely low delinquency rates.[45] What is the connection? These same ethnic groups are often considered drivingly ambitious. Do not their educational aspirations reflect this ambition? Japanese, Chinese, and Jewish parents want to insure their children a share in business and professional occupations; education is the means to this end. Being members of minority groups, they are perhaps more keenly aware of the necessity of education for socioeconomic success, but they are motivated in essentially the same way as white Anglo-Saxon Protestants. The connection between higher education and high-income employment is well understood and provides a principal motivation for college attendance.[46]

---

[45] Jackson Toby, "Educational Maladjustment as a Predisposing Factor in Criminal Careers: A Comparative Study of Ethnic Groups," Ph.D. dissertation, Department of Social Relations, Harvard University, 1950.

[46] Jackson Toby, "The American College Student: A Candidate for Socialization," *American Association of University Professors Bulletin*, vol. 43, June 1957, pp. 319–322.

What about Negroes? Unlike the Japanese, Chinese, and Jews, American Negroes show massive educational disadvantage. But recent studies prove that Negro educational retardation does not reflect lack of interest in education. Negro school children, even though they may be performing poorly in the classroom, are as likely as white children to say that they want to go to college.[47] They are less likely to perceive education as feasible for them; hence they are less likely to plan on going and to put in the consistent studying that can make college attendance a reality. In the light of their underutilization of the educational escalator, it is no coincidence that Negro adolescents have a high delinquincy rate. Whereas education is a legitimate opportunity for Japanese adolescents, delinquency constitutes for Negro adolescents a tempting alternative to poverty—what one sociologist has called an "illegitimate opportunity."[48] It would be oversimplifying to maintain (1) that all delinquents are envious and (2) that they would not be delinquent had they realized that education could get them a high standard of living. Some delinquents are not envious. Some envious adolescents are not delinquent. Some adolescents are not willing or able to wait for the economic payoff of education; they share the sentiments of a famous economist who said, "In the long run we are all dead."

Nevertheless, there is fragmentary but consistent evidence from various industrialized countries that the longer a youngster stays in school the smaller are the chances that he will commit crimes.

.   .   .   .   .

But why does educational commitment have this effect? Criminologists do not know for sure. One likely possibility is that youngsters who pursue successful careers at school are consciously doing so in order to enjoy the "good life" as adults. They desire to share in the material rewards of an affluent society, just as delinquents do, but they utilize a legitimate path to socioeconomic advancement. This is probably not the whole explanation. Whatever the initial motivation for desiring success at school—to please concerned parents, to obtain a well-paying job as an adult, to learn— involvement in the school program has consequences for the student's conception of the world. A relatively uneducated delinquent does not know as much about the pleasures an affluent society can offer as a university student. The university student may obtain pleasure out of reading a book, attending a concert or ballet, visiting a museum, appreciating natural beauty, fighting for social justice—as well as out of driving a powerful car, getting "high," and wearing fashionable clothes. Delinquents in affluent societies characteristically desire material pleasures intensely—so much so that they are willing to risk freedom for them—but they are aware only of a

[47] U.S. Office of Education, *Equality of Educational Opportunity* (Washington: U.S. Government Printing Office, 1966).

[48] Richard A. Cloward, "Illegitimate Means, Anomie, and Deviant Behavior," *American Sociological Review*, vol. 24, April 1959, pp. 164–176.

small part of the opportunities for gratification that their societies offer. Furthermore, opportunities they are unaware of are those that are awakened or cultivated by the educational system. These considerations suggest that another reason that education prevents crime is that education broadens the range of desires of young people and stimulates some desires that bear little relation to money income. This is, of course, speculation. Research is needed to establish the precise mechanism whereby educational achievement prevents crime.

Conclusion

Poverty is nothing new. It is affluence that is new. But the relationship between subjective dissatisfaction and objective deprivation is more complicated than was at first thought. Poverty cannot cause crime but resentment of poverty can, and, curiously enough, resentment of poverty is more likely to develop among the relatively deprived of a rich society than among the objectively deprived in a poor society. This is partly because affluent industrial societies are also secular societies; the distribution of goods and services here and now is a more important preoccupation than concern with eternal salvation. It is also because the mass media—to which television has been a recent but important addition—stimulate the desire for a luxurious style of life among all segments of the population. These considerations explain why the sting of socioeconomic deprivation can be greater for the poor in rich societies than for the poor in poor societies. They also throw light on the high crime rates of affluent societies and on the increase of adolescent delinquency rates with the increase in general prosperity. Relative to adults, adolescents feel like a poverty stricken and powerless minority, and how they feel has consequences for how they behave.

The fact that adolescents mostly go to school and adults mostly go to work helps to explain the phenomenon of "teenage culture." It is not the whole explanation. The affluence of industrial societies creates the material basis for cultural differentiation. That is to say, industrial societies allocate to adolescents substantial discretionary purchasing power, and this enables adolescents to demand (and obtain) distinctive clothing, motion pictures, phonograph records, recreational facilities, and eating and drinking establishments. From the viewpoint of understanding delinquency, however, the extension of formal education is probably more important than the development of the adolescent market. The reason for this is that mass formal education has created serious problems of life goals for adolescents with educational disabilities. For academically successful adolescents, school is a bridge between the world of childhood and the world of adulthood. For children unwilling or unable to learn, school is a place where the battle against society is likely to begin.

Orientation to consumption seems to be an increasing characteristic of industrial societies. It permeates most strata, not merely adolescents, and it contributes to other phenomena besides delinquency, e.g., ostentatious expenditures for food, clothing, travel, housing. However, the impact of commercialism is greatest on working class adolescents because the impact on them of the educational system is less positive than for middle class youth. If they leave school as soon as they legally may, they have less opportunity to experience art, literature, serious music, science, religion, and meaningful work, than they have of being attracted to the gadgets and entertainments available in the marketplace. This isolation of school-leaving youths from what are generally conceded to be the accomplishments of industrial civilization may partially account for violent crimes. As Nelson Algren put it in his paraphrase of a literary idea of Richard Wright, "* * * when a crime is committed by a man who has been excluded from civilization, civilization is an accomplice of the crime."[49] Selective exposure to industrial society is not merely an internal problem. Anthropologists have called attention to the selective "diffusion" of culture traits to underdeveloped societies. Trinkets, tools, hard liquor, and Coca Cola are easier to export than arts and sciences or even religion.

H. G. Wells once remarked, "Human history becomes more and more a race between education and catastrophe." Is delinquency a catastrophe? Some might argue that delinquency is a small price to pay for life in a rich society where most people, including adolescents, have the freedom to choose the direction of their destiny. It is true that delinquency is rare in subsistence economies (where there is less to envy) and in totalitarian states (where social controls coerce would-be rebels). On the other hand, crime does cost a society something, not only the losses to victims but also the wasted years of delinquent youths. Most ex-delinquents regard the years spent in raising hell on the streets as well as those in prison as irretrievable mistakes. Mass education can prevent some of this waste. The appeal of education, like adolescent delinquency itself, is stimulated by affluence. But affluence needs reinforcement if youngsters from homes where parents do not value education are to believe that education is for them too. The primary benefit of education is of course intrinsic: the greater realization of the potentialities of young people. But a secondary consequence is to deflect adolescents from the destructive possibilities open to them in a free society. If the experience of American society with its Japanese, Chinese, and Jewish minorities is any precedent, the indirect consequence of educational upgrading will be the reduction of adolescent delinquency. True, these ethnic groups possessed special cultural values favorable to education, which were transmitted to children without planning. However, it seems likely that planned programs of educational upgrading, adequately financed and enthusiastically publicized, could du-

[49] Nelson Algren, "Remembering Richard Wright," *The Nation*, vol. 192, Jan. 28, 1961, p. 85.

plicate the Japanese, Chinese, and Jewish unintended experiments in delinquency prevention. Is it worth a try?

[*From Jackson Toby, "Affluence and Adolescent Crime," in* Task Force Report: Juvenile Delinquency and Youth Crime, *President's Commission on Law Enforcement and Administration of Justice (Washington: U.S. Government Printing Office, 1967), appendix H, pp. 132–144.*]

4. *Delinquency and the family* ·

Much research has been done by sociologists, psychologists, and psychiatrists concerning the relationship between family and delinquency variables, and many theories have been advanced to explain the relationships found. Due to a severe lack of interdisciplinary communication, however, few attempts have been made to consider both the sociological and psychiatric-psychological aspects of the family's role in delinquency. Axelrad (1965)[1] has pointed to this problem and argued that sociologists should include psychological variables in their studies, in order to provide a more complete analysis of delinquency causation. He comments on the limitations sociological studies incur by not considering the psychic motivations toward deviancy, the internal dynamics of the delinquent, and his family relations. In this context, it is interesting to note that most sociological studies of the family and delinquency have dealt with the outward structure of the family—whether or not it is broken, how large it is, etc.—and most psychiatric studies have dealt with the internal mechanisms of family relationships as they have been uncovered in clinical treatment.

In order to present a more integrated picture of theory and research about the family and delinquency, we will first consider the empirical findings relating to family structure and juvenile delinquency, and then discuss the various sociological and psychiatric theories which relate to the data.

Broken Homes and Delinquency

One facet of family structure which has been the subject of many studies is the broken home. Some researchers have found

[1] Sidney Axelrad (1965), "Juvenile Delinquency: A Study of the Relationship Between Psychoanalysis and Sociology," *Smith College Studies in Social Work*, 35:89–109.

Sidney Axelrad and Selma J. Glick (1953), "Application of Glueck Social Prediction Scale to 100 Jewish Delinquent Boys," *Sociological Quarterly*, 30:27–36.

a very high incidence of broken homes among delinquents and have attributed much significance to broken homes as a cause of delinquency. Others
have given less direct emphasis to the importance of broken homes and
have suggested that the broken home may have a differential effect by
variables such as sex, area, or family cohesiveness. The controversy over the
effect of broken homes on delinquency began with a paper published by
Shaw and McKay (1932),[2] in which they concluded from a study of
Chicago school boys and juvenile court cases that only slightly more broken
homes appeared in the delinquent group than in the control group (42
percent : 36 percent) and that the correlation between high delinquency rate
areas and high broken-home rate areas was small. The data they presented
contradicted several earlier studies, especially one by Burt (1925)[3] in London which had found delinquents coming from broken homes twice as often
as nondelinquents.

Shaw and McKay's study was criticized as unrepresentative, since it made
no attempt to discover delinquents in the control group, and refutations of
it soon appeared. A study by Weeks and Smith (1939)[4] in Spokane, Washington, found that 41.4 percent of the delinquents and only 26.7 percent of
the controls came from broken homes; their correlation between delinquency and broken homes by area was considerably higher than Shaw and
McKay's. Eleanor and Sheldon Glueck (1950)[5], in their monumental study
of 500 matched pairs of delinquents and nondelinquents, found 60.4 percent
of the delinquents and 34.2 percent of the nondelinquents with broken
homes in their backgrounds. More recently, Monahan (1957)[6] reported that
delinquents coming from broken homes were more likely to be recidivists
than delinquents from unbroken homes. Browning (1960)[7] found significantly greater numbers of Los Angeles delinquents coming from "disorganized" homes. Slocum and Stone (1963),[8] using the Nye-Short self-report
delinquency technique, found a significant correlation between broken

[2] Clifford R. Shaw and Henry D. McKay (1932), "Are Broken Homes a Causative
Factor in Juvenile Delinquency?" *Social Forces*, 10:514–524.

[3] Cyril Burt, *The Young Delinquent* (London: University of London Press, 1925).

[4] H. Ashley Weeks and Margaret G. Smith (1939), "Juvenile Delinquency and Broken
Homes in Spokane, Washington," *Social Forces*, 18:48–59.

[5] Eleanor T. Glueck (1963), "Toward Further Improving the Identification of Delin-
quents," *Journal of Criminal Law, Criminology and Police Science*, 54:178–180; Sheldon
Glueck and Eleanor T. Glueck, *One Thousand Juvenile Delinquents* (Cambridge, Mass.:
Harvard University Press, 1934); Sheldon Glueck and Eleanor T. Glueck, *Unraveling
Juvenile Delinquency* (New York: Commonwealth Fund, 1950); Sheldon Glueck and
Eleanor T. Glueck, *Predicting Delinquency and Crime* (Cambridge, Mass.: Harvard
University Press, 1960); Sheldon Glueck and Eleanor T. Glueck, *Family Environment
and Delinquency* (Boston: Houghton Mifflin, 1962).

[6] Thomas P. Monahan (1957), "Family Status and the Delinquent Child: A Reap-
praisal and Some New Findings," *Social Forces*, 35:250–258.

[7] Charles J. Browning (1960), "Differential Impact of Family Disorganization on Male
Adolescents," *Social Forces*, 8:37–44.

[8] Walter Slocum and Carol L. Stone (1963), "Family Culture Patterns and Delinquent-Type Behavior," *Marriage and Family Living*, 25:202–208.

homes and delinquent-type behavior. Peterson and Becker (1965)[9] have referred to other studies that have also found a relationship between broken homes and delinquency.

Many researchers, however, have indicated that broken homes have a differential effect upon children—that the delinquency-producing effect is higher for preadolescents than adolescents and for property offenders than authority offenders. Early studies by Barker (1940)[10] and Weeks and Smith (1939)[11] found significant variations in the correlation between delinquency rates and broken home rates among different areas of a community, and there is similar evidence on rural-urban differences in a study by Ferdinand (1964).[12] But the most common observation about the differential effect of the broken home has been that delinquent girls come from broken homes more often than delinquent boys. An early study by Hodgkiss (1933),[13] which repeated Shaw and McKay's Chicago study on delinquency and broken homes using girls instead of boys, found that 66.8 percent of delinquent girls came from broken homes compared to 44.8 percent of the school girls. Hodgkiss' ratio of 1.49 to 1, delinquent girls to school girls, is considerably higher than the ratio computed by Shaw and McKay (1932)[14] for boys, 1.18 to 1. Wattenberg and Saunders (1954),[15] studying Detroit juvenile delinquents, also found a greater percentage of delinquent girls as compared to delinquent boys coming from broken homes. Monahan (1957)[16] reported much the same results for Philadelphia delinquents—55.4 percent of white girls and 74.3 percent of Negro girls coming from broken homes, compared to 32.2 and 57.9 percent of white and Negro boys, respectively.

Jackson Toby (1957b)[17] has reviewed some of the literature on the differential impact of broken homes, and his paper adds a good deal of clarity to the findings. For example, he introduces age as a differential variable in order to explain the apparent discrepancies between the data of Shaw and McKay and others. He points out that while Shaw and McKay found little overall difference between their delinquent group and control

---

[9] Donald R. Peterson and Wesley C. Becker, "Family Interaction and Delinquency," chapter in Herbert C. Quay, ed., *Juvenile Delinquency: Research and Theory* (Princeton, N.J.: D. Van Nostrand, 1965), pp. 36–99.

[10] Gordon H. Barker (1940), "Family Factors in the Ecology of Juvenile Delinquency," *Journal of Criminal Law, Criminology and Police Science*, 30:681–691.

[11] See *supra* note 4.

[12] Theodore N. Ferdinand (1964), "The Offense Patterns and Family Structures of Urban, Village and Rural Delinquents," *Journal of Criminal Law, Criminology and Police Science*, 55:86–93.

[13] Margaret Hodgkiss (1933), "The Influence of Broken Homes and Working Mothers," *Smith College Studies in Social Work*, 3:259–274.

[14] See *supra* note 2.

[15] William W. Wattenberg and Frank Saunders (1954), "Sex Differences Among Juvenile Offenders," *Sociology and Social Research*, 39:24–31.

[16] See *supra* note 6.

[17] Jackson Toby (1957b), "The Differential Impact of Family Disorganization," *American Sociological Review*, 22:505–512; Jackson Toby (1961), "Early Identification and Intensive Treatment of Predelinquents: A Negative View," *Social Work*, vol. 6, No. 3, pp. 3–13.

group in the percentage of broken homes, some differences do show up when controlling for age. The delinquents were considerably older than the control group, and it turns out that at the older age groups there is little difference between delinquents and controls in the rate of broken homes, while in the younger age groups there is a good deal of difference. Toby reasons that well-integrated American families generally have less control over their older, adolescent sons. As a result, family disorganization (broken homes) would have its greatest impact upon younger, preadolescent sons, where the well-integrated family could generally exert greater control. Toby's data lend support to the hypothesis of differential impact with age, and a similar differential effect was observed by Lees and Newson (1954)[18] in their study of British delinquents.

Toby also applies the same reasoning to account for the differential impact of broken homes on boys and girls—in general the family exercises more control over girls, hence they are more affected by a broken home. Toby presents data showing that, as predicted, the impact of broken homes is greater for girls than for adolescent boys, and further, that urban areas and Negroes, assumed to be more characterized by family disorganization, have a disproportionate number of female (and preadolescent) delinquents. But Toby does not have data on types of offenses, and it appears that the relationship between sex and rate of broken homes is eliminated when one controls for type of offense. Weeks (1940),[19] for example, suggested that the differential effect of broken homes on boys and girls was due to their differential distribution according to type of offense—most girls are arrested for ungovernability, running away, and sex offenses, while most boys are arrested for vandalism, theft, and assault. Testing his theory on Spokane, Wash., delinquents, Weeks found that when type of offense is held constant, delinquent boys and girls come from broken homes in nearly the same proportions. Other studies, by Nye (1958),[20] using his self-report delinquency scale, and Ferdinand (1964),[21] using Michigan court data, have also shown that broken home rates vary according to the type of delinquency, being higher for "authority" offenses such as ungovernability and truancy.

Ordinal Position, Family Size, and Delinquency

Another aspect of family structure which has often been related to delinquency is the ordinal position of the child in the family. Lees and

[18] J. P. Lees and L. J. Newson (1954), "Family or Sibship Position and Some Aspects of Juvenile Delinquency," *British Journal of Delinquency*, 5:46–55.
[19] H. Ashley Weeks (1940), "Male and Female Broken Home Rates by Types of Delinquency," *American Sociological Review*, 5:601–609.
[20] F. Ivan Nye, *Family Relationships and Delinquent Behavior* (New York: John Wiley & Sons, 1958); F. Ivan Nye, James F. Short, Jr., and Virgil J. Olson (1958), Socioeconomic Status and Delinquent Behavior," *American Journal of Sociology*, 63:381–389.
[21] See *supra* note 12.

Newson (1954)[22] made an extensive study of the differences among delinquents which could be attributed to sibling position. Their study showed that intermediates—children having both older and younger siblings—were significantly overrepresented in a group of Nottingham, England, delinquents. The explanation they gave for their finding is that the attention parents often give to oldest and youngest children "squeezes" the intermediates out of the family into the gang. Their study has received some support from the findings of both Nye (1958)[23] and the Gluecks (1950).[24] Nye found both youngest and intermediate children overrepresented in his "most delinquent" group. The Gluecks found that 60 percent of their delinquents were intermediate children, compared to only 47.8 percent of their control group. Thus, there would seem to be greater involvement of middle children in delinquent activities.

Family size has also been cited as a factor which can differentiate between delinquents and nondelinquents, with delinquents seen as more likely to come from larger families. The Gluecks' study gave definite evidence of this, finding that there was a significant difference between a mean of 6.85 children in the delinquents' families and 5.90 in the nondelinquents' families. Nye's "most delinquent" boys were also more often from large families, but he found no such relationship for girls.

This differential in the relationship between family size and delinquency is not restricted to sex differences. Several writers have suggested that large families may have a varying relationship to different types of delinquent offenses. Barker and Adams (1963),[25] for example, report a greater incidence of large families in the background of a group of juvenile glue sniffers than in a control group taken from the general population of a Colorado correctional institution. Over 50 percent of the glue sniffers came from families with more than eight children, compared to 18 percent in the control group. Furthermore, a study by Reiss (1952)[26] of delinquents examined by psychiatrists attached to the Cook County Juvenile Court showed that the psychiatric classifications—integrated, weak ego, weak superego—also differentiated the delinquents according to family size. A greater proportion of weak superego delinquents came from large families.

[22] See *supra* note 18.
[23] See *supra* note 20.
[24] See *supra* note 5.
[25] Gordon H. Barker and W. Thomas Adams (1963), "Glue Sniffers," *Sociology and Social Research*, 47:298–310.
[26] Albert J. Reiss, Jr., "Social Correlates of Psychological Types of Delinquency," *American Sociological Review*, 17:710–718; Albert J. Reiss, Jr., and Albert Lewis Rhodes (1961), "The Distribution of Juvenile Delinquency in Social Class Structure," *American Sociological Review*, 26:720–732; Albert J. Reiss, Jr., and Albert Lewis Rhodes (1963), "Status Deprivation and Delinquent Behavior," *Sociological Quarterly*, 4:135–149; Albert J. Reiss, Jr., and Albert Lewis Rhodes (1964), "An Empirical Test of Differential Association Theory," *Journal of Research in Crime and Delinquency*, 1:5–14.

Maternal Deprivation and Delinquency

One aspect of family structure which has received a great deal of attention, especially from psychiatrists, is that of mother separation—the absence of the mother for a prolonged period of time when the child is young. Although mother separation is generally regarded as a cause of mental illness, one British psychiatrist, John Bowlby, has also attempted to demonstrate its connection with juvenile delinquency. Studying a group of thieves and controls chosen from patients at a child guidance center, Bowlby (1952)[27] found significantly more mother separation among all the thieves, and the statistical significance is even more pronounced among those thieves he classified as "affectionless"—children who were unable to enter into a deep affectionate relationship with anyone. Other studies, of course, have also shown the association between maternal deprivation and an inability to enter an affectionate relationship (Goldfarb, 1943).[28]

Bowlby, however, has been criticized by several investigators for putting too much emphasis on a factor which is often outweighed by others in the process of delinquency causation. Naess (1959),[29] for instance, in her detailed commentary on Bowlby's efforts, accepts the relationship between mother separation and mental illness but criticizes Bowlby for generalizing from his limited data on thieves in a psychiatric clinic to his thesis that mother separation is an important cause of juvenile delinquency generally. Furthermore, she presents evidence from a study of Oslo delinquents and their nondelinquent brothers that no such relationship exists. Robert G. Andry (1957, 1962),[30] the most insistent critic of Bowlby's theory, is unhappy with the emphasis Bowlby gives to the part that mother separation plays in the etiology of delinquency, explaining that the role of the father is of at least equal importance. Michael Hakeem (1958)[31] makes a devastating evaluation of Bowlby's study, criticizing it for a lack of scientific sophistication, for generalizing too much from limited data, and for not attempting to eliminate possible diagnostic biases by proper scientific methods.

In addition, Bowlby also theorized that the younger a child was when he was separated from his mother, the more unfortunate were the effects of

[27] John Bowlby, *Maternal Care and Mental Health* (Geneva: World Health Organization, 1952).

[28] W. Goldfarb (1943), "The Effects of Early Institutional Care on Adolescent Personality," *Journal of Experimental Education*, 12:106–129.

[29] Siri Naess (1959), "Mother-Child Separation and Delinquency," *British Journal of Delinquency*, 10:22–35; New York City Youth Board, *Reaching the Fighting Gang* (New York: New York City Youth Board, 1960).

[30] Robert G. Andry (1957), "Faulty Paternal and Maternal-Child Relationships, Affection and Delinquency," *British Journal of Delinquency*, 8:34–38; Robert G. Andry, "Parental Affection and Delinquency," chapter in Marvin E. Wolfgang, Leonard Savitz, and Norman Johnson, eds., *The Sociology of Crime and Delinquency* (New York: John Wiley & Sons, 1962), pp. 342–352.

[31] Michael Hakeem, "A Critique of the Psychiatric Approach," chapter 4 of Joseph S. Roucek, *Juvenile Delinquency* (New York: Philosophical Library, 1958), pp. 79–112.

that separation; but both Nye (1958) and the Gluecks (1950) found that the child's age at the time of the first break in his home bore no relationship to delinquency. Bowlby's theory of maternal deprivation and delinquency therefore lacks strongly supportive evidence. Maternal deprivation may very well be causally related to delinquency but it is not "foremost among the causes of delinquent character development." (1952, p. 34.)[32] Bowlby himself (Bowlby et al., 1956, p. 242)[33] now speaks more cautiously about the consequences of maternal deprivation.

Family Interrelationships, Family Adjustment, and Delinquency

Studies which have focused upon the internal structure of the family have generally shown greater associations with delinquency than studies focusing upon outward structure. This has led Nye to comment, on the basis of his extensive study of juvenile delinquency, that "the structure of the family 'itself' does not cause delinquency." (1958, p. 34.)[34] Similarly, Browning has concluded, after his study of legally and psychologically broken homes in Los Angeles, that the "broken home, as generally defined, is ineffective and probably meaningless as an indicator of family disorganization and other characteristics of family life known to be associated with deviant behavior. It does not include all homes which are sociologically and psychologically broken nor exclude homes which are well integrated." (1960, p. 43.)[35] McCord and McCord (1959)[36] have indeed shown that quarrelsome and negligent homes lead to more delinquency than broken homes. Nevertheless, we must be careful not to discount the possible influence of a factor like broken homes. As Hirschi and Selvin (1966)[37] have ably documented, it may be true that a broken home is not a sufficient cause of delinquency; it may also be true that other variables are more strongly related to delinquency than broken homes; but such reasons do not permit us to conclude that broken homes are not causally related to delinquency. As a result, we must use statements such as those by Nye and Browning to alert us to the fact that variables measuring the quality of family relationships may be more important in the etiology of delinquency than variables measuring the outward structure of the family, and not to conclude that the latter variables are of no causal importance.

One of the most important aspects of family relations, closely related to

---

[32] See *supra* note 27.

[33] John Bowlby, Mary Ainsworth, Mary Boston, and Dina Rosenbluth (1956), "The Effects of Mother-Child Separation: A Follow-Up Study," *British Journal of Medical Psychology*, 29:211–247.

[34] See *supra* note 20.

[35] See *supra* note 7.

[36] William McCord and Joan McCord, with Irving Kenneth Zola, *Origins of Crime* (New York: Columbia University Press, 1959).

[37] Travis Hirschi and Hanan C. Selvin (1966), "False Criteria of Causality in Delinquency Research," *Social Problems*, 13:254–268.

the concept of broken or unbroken homes, is the quality of parental marital adjustment. Browning (1960) dealt with marital adjustment and family solidarity and found that both of these bore a significant relationship to truancy and auto theft, the two types of delinquency he studied. Nye (1958) reported a very strong association between his self-report delinquency scale and the marital happiness of the child's parents. Among boys and girls from "completely happy" homes—23 and 22 percent, respectively, were "most delinquent"; from "unhappy homes"—46 and 49 percent. The Gluecks (1950),[38] in their research, found that significantly more delinquents than nondelinquents had parents with poor conjugal relations (31.2 percent : 14.9 percent). They also found that marked family cohesiveness was present in 61.8 percent of the nondelinquents' homes but in only 16 percent of the delinquents'. Slocum and Stone (1963),[39] in a self-report study of Washington State schoolchildren, report that 52 percent of the "most delinquent" boys called their families uncooperative, compared to 16 percent of the boys in the "conformist" category. The same relationship, although less pronounced, existed for girls. Dentler and Monroe (1961)[40] report that adolescent theft is related to the "quality of interpersonal relations" in the family. Furthermore, Jaffe (1963)[41] found that family "anomie," measured by the amount of disagreement within the family on selected value questions, was correlated with a high score on a "delinquency proneness" scale. In all of these studies, therefore, we find that reported variables such as marital adjustment, family agreement, and family solidarity are significantly related to measures of juvenile delinquency.

Parental Discipline and Delinquent Behavior

Probably even more important a factor than parental marital relations in delinquency causation is the quality of parent-child relations. The consistency, "fairness," and strictness of parental discipline are among the most important family variables related to delinquent behavior. As Peterson and Becker (1965)[42] say, "If one endorses the common assumption that capacities for internal control are complexly but closely related to previously imposed external restraints, then parental discipline assumes focal significance as a factor in delinquency."

In the Slocum and Stone study (1963),[43] reported fairness of discipline was significantly associated with conforming behavior for boys and for girls.

---

[38] See *supra* note 5.
[39] See *supra* note 8.
[40] Robert A. Dentler and Lawrence J. Monroe (1961), "Social Correlates of Early Adolescent Theft," *American Sociological Review*, 26:733–743.
[41] Lester D. Jaffe (1963), "Delinquency Proneness and Family Anomie," *Journal of Criminal Law, Criminology and Police Science*, 54:146–154.
[42] See *supra* note 9.
[43] See *supra* note 8.

Nye (1958)[44] found that of the children in his study who considered their father's discipline "always fair," only 30 percent of the boys and 20 percent of the girls fell into the "most delinquent" category, while of those who felt their father's discipline was unfair, 55 percent of the boys and 44 percent of the girls fell into the "most delinquent" category. Nye also showed that a relationship existed for girls with regard to the strictness of the mother's discipline, with reported strictness being related to less delinquency.

The Gluecks (1950)[45] found that lax and erratic disciplinary techniques identified a higher percentage of delinquents than did overstrict techniques, and that firm but kindly techniques were practiced much more frequently by the parents of the nondelinquents. McCord and McCord (1959),[46] reviewing the information collected by the Cambridge-Somerville project, concluded that consistent discipline by both parents, whether punitive or love oriented, significantly reduced delinquency. Nye (1958) found that 49 percent of both the boys and girls who reported that their mothers "very often" failed to follow through on threatened punishment were in the "most delinquent" category, compared to 30 percent of the boys and 22 percent of the girls who reported that their mother "never" failed to follow through. The overall relationship is significant for girls but not significant for boys.

Exploring the tendencies for parents to use physical punishment rather than reasoning as a disciplinary method, the Gluecks (1950) found that significantly more parents of delinquents than nondelinquents (mothers, 55.6:34.6 percent; fathers, 67.8:34.7 percent) resorted to physical punishment for discipline, while significantly more parents in the control group than in the delinquent group used reasoning (mothers, 28.2:16.4 percent; fathers, 24.4:11.3 percent). Nye (1958), on the other hand, found no relationship between physical punishment and delinquent behavior. He did, however, find a positive relationship between delinquency and love withdrawal as a disciplinary technique, although this relationship seemed to disappear when the adolescents' feelings of acceptance-rejection were taken into consideration. For example, Nye showed that love withdrawal by mothers made no difference among adolescents when one controlled for their feelings of acceptance or rejection. Since many studies have found a relationship between types of discipline and measures of delinquency, Nye's findings are worth noting. It must be remembered, however, that Nye's study also failed to show the usual relationship between delinquency and low socioeconomic status. Furthermore, Kohn (1963)[47] has questioned the association of class with types of punishment.

In short, the data suggest that the consistency of discipline and its fairness are importantly related to nondelinquency. It must be noted, how-

---

[44] See *supra* note 20.
[45] See *supra* note 5.
[46] See *supra* note 36.
[47] Melvin L. Kohn (1963), "Social Class and Parent-Child Relationships: An Interpretation," *American Journal of Sociology*, 68:471–480.

ever, that most of these studies (the report by McCord and McCord, 1959, is a significant exception) are based upon the perception and recollection of delinquents and controls. It is therefore possible that delinquents and controls perceive their parental discipline differently despite similarities in disciplinary techniques; it is also possible that the actual differences in disciplinary techniques are due to the parents' differential responses to delinquent and nondelinquent behavior, such behavior having been triggered by other variables.

A. H. Maslow and R. Diaz-Guerrero (1960),[48] have pointed to another way in which parental roles and the cultural support for discipline may play a part in the etiology of delinquency. Comparing Mexico and the United States, they suggest that delinquency is much more common in the United States (definitive evidence is lacking, however) despite the greater incidence of poverty and family disorganization in Mexico. They attribute this difference to the fact that parental roles within the family, especially the father's role, are clear cut in Mexico but muddled in the United States. Mexican children are brought up understanding quite clearly the differences between "right" and "wrong," and the father's authoritative and disciplinary role, which the mother supports, fosters the development of strong internal controls in the child which reduce his delinquency. The American father, on the other hand, is faced with a larger number of available roles—friendly, authoritarian, democratic, lenient—and he receives less support from his wife in carrying out his role. As a result, there is more role confusion by the father in the United States, and this creates uncertainty in his children about approved and disapproved behavior. This uncertainty about values, Maslow and Diaz-Guerrero assert, plays a major part in the delinquency of United States adolescents.

Affection, Rejection, and Delinquency

A second aspect of parent-child relations which is often associated with juvenile delinquency is a lack of parental affection. The Gluecks (1950) reported that all the affectional patterns of a home—mother-child, father-child, child-parent, and child-child—bore a highly significant relationship to juvenile delinquency. The most important factor, however, seemed to be the father's affection for the boy—40.2 percent of the delinquents but 80.7 percent of the controls had affectionate fathers. Andry (1957)[49] reported a similar finding in his study of London delinquents and schoolboys, with 54 percent of his delinquents but only 7 percent of his controls expressing the opinion that their fathers ought to love them more. Slocum and Stone (1963) found that 52 percent of the boys in their "delinquent" group came

[48] A. H. Maslow and R. Diaz-Guerrero, "Delinquency as a Value Disturbance," chapter in John G. Peatman and Eugene L. Hartley, eds., *Festschrift for Gardner Murphy* (New York: Harper, 1960), pp. 228–240.

[49] See *supra* note 30.

from unaffectionate families, compared to only 18 percent in the "conformist" group. Nye (1958), choosing acceptance-rejection rather than affection as a variable, found a significant positive correlation between the parents' rejection of their child and the child's delinquency. When mutual rejection between mother and child occurred, 48 percent of the group fell into the "most delinquent" category; with mutual acceptance, 14 percent. McCord and McCord (1964)[50] found that the presence of at least one loving parent, coupled with consistent parental discipline, was enough to mitigate the delinquency-producing effect of a criminal father. More generally, they report that both paternal rejection and the absence of maternal warmth were significantly related to delinquency.

The interplay of affection and discipline in parent-child relationships has been cited by Weinberg (1958)[51] as most important in affecting the personality of the child and predisposing him to select delinquent associates and participate in delinquency. He quotes the Gluecks' study for evidence and then says that the parents of delinquents by "indifference or hostility hindered their children from acquiring positive attitudes towards authority." (1958, pp. 126–127.) Clark and Wenninger's self-report study (1964)[52] of Illinois schoolchildren's attitudes toward the law provides indirect evidence for such a supposition. They found that favorable attitudes toward legal institutions were more closely related to adjustment to maternal and paternal discipline than to social class factors.

Furthermore, Nye (1958) found a strong relationship between the child's acceptance of parental values and the affection of the parent for the child. Finally, the longitudinal data reported by McCord and McCord (1964) show an interesting interaction effect between discipline and affection. With two loving parents, the type of discipline used has no effect upon the delinquency of sons; but with one loving parent, erratic or lax discipline produces significantly more delinquency than consistent discipline.

One way in which child-rearing practices are seen to have an influence upon delinquency is through fostering the development of an aggressive personality. Studying a group of aggressive delinquents and their families, and comparing them to a group of nondelinquent controls and their families, Albert Bandura and Richard H. Walters (1958, 1959)[53] found that a higher proportion of the parents of the aggressive boys had denied the boys

[50] Joan McCord and William McCord, "The Effects of Parental Role Model on Criminality," in Ruth Cavin, ed., *Readings in Juvenile Delinquency* (Philadelphia: J. P. Lippincott, 1964).

[51] S. Kirson Weinberg, "Sociological Processes and Factors in Juvenile Delinquency," chapter 5 of Joseph S. Roucek, *Juvenile Delinquency* (New York: Philosophical Library, 1958), pp. 113–132.

[52] John P. Clark and Eugene P. Wenninger (1964), "The Attitude of Juveniles Toward the Legal Institution," *Journal of Criminal Law, Criminology and Police Science* (55:482–489).

[53] Albert Bandura and Richard H. Walters (1958), "Dependency Conflicts in Aggressive Delinquents," *Journal of Social Issues*, 4:52–65; Albert Bandura and Richard H. Walters, *Adolescent Aggression* (New York: Ronald Ress, 1959).

an opportunity to express dependency feelings. Parental punishment of the boys' strivings for dependency gratification, a form of parental rejection, was significantly higher for the group of delinquent boys. Bandura and Walters went on to show that adolescents whose dependency needs had not been met were also less likely to internalize their parents' standards and values. Becker (1964),[54] reviewing the various studies dealing with the personality consequences of different types of child-rearing practices, put Bandura and Walters' findings in a wider context and showed them to be consistent with several other studies.

The importance of affection within the family thus emerges as an important factor in relation to delinquency. The findings of a number of studies point to the significant differences between delinquent and nondelinquent groups in terms of the patterns of affection within the family. In addition, several studies point out that affection is related to the child's internalization of parental values. Assuming that parental values support conventional rather than deviant behavior, it appears that an affectionate parent-child relationship promotes the internalization of conventional values and thus insulates a child against delinquent behavior. Of course, affectionate family patterns may also operate in other ways to reduce delinquent behavior.

Some Psychiatric Theories of Delinquency

The problem of relating the wealth of available data on the association between family variables and juvenile delinquency has been approached theoretically in many ways. Psychiatrists, psychologists, and sociologists have all tried their hand at explaining the connection, with differing degrees of success. We will start our discussion by reviewing several psychiatric theories of delinquency.

One theory, the "superego lacunae" theory put forward by Adelaide M. Johnson (1949),[55] considers only the delinquencies "arising in 'apparently normal families of good reputation' unassociated with the influence of sociologic gangs." She suggests that inconsistent discipline in many middle class families deprives children of an important part of their security (Johnson and Burke, 1955).[56] Furthermore, this inconsistency is often the manner in which parents unconsciously foster delinquency in their children. These children grow up with gaps or lacunae in their superego, and play a scapegoat role in their families—the parents project their own problems

---

[54] Wesley C. Becker, "Consequences of Different Kinds of Parental Discipline," chapter in Martin L. Hoffman and Lois Hoffman, eds., *Review of Child Development Research* (New York: Russell Sage Foundation, 1964), pp. 169–208.

[55] Adelaide M. Johnson, "Sanctions for Superego Lacunae of Adolescents," in K. R. Eissler, ed., *Searchlights on Delinquency* (New York: International Universities Press, 1949), pp. 225–246.

[56] Adelaide M. Johnson and Edmund C. Burke (1955), "Parental Permissiveness and Fostering in Child Rearing and Their Relationships to Juvenile Delinquency," *Proceedings of the Staff Meetings of the Mayo Clinic*, 30:557–565.

onto their child and derive vicarious pleasure from the child's delinquency.

Although the theory may have some validity when it is limited to middle class nongang delinquents, other psychiatrists have extended it almost beyond reason. Ruth S. Eissler (1949),[57] for instance, claimed that not only do the parents of delinquents need and foster delinquency in their children, but also that the whole society needs and fosters such delinquency, as a societal scapegoat. Matza and Sykes (1961)[58] have suggested that many of the values held by delinquents are actually subterranean values held by certain segments of society; but Eissler's extreme position claims that society needs criminal or delinquent scapegoats, that it seduces individuals into delinquent behavior, and that it interferes with programs which promise to prevent delinquency.

Hakeem (1958)[59] has pointed to several weaknesses of the "superego lacunae" theory. He points out that no experimental or predictive studies have tested it and that no scientific evidence has been put forth to support it. It is merely based upon case studies that have been presented by the theorists. Moreover, these case histories usually deal with emotionally disturbed children whose delinquency is a secondary problem.

David Abrahamsen (1949, 1960)[60] has presented another theoretical view of the connection between the family and crime or juvenile delinquency. According to him all delinquents are emotionally disturbed, and their disturbance results from tensions in the family. Although his position has changed somewhat between 1949 and 1960 so that he acknowledges multiple factors in the causation of delinquency and crime, he still stresses deformed character structure as a basic causal factor, whether dealing with individual delinquents or gang delinquents, lower class delinquents or middle class delinquents. There is little evidence to support his position, however. The Gluecks (1950), for instance, found only 36 psychopaths in their group of 500 delinquents. This finding hardly supports the statement, as Abrahamsen (p. 82) suggests it does, that "basically the persistent juvenile delinquent has a deformed character structure." Furthermore, Abrahamsen's own evidence in support of his theory about family tension and emotional disturbance is sketchy and unconvincing. He refers to a comparative study he made of 100 criminals and 100 noncriminals who needed treatment. Using data from psychiatric interviews with the criminals and the controls, along with Rorschach tests administered to 31 criminals and 29 of their family members, he concluded that there was much more family tension in the criminal group than in the control group;

[57] Ruth S. Eissler, "Scapegoats of Society," chapter in K. R. Eissler, ed., *Searchlights on Delinquency* (New York: International Universities Press, 1949), pp. 288–305.

[58] David Matza and Gresham M. Sykes (1961), "Juvenile Delinquency and Subterranean Values," *American Sociological Review*, 26:712–719.

[59] See *supra* note 31.

[60] David Abrahamsen (1949), "Family Tension, Basic Cause of Criminal Behavior," *Journal of Criminal Law, Criminology and Police Science*, 40:330–343; *The Psychology of Crime* (New York: Columbia University Press, 1960).

moreover, he found that criminals always manifested emotional disturbance. Unfortunately, the author worked with knowledge of who was in the delinquent group and control group; he did not attempt to collect similar information from the two groups; and the representativeness of these clinical groups leaves something to be desired. Finally, the author's acknowledgment that some differences between the groups were not easy to detect except through skilled interviewing and interpretation necessarily puts us on guard about the possible operation of subjective bias.

In general it can be said of the psychiatric theories of delinquency that they are based almost entirely on the subjective clinical experience of the theoretician rather than on objective evidence. Furthermore, they probably apply mainly to that small proportion of the delinquent population which can be termed "psychopathic." Estimates differ on the size of this "psychopathic" group, usually depending upon the diagnostic methods and categories used. As examples, the Gluecks (1950) report 7 percent of their delinquents have serious personality disorders while Reiss (1952)[61] reports over 20 percent with some degree of pathology.

Containment and Control Theories

The other set of theories dealing directly with the family and delinquency is sociological in nature, and describes the family's main function as one of control—preventing the child, directly and indirectly, from participating in delinquent acts. Albert J. Reiss, Walter C. Reckless, and F. Ivan Nye are the main proponents of these control theories, but numerous others have also contributed to this line of theoretical development.

Reiss (1951)[62] hypothesized that delinquency is likely to result when personal and social controls break down. He distinguished between delinquent recidivists and nonrecidivists on the basis of various indicators of primary group controls, community and institutional controls, and personal controls. Family's socioeconomic status, parental income, parents' marital status and adjustment, and parental moral ideals and techniques of discipline were used as indicators of primary group controls. The amount of delinquency in the neighborhood, measures of school adjustment, family home ownership, and residential stability were used as indicators of community controls. Finally, psychiatric and casework diagnoses and treatment recommendations were used to classify delinquents as exhibiting either relatively strong ego or superego control, or relatively weak ego or superego control. All of these variables were significantly associated with probation outcome, but the most efficient predictor variables turned out to be the "measures of the adequacy of personal controls of the individual and his

---

[61] See *supra* note 26.
[62] Albert J. Reiss, Jr. (1951), "Delinquency as the Failure of Personal and Social Controls," *American Sociological Review*, 16:196–207.

relation to social controls in terms of the acceptance of or submission to social control" (1951, p. 206).

Nye (1958) proposed a theory quite similar to Reiss' and then tested it, using extensive data from a self-report delinquency study. He suggested that four attitude and behavior patterns are influential in controlling juvenile delinquency: "(1) Direct control imposed from without by means of restriction and punishment, (2) internalized control exercised from within through conscience, (3) indirect control related to affectional identification with parents and other noncriminal persons, and (4) availability of alternative means to goals and values" (1958, p. 5).

Nye differs from Reiss in two important ways. First, he introduces the concept of indirect control, which he defines as the consideration adolescents show their parents or other adults by avoiding activities that would embarrass them. This indirect control is based on an affectional relationship between the adolescent and the adult involved. Nye tested this aspect of control by examining the mutual acceptance-rejection pattern between parents and children. He found an orderly progression from least to most delinquency as the acceptance-rejection matrix went from mutual acceptance to mutual rejection.

Secondly, Nye indicates that adolescents may be motivated toward delinquent behavior because such behavior satisfies certain of their needs. He cites William I. Thomas' list of four needs as good examples of the type that may motivate delinquents: affection, recognition, security, and new experiences. Thus, Nye takes psychological motivations for delinquent behavior into account. In this he differs from most other containment theorists; but he nevertheless does propose that in the absence of controls every child would be "delinquent."

Reckless (1961),[63] in the third edition of *The Crime Problem,* reviewed the work of both Nye (1958) and Reiss (1951), and then, citing work by himself (1956)[64] and by Redl and Wineman (1951),[65] developed his own theory of social and personal control, which he terms "containment theory." He pointed to social disorganization—living in a slum or high-delinquency area or being an immigrant or migrant—as the breakdown of social controls and a cause of delinquency. The absence of effective discipline was an indicator of family disorganization and another form of social control failure. But most of Reckless' emphasis is concerned with the factor of inner control, the development of a child's self-concept and superego. He and various associates have made intensive longitudinal studies of boys in a high-delinquency slum area who do not become delinquent (Dinitz, et al.,

---

[63] Walter C. Reckless, *The Crime Problem* (3d ed., New York: Appleton Century Crofts, 1961).

[64] Walter C. Reckless, Simon Dinitz, and Ellen Murray (1956), "Self Concept as an Insulator Against Delinquency," *American Sociological Review,* 21:744–746.

[65] Fritz Redl and David Wineman, *Children Who Hate* (Glencoe, Ill.: The Free Press, 1951).

1962;[66] Reckless, et al., 1956; Scarpitti, et al., 1960;[67] Simpson, et al., 1960[68]). These boys, chosen by their teachers, were compared over a period of years with a group of delinquents. The "good" boys, Reckless concluded, were marked especially by an excellent self-concept—they evaluated their families favorably; they evaluated their school experiences favorably; and they were confident of their ability to stay out of trouble.

Reckless also showed how the extensive work reported by Redl and Wineman (1951) on ego and superego development fits in with the "inner control" part of his containment theory. An adequate ego and superego, lacking in the young, hyperaggressive delinquents Redl studied, were considered by Redl to be necessary for good behavior control. Reckless suggests that Redl's psychiatric formulation is equivalent to his own formulation of inner control based upon a good self-concept. Thus, Reckless attempted to show that "containment theory" is amenable to certain psychiatric findings about the nature of juvenile delinquency as well as to sociological ones. Furthermore, Ball (1966),[69] after successfully testing Sykes and Matza's (1957)[70] theory of neutralization techniques, suggested that the use neutralization by delinquents is symptomatic of the breakdown of internal controls and, in that sense, is a specific instance of the more general "containment theory."

In line with the comments by Ball (1966) and Matza (1964[71]), it is possible to see most of Matza's theory, developed in *Delinquency and Drift*, as another example of a containment theory. Matza explains that the development of neutralizing techniques, learned in an individual's family or social situation, and derived from a sense of injustice common to the lower class, sets the adolescent free from the normal moral ties to conventional behavior. Once the adolescent is in this uncommitted moral position he may drift into delinquency. The formulation presented by Matza assumes that adolescents will vary in the degree to which they have been able to neutralize the conventional norms so as to be available for delinquent acts. This may account for the differential participation in delinquent gangs and in delinquency which Yablonsky[72] reported in his study of the gang as a near-group. Since neutralization techniques have been learned, neutraliza-

---

[66] Simon Dinitz, Frank R. Scarpitti, and Walter C. Reckless (1962), "Delinquent Vulnerability: A Cross Group and Longitudinal Analysis," *American Sociological Review*, 27:515–517.

[67] Frank Scarpitti, Ellen Murray, Simon Dinitz, and Walter C. Reckless (1960), "The 'Good' Boy in a High Delinquency Area: Four Years Later," *American Sociological Review*, 25:555–558.

[68] John E. Simpson, Simon Dinitz, Barbara Kay, and Walter C. Reckless (1960), "Delinquency Potential of Pre-Adolescents in High-Delinquency Areas," *British Journal of Delinquency*, 10:211–215.

[69] Richard A. Ball, "An Empirical Exploration of Neutralization Theory," paper presented at Ohio Valley Sociological Society Meeting, Dayton, *Criminologica* (1966).

[70] Gresham M. Sykes and David Matza (1957), "Techniques of Neutralization: A Theory of Delinquency," *American Sociological Review*, 22:664–670.

[71] David Matza, *Delinquency and Drift* (New York: John Wiley & Sons, 1964).

[72] Lewis Yablonsky, *The Violent Gang* (New York: Macmillan, 1962).

tion theory is also akin to differential association theory, although the former stresses the essential similarity of delinquent and conventional values while the latter stresses their dissimilarity.

One criticism that has been leveled against social control theories is that they take the potential delinquent to the point where he is relatively free of social and personal control, but that they do not actually lead him into delinquent behavior. As Matza puts it, the potential delinquent may be in drift and not subject to social control, but he need not then engage in delinquent behavior. The actual motivational thrust to delinquency is missing.

Different containment theorists have dealt with this problem in different ways. Nye, aware of this problem, suggested the four wishes of W. I. Thomas as possible examples of the motivational forces leading to delinquency. Reckless does not deal with the problem directly in terms of his containment theory, but rather views his containment theory as a central one within a list of other theoretical approaches, some of which emphasize the inner motivational thrust. Matza resurrects the concept of "will" to provide the element of thrust. According to his formulation, the will to engage in delinquent behavior is activated under two kinds of circumstances: (1) when the adolescent is able to manage both the technical skills and the apprehension associated with a delinquent act; (2) when a sense of desperation, of "being pushed around," heightens the value of a delinquent act—for it can set things in motion and thereby provides the adolescent with a means of demonstrating his potency.

However, there is probably a simpler way of phrasing the problem of motivational thrust. Torgoff (1965),[73] for example, has conceptualized the problem of deviant behavior in terms of the interplay between temptation and control, and this approach provides an answer to the question of motivational thrust that has plagued the social control theorists. According to Torgoff, the situation can be seen in terms of two factors—the strength of the temptations and the strength of the controls. How much of a temptation is the radio in a store window to the adolescent? How strong are the internal and external controls against stealing the radio? Whether or not the adolescent steals the radio is a function of the balance of the forces of temptation and control. The stronger the adolescent's internal moral controls, or the stronger the external social constraints, the less likely is he to succumb to a given level of temptation. Viewed in this way, there is no need to try to bootleg a quantum of motivational thrust into one's control theory; the presence of motivational and control elements can be assumed from the start.

Martin Gold (1963)[74] has also developed a theory of delinquency that is

[73] Irving Torgoff, "Achievement Motivation, Morality, and Conflict: A Study of Italian Working-Class Apprentices," presented at the Society for Research in Child Development meetings, Minneapolis, 1965.

[74] Martin Gold, *Status Forces in Delinquent Boys* (Ann Arbor: University of Michigan Press, 1963).

based upon two forces—control forces that inhibit delinquency, and provoking forces that lead toward delinquency. Controlling forces are conceptualized as stemming from the attractions that adolescents have toward individuals and organizations that support conventional norms. Gold's research has underlined the important role of the family in this connection. Provoking forces are seen in terms of the problem of status deprivation, derived from the work of Cohen (1955)[75]: "Delinquency is an ideal solution for status deprivation problems because * * * delinquent behavior simultaneously repudiates the societal values by which boys are to regard themselves as failures and wins status for boys among peers who share these status problems" (Gold, 1963,[76] p. 182).

One can readily recast Matza's and Nye's analysis to fit Torgoff's or Gold's analysis. For example, Matza's discussion of "will" contains references to temptations based upon internal personality dynamics and external constraints. Jackson Toby's (1957a)[77] formulation is also related. He provided an early statement of social control theory in which the relative ineffectiveness of parental control and community control were singled out as major causes of lower class delinquency. In addition, he referred to the individual's "stake in conformity" to account for individual differences within a community. For example, a youngster who is doing well in school and looking forward to occupational success has a greater stake in conformity—he has more to lose through delinquent behavior. A youngster doing poorly in school and without hope for any kind of occupational success has less to lose, and might therefore be more tempted to gain prestige within a group of delinquent peers.

In addition to the element of inner motivation, social control theories must also handle the related element of situational context. In other words, delinquency arises out of situations that are conducive to it. Briar and Piliavin (1965)[78] have referred to this as "situational inducement" and suggest that it is an important variable in delinquency causation. Case histories presented by Spergel (1964),[79] Short and Strodtbeck (1965),[80] and Karacki and Toby (1962)[81] appear to bear this out. The nature of the

[75] Albert K. Cohen, *Delinquent Boys* (Glencoe, Ill.: The Free Press, 1955).

[76] Martin Gold (1966), "Undetected Delinquent Behavior," *Journal of Research in Crime and Delinquency*, 3:27–46.

[77] Jackson Toby (1957a), "Social Disorganization and Stake in Conformity: Complementary Factors in the Predatory Behavior of Hoodlums," *Journal of Criminal Law, Criminology and Police Science*, 48:12–17.

[78] Scott Briar and Irving Piliavin (1965), "Delinquency, Situational Inducements and Commitments to Conformity," *Social Problems*, 13:35–45.

[79] Irving Spergel, *Racketville, Slumtown, Haulburg* (Chicago: University of Chicago Press, 1964).

[80] James F. Short, Jr. (1960), "Differential Association as a Hypothesis: Problems of Empirical Testing," *Social Problems*, 8:14–25; James F. Short, Jr., and F. Ivan Nye (1957–1958), "Reported Behavior as a Criterion of Deviant Behavior," *Social Problems*, 5:207–213; James F. Short, Jr., and Fred L. Strodtbeck, *Group Process and Gang Delinquency* (Chicago: University of Chicago Press, 1965).

[81] Larry Karacki and Jackson Toby (1962), "The Uncommitted Adolescent: Candidate for Gang Socialization," *Sociological Inquiry*, 32:203–215.

inducement would stem not only from the circumstances of the situation but also from the definition of the situation by the adolescent.

In their critical commentaries on social control theories, Cohen and Short (1958)[82] reject the idea that delinquency is a potential of human nature. Matza (1964)[83] considers the same idea, hesitates, and also rejects it as the answer to the appearance of delinquent behavior. But perhaps the answer to the motivational dilemma of social control theory lies, as suggested above, in a slightly different direction. It is not that "delinquency" is built into human nature; rather, "temptation to commit delinquent acts" is built into the process of interaction between an individual and his environment.

Although there are clearly weaknesses in the various containment or control theories that have been offered, they nevertheless do provide a point of departure for further empirical work. Containment theory, stated very generally, seems to fit a good deal of the empirical evidence of delinquency, and it is unfortunate that the various containment theories have received heretofore relatively little attention compared to other theories on the etiology of delinquency.

. . . . .

_ Social Class, Delinquent Gangs, and Family Variables

The review of research makes it clear that many variables are related to delinquency. Family variables, particularly parental affection and parental discipline, are among the most important variables. It is possible, of course, that the rather clouded multicausal picture which emerges from the research may be cleared somewhat by attention to "types" of delinquency rather than through dealing grossly with "delinquency" as a variable. But much further research remains to be done for this kind of clarification to emerge.

The research carried out by the Gluecks (1950)[84] is among the most important in demonstrating the potential etiological importance of family variables. This research has been criticized, however, for its lack of attention to social and cultural variables. Since their design involved matching delinquents and nondelinquents on social class, they were unable to examine the independent contribution that social class variables might make to delinquency. They concentrated upon personality and family variables.

Nye (1958)[85] has also demonstrated the importance of family variables for delinquent behavior, and he carried this out within a study that did include social class as an independent variable. Since he found that social

---

[82] Albert K. Cohen and James F. Short, Jr. (1958), "Research in Delinquent Subcultures," *Journal of Social Issues,* 14:20–36.

[83] See *supra* note 71.

[84] See *supra* note 5.

[85] See *supra* note 20.

class variables were not related to delinquent behavior—measured from data obtained on self-report questionnaires—his finding that family variables were importantly related to delinquent behavior takes on added weight.

More recently, Gold (1963) has suggested that even Nye's data indicate that there is at least a slight association between social class and delinquent behavior, and Gold also presents his own data to demonstrate such a relationship. At the same time Gold is in agreement with Nye that studies based upon officially adjudicated delinquents exaggerate the relationship between class and delinquency because of the biases operating in police and court procedures. Gold presents data that demonstrate the operation of these biases.

For the most part sociologists and anthropologists have focused upon social class and delinquent gangs as etiological variables, while psychiatrists and psychologists have focused upon family and personality variables. It is curious that the study of the family, which has been primarily pursued by sociologists and anthropologists, should so largely be ignored by them in relation to delinquency. The sociologist has generally viewed delinquency as a kind of normal social functioning, and has therefore looked to differential social class or peer group patterns that might support such behavior. He has not been able to turn to the family because there is little evidence suggesting socialization to, or overt support for, delinquent patterns within the family. The psychiatrist, however, has generally viewed delinquency as a kind of disturbed personality functioning, and has looked to early family relationships for the origins of this disturbance. Neither approach by itself is totally adequate, although each may be most relevant for the explanation of certain types of delinquency. But what is of special interest is the recent work of a number of investigators with a social psychological orientation who have been developing a number of related "control" theories of delinquency. These theories focus upon personal and social controls, and are therefore able to give a central place to family relationships and personality functioning as well as to social class and to peer groups.

Many independent variables have been related to measures of delinquency, but a narrow disciplinary orientation and a lack of methodological sophistication have kept the study of the simultaneous effect of two or more variables to a minimum. For example, it is possible that the presence of at least one "control" variable, whether personal or social, would significantly inhibit delinquency; the presence of additional "control" variables have an additive or a multiplicative effect. Information of this sort could have strong practical implications. But the amount of research that remains to be done on the simultaneous effect of different combinations of independent variables upon different measures of delinquency for different groups is enormous.

One study done with a cohort of schoolboys reports an additive effect between social class status and truancy record (Robbins, 1965)[86]—14 percent of the boys who were not of lower class status and who showed no truancy record were delinquent; 25 percent of the boys with either characteristic were delinquent; and 42 percent of the boys with both were delinquent. School retardation was slightly associated with delinquent behavior, and father's presence or absence was not at all associated with delinquent outcome.

A report by Stanfield (1966)[87] presents some suggestive data on the interaction of several key variables from the Cambridge-Somerville Youth Study. Low social status, erratic or lax discipline by father, and frequent peer activity were all significantly related to delinquency. Examining the combined influence of these variables, taken two at a time, the following interesting interaction effects emerge: (1) Erratic or lax discipline by father is more strongly associated with delinquency in low status than in high status families; (2) frequent peer activity is more strongly associated with delinquency in high status than in low status families; (3) frequent peer activity is more strongly associated with delinquency among those boys where father's discipline is erratic or lax than where it is consistent. Further, in examining the interaction of all three independent variables, it turns out that lower class boys with frequent peer activity who are subjected to consistent discipline by their fathers show a surprisingly low proportion of delinquency. It therefore seems that consistent discipline by the father can offset the influence toward delinquency of low status and high peer activity. Conversely, erratic or lax discipline makes boys of lower status more vulnerable to the influence of a delinquent subculture than boys of higher status.

Palmore and Hammond (1964)[88] also present interesting information on the interaction of variables. Working with a sample of deprived children, they first demonstrated that delinquency was higher for Negroes than whites, for boys than girls, and for those failing at school than for those succeeding. Further, they pointed out the following: "(1) A deviant family background increases Negro, but not white, delinquency. (2) A deviant neighborhood increases male, but not female, delinquency. (3) Either kind of deviant influence increases delinquency more among those failing in school than among those succeeding" (p. 851). Palmore and Hammond point out that these interactive findings lend support to one aspect of the Cloward and Ohlin (1960)[89] delinquency theory on the combined influence

[86] Lee N. Robbins, "Assessing the Contribution of Family Structure, Class, and Peer Groups to Juvenile Delinquency," paper presented at the Fifth International Criminological Congress, Montreal, 1965.

[87] Robert Everett Stanfield (1966), "The Interaction of Family Variables and Gang Variables in the Aetiology of Delinquency," *Social Problems*, 13:411–417.

[88] Erdman B. Palmore and Phillip E. Hammond (1964), "Interacting Factors in Juvenile Delinquency," *American Sociological Review*, 29:848–854.

[89] Richard A. Cloward and Lloyd E. Ohlin, *Delinquency and Opportunity* (Glencoe, Ill.: The Free Press, 1960).

of the lack of legitimate, and the availability of illegitimate, opportunities. They suggest that family deviance or neighborhood deviance are indicators of the opportunity to learn illegitimate behavior; that being Negro, or a boy, or showing school failure are indicators of fewer legitimate opportunities. Hence the greater impact of family deviance or neighborhood deviance upon Negroes, upon boys, and upon those failing at school.

A Paradigm for Delinquency

Based upon the theory and research we have reviewed, the following is offered as a schematic paradigm on the etiology of delinquency, particularly of the adjusted-habitual-gang type of delinquency. Although many references would be appropriate at each step of the paradigm, we shall generally content ourselves with listing only a single reference.

1. *The community's limited ability to provide opportunities to achieve in accordance with middle class values.*—Living in a lower class community—
   (a) lessens legitimate opportunities and lessens the possibility of achievement in accordance with middle class values (Cloward and Ohlin, 1960);
   (b) makes illegitimate or "delinquent" behavior likelier (Merton, 1957);[90]
   (c) makes it likelier that groups or gangs will develop in which there is social support for delinquent behavior (Cohen, 1955);[91]
   (d) leads to a discrepancy between middle class values and actual behavior so that pressure is exerted to modify the middle class values in some way; this may take the form of reaction formation (Cohen, 1955), of neutralization (Sykes and Matza, 1957),[92] of value stretch (Rodman, 1963),[93] or of a completely separate lower class culture in which the middle class values are not taken as a baseline (Miller, 1958).[94]

One result is that groups with modified values, such as delinquent gangs, are likelier to arise in lower class communities.

[90] Robert K. Merton, *Social Theory and Social Structure* (Glencoe, Ill.: The Free Press, 1949), ch. 4, pp. 125–149; rev. and enl. ed. 1957), ch. 5, pp. 161–194.
[91] See *supra* note 75.
[92] See *supra* note 70.
[93] Hyman Rodman (1963), "The Lower-Class Value Stretch," *Social Forces*, 42:205–215; "Illegitimacy in the Caribbean Social Structure: A Reconsideration," *American Sociological Review*, October 1966.
[94] Walter B. Miller (1958), "Lower Class Culture as a Generating Milieu of Gang Delinquency," *Journal of Social Issues*, 14:5–19; Walter B. Miller (1959), "Preventive Work with Street-Corner Groups: Boston Delinquency Project," *Annals*, 322:97–106; Walter B. Miller (1962), "The Impact of a 'Total-Community' Delinquency Control Project," *Social Problems*, 10:168–191; Walter B. Miller (1966), "Violent Crimes in City Gangs," *Annals*, 364:96–112; Walter B. Miller, *City Gangs* (New York: John Wiley & Sons, 1966).

2. *The family's limited ability to maintain external controls.*—Growing up in a lower class family involves—

(a) social, economic, and occupational deprivation (by definition);

(b) lesser attraction for the family, and for one's father, given the emphasis that is placed upon the man's occupational position and earning power (Gold, 1963);[95]

(c) a lower concept of personal and family worth (Reckless, 1961);[96]

(d) a lesser ability of parents—stemming from limited resources which make the manipulation of rewards and punishments more difficult—to maintain external controls over their children, especially in anonymous urban areas (Hylan Lewis, 1965;[97] Sherwood and Sherwood, n.d.);[98]

(e) a lesser degree of attractiveness of community agencies—for example, schools—and therefore their lesser ability to maintain external controls (Toby, 1957a).[99]

One result is that individuals less subject to external controls are likelier to come from lower class families.

3. *The family's limited use of child-rearing techniques that lead to effective internal controls.*—Living in a lower class family involves—

(a) more family disharmony and instability, stemming from the members', and especially the father's, greater difficulty in fulfilling expected roles;

(b) a greater likelihood of lax or inconsistent discipline and of discipline focused upon the child's actions rather than intentions—stemming in part from the constraining situation represented by lower class occupations (Kohn, 1963);[100]

(c) a lesser degree of affection within the family, stemming from the pressures imposed upon the family by the need to adapt to deprived circumstances (Nye, 1958);[101]

(d) a lesser degree of identification with parents or of internalization of parental norms (McCord and McCord, 1959).[102]

One result is that individuals less subject to conventional internal controls are likelier to come from lower class families.

Thus, according to section (1) of the paradigm, the lower class community's limited ability to provide opportunities to achieve in accordance with

[95] See *supra* note 74.

[96] See *supra* note 63.

[97] Hylan Lewis, "Child Rearing Among Low-Income Families," in Louis A. Ferman, Joyce L. Kornbluh, and Alan Haber, eds., *Poverty in America: A Book of Readings* (Ann Arbor: University of Michigan Press, 1965), pp. 342–353.

[98] Clarence C. Sherwood and Sylvia Sherwood (n.d.), "Deviancy and Family Control," mimeograph.

[99] See *supra* note 77.

[100] See *supra* note 47.

[101] See *supra* note 20.

[102] See *supra* note 20.

middle class values makes it more likely that delinquent gangs with modified values will arise. According to section (2), lower class status directly influences the family's (and the community's) transactions with its children because of the lesser degree of attraction it has for them. According to section (3), lower class status indirectly influences the family's transactions with its children because of its influence over the child-rearing techniques that are used. As a result of the low degree of attraction for the family and of the kind of child-rearing techniques used, a greater proportion of children who grow up in lower class families are less subject to conventional personal and family controls. The overall result is that within the lower class community there are more individuals who frequently interact in gangs, who behave in ways that do not accord with evaluated middle class values, and who have modified the middle class values so that the gang provides support and status for its members.

What we have covered in the above paradigm centers specifically upon lower class families, lower class communities, lower class gangs, and lower class delinquency. It helps us to understand the higher rate of delinquency within the lower class. But it does not specifically address itself to variations within the lower class. It is only by inferring the differential availabilities of opportunities within the lower class, or the differential attractiveness of families or of affection within parent-child relationships, that we can begin to deal with such variations.

The above paradigm also does not address itself directly to middle class delinquency. Gold (1963) has suggested that some of the same factors that lead to lower class delinquency also account for middle class delinquency; this would principally involve the child-rearing variables listed in section (3), although such matters as lax discipline or low affection within middle class families would presumably stem from something other than deprived circumstances.

The paradigm, of course, is highly tentative, and is merely presented as a way of coordinating some of the theories and data we have reviewed. As additional data and theoretical interpretations are made available, modifications will become necessary, and these . . . [may] be in the direction of turning the loosely organized paradigm into a more tightly conceived theoretical structure.

. . . . .

[*From Hyman Rodman and Paul Grams, "Juvenile Delinquency and the Family: A Review and Discussion,"* in Task Force Report: Juvenile Delinquency and Youth Crime, *President's Commission on Law Enforcement and Administration of Justice* (Washington: U.S. Government Printing Office, 1967), *appendix L, pp. 195–202, 209–211, 218–219.*]

5   Delinquency and the schools

In considering changes in social conditions that will prevent and reduce delinquency, we are immediately faced with this question: What existing conditions around certain youth heighten their attraction to delinquency? Most who have studied the problem agree that commitment to illegitimate rather than legitimate patterns of behavior results from a multitude of conditions and forces: defective families, overcrowded housing, adult criminal influences, access to automobiles, poverty and lack of economic opportunity, decline of influence of the church, and many others. Most also agree that anything approaching complete elimination of delinquency rests on major social changes at each of these and other points.

At the same time, available evidence strongly suggests that delinquent commitments result in part from adverse or negative school experiences of some youth, and, further, that there are fundamental defects within the educational system, especially as it touches lower income youth, that actively contribute to these negative experiences, thereby increasing rather than decreasing the chances that some youth will choose the illegitimate alternative. Despite the fact that the schools are meant to be the major agency for promoting progress along legitimate avenues to adulthood, prevailing conditions in education deter such progress for some youth and make the delinquent alternative more attractive. Evidence also suggests that because of its central and strategic place in the lives of youth, the school has the potential to at least partly off-set or neutralize pressures toward delinquency set in motion by noneducational forces in the family and community, but that this potential is not now being realized.

If these positions are valid, then major educational changes are crucial for large-scale and effective prevention and reduction of delinquency. Because of the size of the present problem, such changes must be aimed at reducing law violations among currently delinquent and predelinquent youth; but, at the same time, large-scale prevention calls for broad educational changes that will reduce pressures toward delinquency in the first place.

We believe that unless these underlying educational conditions that help produce delinquency are altered, efforts to deal with particular delinquent or delinquency-prone youth will have little effect in the long run.

. . . . .

Juvenile Delinquency and Shortcomings in Education

We believe that the public schools are not adequately fulfilling these responsibilities, one result of which is heightened delinquency. It hardly need be said that this is a period of extremely rapid change in noneducational areas of American life. We have already seen that technological and economic shifts have resulted in a changed occupational structure and new manpower demands. Moreover, past decades have seen major shifts in the American population. More and more families have moved off the farm, many of them resettling in metropolitan areas. Expansion has not been uniform within those areas, however, as urban fringes have experienced rapid growth, while central cities have remained stable in size or have actually declined. Nor has the distribution of economic and racial groups within large cities remained stable. Rather, central cities have increasingly come to be made up of lower income and non-white families, at the same time that suburbs have remained or become predominantly white, middle class. Accompanying these economic, social, and population changes has been a reawakening in this country in regard to equal educational and economic opportunity.

These changes, as well as others, have combined to place new demands on the educational system and have called for major adaptations by the public schools. It is our contention that, although there is a stir in the air, the schools—and the public that supports them—have largely failed to respond, resulting in serious lags between the educational system and other parts of the society. As a step toward identifying the particular linkages between these institutional shortcomings and delinquency, we will briefly review several sociological theories of delinquency in the next section.

. . . . .

The School Career and Delinquency

In order to understand how the shortcomings of public education suggested earlier get translated into heightened delinquency, we must seek to answer the following questions. . . . According to best evidence, what school experiences contribute to delinquency? What conditions and practices in the schools contribute to those predelinquent experiences or directly to delinquency? In this section we will review available evidence pertaining to the first question.

. . . . .

Accumulation of Educational Failure,
Combined with a Desire for Success

Considerable research shows that most children and youth are exposed to strong pressures to seek after middle or high ranking occupations and to obtain at least a high school if not a college education as a means to that end. Moreover, most parents place considerable importance on their children obtaining middle or high levels of academic achievement.

Widespread stress among parents on educational attainment has been reported in numerous studies in the past, as well as in the recently released national study of *Equality of Educational Opportunity*, which was commissioned by Congress in the Civil Rights Act of 1964, and was directed by James S. Coleman in conjunction with the U.S. Office of Education. This study of over 645,000 students found that in general parents were . . . "highly interested in their (childrens') educational success . . ."[1]

Although there are differences in the degree to which education is stressed by parents, several studies show that even most lower status and minority groups parents place a high value on school achievement for their children. Reissman reported, for instance, that when

> . . . interviewees were asked the question, "what do you miss most in life that you would like your children to have," over 50 percent of the white lower socioeconomic group (and 70 percent of the Negro group) said "education." Even more significant is the fact that the respondents supplied the word education: they did not select it from a list of possible choices provided by the interviewer . . . This would seem to mean that education, at some level, not only is important to this group but also is in the forefront of their minds.[2]

More recently, Cloward and Jones reported that in a study in the Lower East Side of Manhattan, as many parents from the "lower" as from the "middle" class said education came to mind when thinking of the good life for their sons or daughters.[3] In fact, more from the in-between "working" class than from the "middle" class gave this response. Finally, the Coleman Report found that, according to student responses, nonwhite parents placed just as much emphasis as white parents on educational attainment.[4] At the secondary level, in fact, higher percentages of nonwhite than white fathers wanted their children "to be one of the best students in the class." These

---

[1] James S. Coleman and others, *Equality of Educational Opportunity* (Washington: U.S. Government Printing Office, 1966), p. 192. In subsequent references, we will refer to this document as the Coleman Report.

[2] Frank Reissman, *The Culturally Deprived Child* (New York: Harper and Row, Publishers, 1962), p. 10.

[3] Richard A. Cloward and James A. Jones, "Social Class: Educational Attitudes and Participation," in A. Harry Passow, editor, *Education in Depressed Areas* (New York: Teachers College Press, Columbia University, 1963), p. 203.

[4] *Coleman Report, op. cit.,* p. 192.

and other studies, then, suggest the conclusion that educational attainment and success are stressed to a considerable extent by most parents, whatever their economic position or race.

Parental emphasis on education is continually enforced and supplemented by the mass media and, to an even greater extent, by the schools themselves. When all of these influences are combined, there is little doubt that most children and youth live in a world in which educational success and attainment are strongly stressed and that, while there are differences in degree, this is true of the slum as well as the suburb.

Of even greater importance is that this emphasis is learned by most youngsters, regardless of social or economic background. For example, in a study of Michigan students, Vinter and Sarri found that almost all the youngsters placed a high value on passing courses.[5]

Similarly, in a study of Los Angeles area high school students, Ralph Turner found that all boys and girls in his sample aspired to at least finish high school and 85 percent of the boys and 75 percent of the girls hoped to acquire some post–high school training.[6] Albert J. Reiss, Jr., after studying all youth enrolled in junior and senior high schools in and around Nashville, Tennessee, concluded, "adolescents on the whole accept the success goals of education in our society."[7] His research showed that not all youth accept educational goals to the same degree but, contrary to usual belief, Negro and lower income students place a higher value on education than do white and higher income pupils.[8] Finally, the Coleman Report also found that when asked the question, "If something happened and you had to stop school now, how would you feel," 81 percent of the sample said they would "try hard to continue" (36 percent) or would "do anything to stay in school" (45 percent).[9] Negroes gave these responses just as often as whites and, in fact, reported more often than whites that they wanted to be "one of the best students in the class."[10]

At the same time that most students are exposed to outside pressures to achieve and place a high personal interest on school themselves, not all of them succeed in meeting school standards of performance and progress. For reasons that will be discussed later in the paper, lower income and non-white students are most often unsuccessful in school, whether the indicator

[5] Robert D. Vinter and Rosemary C. Sarri, "Malperformance in the Public School: A Group Work Approach," *Social Work*, Vol. 10 (January 1965), pp. 3–13.

[6] Ralph Turner, *The Social Context of Ambition* (San Francisco: Chandler Publishing Company, 1964), p. 43.

[7] Albert J. Reiss, Jr., and Albert Lewis Rhodes, *A Sociopsychological Study of Adolescent Conformity and Deviation* (United States Office of Education, Co-operative Research Project Number 507, 1959); also see Reiss and Rhodes, "Are Educational Norms and Goals of Conforming, Truant, and Delinquent Adolescents Influenced by Group Position in American Society?" *Journal of Negro Education*, XXXVII, Summer 1959, pp. 252–267.

[8] *A Sociopsychological Study, ibid.*

[9] *Coleman Report, op. cit.*, p. 278.

[10] *Ibid*, p. 278.

of failure is achievement test performance, academic grades, nonpromotion, or dropping out of school. For example, Sexton found in "Big City" that almost one-third larger proportion of high school students in the lowest income schools than from the highest failed one or more subjects.[11] She also reported that in the eighth grade the highest income schools were on the average two full years ahead of the lowest in achievement test scores.[12] Finally, she found dropout rates six times greater in the lowest than the highest income schools.[13] A similar pattern was reported for nonpromotions.[14]

Schafer found similar differences in two Michigan high schools. For example, he reported that 35 percent of working class students were in the bottom quartile of their graduating class in academic achievement, while the comparable middle class figure was 15 percent.[15] In addition, middle class students dropped out only one-fourth as often as working class students.[16] Differences in reading test scores were just as striking.[17] Finally, Reiss found that in his Nashville sample, over twice as many low status students received a D or E in English, while in an Oregon study of high school students, Polk and Halferty found that over five times as many blue collar than white collar boys received a modal grade of D or F.[18] Hollingshead, Abrahamson, Havighurst and many others have reported similar findings for many different types of schools and communities.[19]

Similar differences have been reported between whites and nonwhites. In the New York City schools, for example, Puerto Rican and Negro elementary children were considerably lower than white pupils in reading test scores.[20] The Coleman Report describes similar patterns on a national scale with respect to tests of verbal ability, nonverbal ability, reading comprehension, mathematics, and general information.[21]

[11] Patrica C. Sexton, *Education and Income* (New York: The Viking Press, 1966), p. 163.

[12] *Ibid.*, p. 28.

[13] *Ibid.*, p. 201.

[14] *Ibid.*, p. 54.

[15] Walter E. Schafer, "Student Careers in Two Public High Schools: A Comparative Cohort Analysis" (unpublished doctoral dissertation, University of Michigan, 1965), p. 88.

[16] *Ibid.*, p. 179.

[17] *Ibid.*, p. 68.

[18] Reiss and Rhodes, see *supra* note 7; Kenneth Polk and Daniel Halferty, "Adolescence, Commitment and Delinquency," *Journal of Research in Crime and Delinquency,* July 1966, pp. 82–96.

[19] A. B. Hollingshead, *Elmtown's Youth* (New York: John Wiley & Sons, 1949), p. 172; Stephan Abrahamson, "Our Status System and Scholastic Rewards," *Journal of Educational Psychology,* 25 No. 8, April 1952; Robert J. Havighurst, Paul Hoover Bowman, Gordon P. Liddle, Charles V. Matthews, and James V. Pierce, *Growing Up in River City* (New York: John Wiley & Sons, 1962), p. 38.

[20] Miriam L. Goldberg, "Schools in Depressed Areas," in Passow, p. 83; *Youth in the Ghetto* (New York: Harlem Youth Opportunities Unlimited, Incorporated, 1964), pp. 189–195.

[21] *Coleman Report, op. cit.,* p. 219.

As we will see later, a very important feature of achievement differences between pupils from varying economic and social backgrounds is that the gaps increase over time, as lower income and nonwhite pupils fall progressively farther beyond.

Educational failure, whether experienced by lower or higher income pupils or by whites or nonwhites, often begins early, then builds up and accumulates, setting into motion a series of reactions both among others and within the student himself that sometimes leads to delinquency. Perhaps the most important consequence of failure is the reactions of others.

> In the eyes of the school and the outside world the pupil who receives certain 'low marks' is regarded as a failure and treated accordingly, regardless of whatever other assets he may have or whatever satisfactory growth he may achieve in his other activities.[22]

The effect of these reactions was graphically described to the authors by one of several former delinquents we recently interviewed who had dropped out of school in a major Eastern city, but are now employed as community workers in the Poverty Program.[23]

> (What would the school make him feel like before he dropped out? Would it make him feel like something or would it make him feel differently?) That would depend on how his standing is in that school. If he's intelligent, he has his standing, he wants to go along with the school. The school's going to put his name up on the board and say—"honor roll student" and things like that. Teachers come by and look at him—"he made the honor roll." If he's got low standing and every teacher every time they see him say, "Get out of here," and "I don't want you in my class" and things like that, he's going to come on out (drop out).

Students who fail are not only likely to be perceived and defined as "failures," "slow learners," or "goof-offs," but there are likely to be more objective negative consequences as well, both among peers and teachers. Vinter and Sarri recently reported, for instance, that:

> Those who performed below a certain standard received adverse grades and might *also* be denied, as a direct consequence, a wide variety of privileges and opportunities within the school. They lost

[22] William C. Kvaraceus, *Juvenile Delinquency and the School* (New York: World Book Company, 1945), p. 140.

[23] We wish to thank Mr. Karl Gudenberg of the United Planning Organization of Washington, D.C., Mrs. Terry Alt of the United States Office of Education, and Mr. Martin Timin of the National Crime Commission staff for arranging and participating in the group interviews from which the following quotation is taken. Above all, we owe a great debt to the members of Rebels with a Cause from Washington, who participated in the interviews. Uncited quotations throughout the rest of this paper are from these interviews.

esteem among their classmates, they were seldom chosen for minor but prestigeful classroom or school assignments, and they were excluded from participation in certain extra-curricular activities. This process, in turn, often subjected such students to negative parental responses, representing a third penalty.[24]

In addition, students who fail may be assigned to a special track or classroom for "slow learners," usually resulting in decreased expectations and attention, not increased educational service.

These findings, which have been closely paralleled by those of Polk in the study of Oregon pupils,[25] clearly suggest that as a result of being negatively perceived and evaluated, students who fail tend to be progressively shunned and excluded by other achieving students, by individual teachers, and by the "system as a whole." Partly as a result of the internal frustrations generated by blocked goal attainment and partly as a result of the stigma which others tend to attach to educational failure, failing students' own assessment of themselves, their place in the world, and their future tend to progressively deteriorate and, understandably, the school experience becomes highly unsatisfying, frustrating, and bitter. The frequent result, as reported by Polk, Vinter and Sarri, Gold, and others, is an increase in negative attitudes toward school performance, rules, and activities; devaluation of the importance of education; and turning toward other youths who have also failed.[26] The consequence, in turn, is often the collective substitution or acceptance of alternative standards of conduct that are more easily reached.

Commitment to these new standards or norms often produces behavior that immediately is far more rewarding and satisfying, but that sometimes violates community laws and comes to be defined as delinquent. Such behavior may represent an attack, through some such psychological process as reaction-formation, on the system that labeled them as "failures"; or it may simply be conformity to new standards that are illegitimate or delinquent but that to delinquents themselves do not represent a direct attack against the school or the middle class community.

Miriam Goldberg has clearly summarized these connections between educational failure and delinquency, especially among disadvantaged projects, as follows:

> Early difficulty in mastering the basic intellectual skills which the schools and thus the broader society demand leads to defeat and failure, a developing negative self-image, rebellion against the increasingly defeating school experiences, a search for status outside the school together with an active resentment against the society

[24] Vinter and Sarri, *op. cit.*, p. 9.

[25] Kenneth Polk and Lynn Richmond, "Those That Fail," unpublished paper (Lane County Youth Project, Eugene, Oregon, 1966).

[26] Vinter and Sarri, *op. cit.*; Polk and Richmond, *ibid.*; Martin Gold, *Status Forces in Delinquent Behavior* (Ann Arbor: University of Michigan, 1963).

which the school represents. The child early finds status and protection in the street and the gang which requires none of the skills which are needed in school but makes heavy use of the kinds of survival skills which he learned in his early home and street experiences.[27]

While there are relatively few studies that trace these social and psychological processes through time, there is considerable evidence that failure and delinquency are associated. In a study of delinquents and nondelinquents in Flint, for example, Gold found no difference between the two groups in concern about future jobs and belief in the importance of education for future opportunities.[28] Despite this, and the additional fact that delinquents and nondelinquents were matched to within ten points on measured intelligence, delinquents had significantly lower grade point averages than nondelinquents prior to first police contact, as well as more negative attitudes toward school.[29] Short also found an association of poor "educational adaptation" with delinquency in a study of Chicago gangs.[30] Regardless of educational aspirations or occupational level of parents, both Negro and white youth who were unsuccessful in school had higher delinquent rates than those who were successful. Short points out, however, that delinquency did not represent a total rejection of legitimate standards of school and community and a total commitment to the illegitimate alternative, but rather was an on-again, off-again pattern at the same time that a basic commitment to education and the "legitimate system" was retained.[31]

In an earlier investigation, Kvaraceus found that a disproportionate number of delinquents in his New Jersey sample received failing or inferior grades in comparison with nondelinquent youth in the same community.[32] Similarly, Toby and Toby state that:

> . . . the kind of school status that was most strongly related to delinquent outcomes was intellectual status—whether measured by teacher placement in bright or slow classes, by academic grades, or by student votes as the "smartest, most intelligent boy in the grade."[33]

Finally, Polk found that boys from white-collar homes had five times a greater chance of becoming delinquent than those who did not fail, while boys from blue-collar backgrounds who failed were delinquent almost seven times more often than those who did not fail.[34]

[27] Goldberg, in Passow, *op. cit.*, p. 87. Reprinted with permission of the publisher (Teachers College, Columbia University, 1963).

[28] Gold, *op. cit.*, pp. 154, 161.

[29] *Ibid.*, p. 163.

[30] James F. Short, Jr., "Gang Delinquency and Anomie," in Marshall B. Clinard, ed., *Anomie and Deviant Behavior* (New York: Free Press, 1964), p. 107.

[31] *Ibid.*, p. 115.

[32] Kvaraceus, *op. cit.*, p. 141.

[33] Jackson Toby and Marcia Toby, "Low School Status as a Predisposing Factor in Subcultural Delinquency" (United States Office of Education, Cooperative Research Project, No. 526, 1961).

[34] Polk and Richmond, *op. cit.*

Cooper has clearly summed up the literature on educational attainment and delinquency as follows:

> The educational status of offenders is inferior on the whole to that of the general population, tending to be slightly inferior in respect to illiteracy, somewhat inferior in respect to amount of schooling, decidedly inferior in repeat and school progress, and clearly inferior in respect to educational achievement.[35]

The evidence suggests, then, that educational failure is one experience, especially when combined with a desire for success, that contributes to delinquency. While such failure has been shown to relate to delinquency regardless of family status there are at least two reasons why lower income youth are especially susceptible to this influence toward illegitimate behavior. First, they fail more often, as noted earlier; and, second, students from higher status backgrounds who fail are likely to be "held into" the legitimate system by greater pressures from parents and achieving peers and by less accessibility to delinquent or criminal subcultures.

These questions immediately arise from these findings and arguments: How might the school itself contribute to this deepening cycle of failure, alienation, and delinquency? What educational changes can be made that will prevent the cycle from starting and, if started, from culminating in delinquency? As we will see in greater detail below, there are at least two major ways in which the school inadvertently contributes to delinquency insofar as it results from this set of experiences. First, certain conditions and practices, especially as they affect lower status and nonwhite pupils, tend to contribute directly to educational failure. Therefore, identification and change of those conditions and practices are likely to help prevent delinquency. Second, certain current patterns of school responses to failure increase rather than decrease the chances that delinquency will result. As suggested above, there is evidence that the sanctioning system often tends to push away, exclude, and lower involvement and interest of the student in education, rather than to "rescue," or upgrade instruction and involvement. Thus, changes in some of the ways the school reacts to failing students are also likely to prevent and reduce delinquency.

Perceived Irrelevancy of Education

A second school experience that is often associated with delinquency is the sense that education is fundamentally irrelevant to later life. Because school tasks, demands, and rewards are seen as having no payoff in the future, the school career becomes meaningless and empty. As a result, the illegitimate alternative becomes increasingly attractive and delinquency sometimes results.

[35] Clara Chassell Cooper, *A Comparative Study of Delinquents and Non-Delinquents* (Portsmouth, Ohio: The Psychological Service Center Press, 1960), p. 207.

Among some youth this experience is closely tied to educational failure. If they are not achieving, it is only reasonable to expect that their perceptions of future occupational payoff will be highly pessimistic, not only because anything but low status, low paying jobs require at the least a good high school record and a diploma, and at the most college training, but also because most students know this. Thus, Gold reported that the higher a boy's academic achievement, the better he saw his chances for getting the job he wanted, except for white collar delinquents, whose aspirations and expectations were probably bolstered by peer and parental pressures.[36] Similarly, Vinter and Sarri and Polk both noted that low achieving students who became delinquents tended to give negative assessment of later job chances.[37]

At the same time there is evidence that the relationship between perceived irrelevancy and educational failure is sometimes reversed. That is, educational failure sometimes results from the belief that there will be no real rewards after high school, regardless of current efforts or attainment. In the words of Arthur Pearl, ". . . growing failure may be also in part due to a growing recognition that there is no payoff in the system for them."[38] In addition, there is evidence that perceived irrelevancy of education exerts an independent influence on delinquency. Main support for this position comes from a study of California high school students by Arthur Stinchcombe.[39] He found that students who were not taking college preparatory work tended to believe that regardless of their present efforts or achievement, the system was not going to come through with anything but low status, low paying jobs after high school.[40] As a result, present tasks and demands of the school had little meaning or payoff. Thus, perceived prospects for future occupational status was found to be a far more important determinant of "rebellion" than social or economic origin.[41]

. . . . .

While Stinchcombe's study is probably the most definitive in supporting the linkage between perceived irrelevancy and delinquency, there are others that also suggest the same conclusion. For example, Short found that poor "articulation between school experience and future orientation" was associated with high rates of delinquency.[42] Similarly, Polk found that delinquency was greater among noncollege bound than college bound students, even when grades were the same.[43]

More indirect evidence is contained in a number of studies which show

[36] Gold, *op. cit.*, p. 213.
[37] Vinter and Sarri, *op. cit.*; Polk and Richmond, *op. cit.*
[38] Arthur Pearl, "Youth in Lower Class Settings," in Muzafer Sherif and Carolyn W. Sherif, eds., *Problems of Youth* (Chicago: Aldine Publishing Co., 1965), p. 95.
[39] Arthur L. Stinchcombe, *Rebellion in a High School* (Chicago: Quadrangle Books, 1964), p. 70.
[40] *Ibid.*, p. 70.
[41] *Ibid.*, p. 5.
[42] Short, *op. cit.*, p. 114.
[43] Kenneth Polk, unpublished data (Lane County Youth Project, Eugene, Oregon, 1966).

that the greater the extent to which youth perceive future opportunities as closed, the greater the delinquency. Short, for example, also reported that delinquents saw educational and occupational opportunities as more limited than nondelinquents, while Polk found that perception of limited opportunity in the local community and in the system in general were associated with high delinquency rates.[44] Finally, Elliott reported that "delinquents (from both lower and middle status) quite uniformly perceive lower opportunities to achieve success goals than nondelinquents."[45] We suggest that these wider patterns of perceived lack of opportunities partly reflect the lack of connection seen between the current school career and later outcomes.

It seems likely, then, that perceived irrelevancy of education for the future is one of the factors contributing to delinquency, at times independently of low achievement, especially among the non–college bound and among nonwhite and lower income students who live in slums, since their chances of going to college or obtaining a good job as a result of striving or succeeding are remote. We suggest that perceived irrelevancy may partly account for the finding of the Coleman Report that considerably higher proportions of metropolitan Negroes (most of whom live in ghettos) than metropolitan whites agree with the statement, "Every time I try to get ahead, something or somebody stops me."[46] As a Washington, D.C. dropout put it, "all you have to do is look around at your older friends and brothers, your dad, and your neighbors to know it doesn't make any difference."

At the same time, Stinchcombe's evidence shows that some higher status students take noncollege preparatory work, perceive a lack of payoff, and turn to delinquency as an alternative. This form of "blocked goal attainment," then, sometimes contributes to middle class delinquency as well.

Here, too, the evidence and arguments generate questions about the role of the school in contributing to and preventing delinquency. In his conclusion, Stinchcombe leaves little doubt that the emptiness that some students feel in relation to the school experience is largely based on an accurate assessment of the way the noncollege bound curriculum links up with the job market.[47] He contends that rebellion is an understandable response to the false promises of education, since most of these youth can only look forward to unskilled jobs that are rapidly disappearing, and since they are virtually locked out of better paying, more rewarding occupations. As Arthur Pearl puts it, such students have a "fair fix on reality."[48]

[44] Kenneth Polk, "An Exploration of Rural Delinquency," in Lee Burchinal, ed., *Youth in Crisis: Facts, Myths, and Social Change* (Washington: U.S. Government Printing Office, 1965), pp. 221–232; Short, *op. cit.*, p. 114.

[45] Delbert S. Elliott, "Delinquency and Perceived Opportunity," *Sociological Inquiry,* XXXII (Spring 1962), pp. 216–222.

[46] *Coleman Report, op. cit.*, p. 202.

[47] Stinchcombe, *op. cit.*, p. 179.

[48] Pearl, in Sherif and Sherif, *op. cit.*, p. 93.

We believe this source of delinquency in part is avoidable through the updating and modification of noncollege preparatory training so that more youth will be fed into the labor market at middle rather than low levels and will be prepared for upward mobility through channels other than the traditional one of college graduation. We recognize that aspirations of some youth will always be frustrated by lack of occupational opportunities or by their own lack of potential and that some delinquency will almost certainly remain even after changes are made. But we hold that the magnitude of the problem can be reduced with a better fit between the secondary school curriculum and labor market demands that will in turn produce a closer fit between student aspirations and occupational outcomes. This, too, is Stinchcombe's position.[49]

.   .   .   .   .

Lack of Commitment

. . . [T]he theories of Karacki and Toby and of Miller take the position that delinquency is sometimes the result of lack of commitment to adult roles, school standards, and community laws. That is, they contend that some delinquent youth, for different reasons in working and middle classes, tend to develop early and continuing loyalties to standards and activities outside the normal, legitimate stream of things.

Miller contends that uncommitted working class youth sometimes adopt these illegitimate orientations and behavior patterns because they have been acculturated into a lower class pattern of life that includes in the natural course of events engagement in activities that sometimes are defined by the larger system as unacceptable or delinquent.[50] Karacki and Toby, on the other hand, argue that some middle class youth fail to develop a commitment to the legitimate system early in adolescence because of imperfect socialization by the adult world or because of plain choice.[51]

There is some evidence that the uncommitted are in fact "candidates for delinquency." Karacki and Toby, for example, reported that the middle class gang they studied did not get "hooked into" the legitimate system in early adolescence.[52]

.   .   .   .   .

In a different context, Miller reported that the lower class street gangs he studied in Boston tended to be drawn into a culture with a greater emphasis on "trouble, toughness, smartness, excitement, fate, and autonomy" than on

[49] Stinchcombe, *op. cit.*, p. 179.
[50] Walter B. Miller, "Lower Class Culture as a Generating Milieu of Gang Delinquency," *Journal of Social Issues*, 14:5–19:No. 3, 1958.
[51] Larry Karacki and Jackson Toby, "The Uncommitted Adolescent: Candidate for Gang Socialization," *Sociological Inquiry*, 32 (Spring 1962), p. 207.
[52] *Ibid.*, p. 207.

conformity to community laws or achievement in school.[53] Finally, Polk and Halferty recently reported an association between lack of commitment and delinquent involvement.[54]

. . . . .

It should be clear from our earlier argument that lack of commitment is sometimes likely to be a reaction to educational failure and perceived irrelevancy of education. We argued in both of the above sections that those experiences sometimes lead to alienation from school personnel, activities, and demands and a turning toward substitute or rebellious behavior. Part of this process is likely to be withdrawal of a basic legitimate commitment. Yet Karacki and Toby are quick to point out that among the middle class boys in their samples, lack of commitment seemed to develop prior to low achievement. The problem seemed to be that they "were unable or unwilling to devote themselves to school or work . . . thus, one Duke in explaining his lack of concern for school commented, 'I wanted fun more than I wanted to go to school.' "[55]

This raises an important question about the possible role of the school itself in deterioration or lack of commitment. While both Miller and Karacki and Toby attribute lack of commitment to socialization patterns in the family and neighborhood, we believe that the school itself plays an essential role in the motivational and behavioral disengagement of some youth from the legitimate system. We contend that the character of the authority system, the decision-making process, and the basic teaching-learning structure in most public secondary schools limit the chances for most youth, especially if they are not involved in extracurricular activities, to become actively engaged in the educational process. That is, there are fewer opportunities than there might be for youth, in both lower and middle class schools, to get "hooked into" the legitimate system of conformity and achievement. In short, we suggest that lack of commitment may result from the fact that, as a result of some of the essential characteristics of the school structure, the educational system is sometimes unable either to "hold" middle class youth within normal channels of development and commitment or to draw the lower class "unacculturated" pupil toward legitimate paths of learning and development. Specific defects contributing to delinquency in this way are discussed below.

Misconduct in School

Finally, there is considerable evidence that students who violate school standards pertaining to such things as smoking, truancy, tardiness, dress, classroom demeanor, relations with peers, and respect for authority are more likely to become delinquent than those who conform to such stand-

---

[53] Miller, *op. cit.*
[54] Polk and Halferty, *op. cit.*, p. 93.
[55] Karacki and Toby, *op. cit.*, p. 210.

ards. This finding has been reported by Healy and Bronner, the Gluecks, Havighurst, and others.[56]

It is likely, of course, that violations in both the school and the community represent a single pattern of rebellion, rejection, or lack of commitment. Available data, however, show that misconduct in school frequently but not always precedes delinquency in the community. We take the position, therefore, that there is not a necessary linkage of misconduct in school with delinquency and that one of the determinants of whether or not delinquency follows is the way the school itself reacts to students who get into trouble.

As noted in an earlier part, one of the determinants of whether deviance will be reduced or repeated and widened are the effects on the deviant and his circumstances of the group's labelling process and subsequent sanctions. The relevance of this general principle to the problem at hand is evident. One of the factors affecting the chances that misconduct in the school will be reduced or will be repeated and extended to include misbehavior in the community is the character and effect of the school's sanctioning system. On one hand, the school can prevent behavior problems from re-occurring by imposing firm sanctions, while at the same time involving the student in the legitimate system, rewarding him for conforming behavior, and developing academic and social competencies. On the other hand, the school can inadvertently push the student toward illegitimate commitments by imposing overly punitive sanctions in a degrading way; by locking the individual out of the legitimate system through such mechanisms as expulsion, suspension, withdrawal of extracurricular privileges, and placement in a special classroom for the "emotionally disturbed."

It is our position that the balance has traditionally been on the side of debasement, exclusion, and locking out, rather than on the side of respect, reinvolvement, and recommitment of the misbehaving student.

.   .   .   .   .

[*From Walter E. Schafer and Kenneth Polk, "Delinquency and the Schools," in* Task Force Report: Juvenile Delinquency and Youth Crime, *President's Commission on Law Enforcement and Administration of Justice (Washington: U.S. Government Printing Office, 1967), appendix M, pp. 223, 225–226, 228–234.*]

[56] Havighurst, Bowman, Liddle, Matthews, and Pierce, *op. cit.*, p. 75; William Healy and Augusta F. Bronner, *New Light on Delinquency and Its Treatment* (New Haven: Yale University Press, 1963); Sheldon and Eleanor Glueck, *Unravelling Juvenile Delinquency* (New York: The Commonwealth Fund, 1950); William Wattenburg, "Relationship of School Experience to Repeated Delinquency Among Boys with Intelligence in the Bottom Fifth of the Population," United States Office of Education Cooperative Research Project No. 201 (1960); Kvaraceus, *op. cit.*, p. 148; Polk and Richmond, *op. cit.*; Toby and Toby, *op. cit.*; Alfred E. Simone and Nelson S. Burke, "The Probable Syndrome in Terms of Educational Experience Which Precipitates Dropouts, Delinquency, and Eventual Incarceration," *Journal of Negro Education* 35:1 (Winter 1966), pp. 27–34. For a view of literature on school experiences and delinquency, see Maynard L. Erikson, Max L. Scott, and LaMar T. Empey, *School Experiences and Delinquency* (Provo, Utah: Brigham Young University, 1964).

6   *Police treatment of juveniles*

San Diego—A Case Study

A. Introduction

At the time of this study, the Juvenile Bureau of the San Diego Police Department consisted of forty-one personnel. Commanded by a Captain, the Bureau included the following sworn personnel: one Lieutenant, three Sergeants, twenty-five Patrolmen, and five Policewomen. The remainder were assigned to clerical functions.

Organizationally, the Bureau is placed under the command of the Inspector of the Investigations Division. Other units in the same Division are the Detective Bureau, Vice Squad, License, Intelligence, and Narcotics Details.

Departmental publications give the Juvenile Bureau the following responsibilities:

1. The investigation of all crimes in which juveniles are listed as the actual or suspected violators.
2. The investigation of school, recreation department, and child care center burglaries.
3. Processing of adult persons charged with or suspected of a violation of 272 P.C. (Contributing to the Delinquency of a Minor).
4. Neglected or abandoned children.
5. Investigation of battered child complaints along with the taking of appropriate criminal action when indicated.
6. Investigation of missing and runaway juveniles. Maintain appropriate files on same.
7. Make referrals or other suitable disposition of juvenile offenders.
8. Maintain bicycle registration files and provide a limited bicycle license service in conjunction with the Fire Department Program.
9. Supervise and regulate teenage dances (excluding licensing).
10. Provide, in cooperation with other community agencies, a program of delinquency control and prevention.
11. Discovery and elimination of community hazards such as caves, etc.
12. Stolen and recovered bicycles.
13. Checking crime-prone areas, hangouts, etc.
14. Counseling with parents and children.

Although the Juvenile Bureau does not have primary responsibility for the issuance of licenses for teenage social events, it does take an active part in the investigation which precedes such licensing. The attitude of the police toward such events will be analyzed later in this chapter.

One can observe from the above list of functional responsibilities, that the Bureau is "protection" and "enforcement" oriented. The bulk of its work could justifiably be classified as falling within the generic term of "investigatory." That this is a correct judgment of the Bureau's philosophy and orientation is verified not only by administrative analysis, but also by observation and by the data accumulated in interviews with Departmental personnel. This is further verified by the study of the other agencies involved in the administration of juvenile justice.

The two agencies in the city which deal most frequently with "delinquent" youth—the police department and the County Probation Department—tend to "compartmentalize" their processing and handling of the youth. There appears to be almost no overlapping of functions between these two agencies, as if by rigid and formal agreement the two agencies had agreed to "which was to have what." Furthermore, during the entire time the research staff was in San Diego it appeared that there was at least a tacit agreement that neither agency would comment upon the work of the other. In fact, the head of the Juvenile Division of the Probation Department candidly told a member of the research staff that neither he nor any of his employees would discuss police procedures with juveniles. As far as his "official" view was concerned, the Police Department was doing an effective job of dealing with youths. Other agencies dealing with youth—schools, recreations, etc.—spoke freely of their associations with the Police and Probation Departments.

B. Enforcement Policies and Practices

1. THE CURFEW ORDINANCE

A municipal ordinance provides that it is unlawful for a minor under the age of 18 years to be on the streets or in other public places between 10 P.M. and daylight, unless accompanied by an adult, or involved in some other clearly permissible activity. Involvement in only certain types of activities excludes a juvenile from application of the curfew; consequently, the Department realizes that care and caution must be exercised in the enforcement of the ordinance. Departmental policy states that policemen are ". . . NOT to use this ordinance as strictly interpreted but to employ it as a LOITERING control ordinance." It then cautions officers to make reasonable use of the ordinance:

> The Curfew Ordinance and other laws are reasonable and enforcible only so long as the majority of parents and public agree with them. If overenforcement creates a vindictive attitude on the part of

the public, it would only be a matter of time before the Curfew Ordinance would be drastically amended or repealed, and thus lose its value as an antiloitering tool.

The Curfew Ordinance can be of great value if enforced properly. It gives the Police Department a valuable tool with which to control the activities of individuals and groups hanging around the street corners, businesses, or other places where their purpose or intention is questionable or a source of annoyance to other citizens.

In the event that a juvenile is detained for violation of the curfew, officers are advised that the juvenile may be placed in Juvenile Hall "only in aggravated cases." For less serious matters, the juvenile is to be brought to central police headquarters, where the Commanding Officer will contact the parents and require them to come for the child. In routine cases, it is permissible for the officer to take the juvenile home and release him to his parents.

2. ETHNIC FACTORS IN THE JUVENILE PROBLEM

Officially, the police state that race is *not* a significant factor in the juvenile problem. According to them, "all areas yield between one and two percent delinquent." Also, "juvenile problems should be handled like any other disturbance, regardless of what race of people are involved." The Police Department reports that Logan Heights, primarily a Negro district, does not have the highest rate of delinquency. The private expressions of policemen dispute this statement, however.

In contrast to the official police viewpoint, the individual patrolman expresses a different attitude. One officer explains when trouble will arise:

> We have problems when the colored schools play together or when they play a white school—we always have a fight—it's automatic that we're going to have a beef afterwards—where we have two other schools and we don't have a beef.

Other comments indicate similar concerns about Negro teenagers:

> Negroes dislike authority . . . they have little or no supervision at home. They hate policemen.

> Maybe it's their upbringing, maybe it's because of this civil rights movement where they've got such a chip on their shoulder that policemen will walk up to one and say, "You're causing a disturbance—out!" "You're pickin' on me 'cause of my color of my skin!" "That's the only reason you're kickin' me out is because I'm a Negro!"

> And it never fails, if we have a school that is predominantly colored, we will have a problem policing that school in their sporting activities.

As can be detected from the above quotations, the individual Caucasian police officer believes race *is* very much a factor in juvenile delinquency. Negro police officers express a different attitude.

> The racial overtones . . . may start if the number of policemen increases, the number of bystanders also increases. And then you have the racial overtones built up. But actually, I would think, in a lot of instances, it's built up by us as policemen.

They believe that many times the attitude of the Caucasian officer influences, in a negative manner, the relationship between the Negro and the police. . . .

3. THE JUVENILE SOCIETY

The police see a difference between the role of enforcement in the past and at the present time. Accordingly, years ago juveniles could be handled informally.

> . . . the policeman on the beat caught him doing something, grabbed him by the scrub of the neck, and shook him a few times and gave him a size 9-D in a soft spot, and maybe later if he saw my grandfather, then he told him, 'I caught your boy down here where he shouldn't be,' and that was it. He not only got it from the policeman on the beat, but he got it from his dad when he got home. Now, without going into any sociological subjects, I think parents have a different outlook on home discipline than they did years ago. We could always get back to the root of the thing and say it belongs at home.

Policemen believe the difference exists as a result of modification in family structure and in the degree of home discipline.

The general police attitude regarding gangs in San Diego is as follows: "I don't believe that we do have gangs as such; we have individual cliques." But while actual gangs are not a problem, the police realize there are troublemakers.

> As a police officer you work in the community and know the people. And if you see particular individuals from a community going to a dance, you know whether they're troublemakers or whether they're not troublemakers . . . you know that something's going to start.
>
> Now, certainly some organizations have better reputations than others, irrespective of race.

Despite the racial overtones of any public gathering or event, the police are adamant that order be maintained. If trouble is continuously a problem with a particular juvenile social function, then, ". . . that event should be eliminated until people demonstrate that they can conduct themselves like normal human beings and obey the law!"

The police attitudes toward the juvenile society appears, therefore, to be of two types: first, the official viewpoint that there is no racial component to juvenile problems and, second, the officer's private viewpoint that the Negro juvenile definitely *does* constitute a special police problem.

4. POLICE RESPONSIBILITY FOR JUVENILES

The police believe that many youngsters "require supervision, not only from parents but from the police." It is considered a police responsibility "to direct youngsters who are otherwise directionless." It is due to this type of reasoning that the police justify such activities as licensing of social events.

> I think it [licensing] is one of the forerunners of control; and, if you have a troublesome group that has been troublesome to the community, the Department or any other organization, if you can prevent them from staging one of these affairs . . . then half the problem would be solved.

In addition to control, it is believed that through licensing the protection of the juveniles can be accomplished.

> Imagine a situation where perhaps a person who has been in the business of prostitution or the illegal sale of alcoholic beverages wants to conduct such a dance for children. If it were not a Police Department licensing the situation, it could well be that they would be able to license such a place.

Recommendations about the granting of a license for a social event involving juveniles are made by the Juvenile Division. Since this constitutes an administrative decision, personnel of the Division were asked what appeal a person had if the Division had not recommended the granting of a permit. At first, the answer was, "None." Pursuing the question, a researcher asked the officer-in-charge who had the ultimate decision. His response was, "I guess the Chief has the final say in the matter." Asked if the Chief had ever overturned one of his recommendations, this officer stated, "I have been making these recommendations for a number of years and I don't think the Chief has ever gone against one of my recommendations. Of course, that's primarily because I am cautious in making my recommendations to the Chief!"

That the police believe they have a responsibility to juveniles is also illustrated by their maintenance of a Border Check Station, the operation of which is discussed in detail, below. At the station unescorted juveniles without written parental permission are turned back to prevent their exposure to the immorality of the Mexican border towns.

It is the opinion of the police that if the parents were aware of juveniles' activities, some of the problem would be eliminated. It is suggested that "an effort should be made . . . through our community relations program to . . . leaders of the community . . . they could advise the parents of just what these kids were doing." It is clear that the police believe they have a definite responsibility in the supervision of juveniles.

5. POLICE ATTITUDE TOWARD SOCIAL AGENCIES

In general, the police attitude toward other social agencies can be summarized in the following statement: ". . . the rehabilitation efforts on the part of probation and parole agencies were not effective in this area [juvenile delinquency]."

Much has been written about police attitudes toward the courts, and nothing has been found to contradict the generally accepted viewpoint that police believe courts are overly concerned with the rights of the individual and not enough concerned with the protection of society. "I think they [the courts] are putting more restrictions on the police . . ." is a typical statement.

6. TECHNIQUES OF ENFORCEMENT

In addition to standard enforcement procedures, the Police Department utilizes a number of other techniques to handle the juvenile problem. (Only those procedures dealing for the most part with juveniles will be discussed in this section.) The police recognize that it is important for them to be in contact with juveniles in other than negative circumstances.

> . . . administratively the Department established a policy of the patrol units and traffic the same way, making a routine of getting acquainted at the recreation centers, playgrounds, the locations where youngsters congregate—maybe it's the malt shop or the drive-in—to get to know those people. This policy started with the Chief of Police. He says, "I want those men to get acquainted, to get to know them, to make friends out of those individuals."

Individual officers point out, however, that the main problem seems to be one of finding the time and the opportunity for these positive, nonofficial contacts.

The use of the patrol car and the subsequent elimination of the foot patrolman, however, significantly reduced these more informal contacts.

> I think the administration in the past few years has emphasized mechanized equipment, and you get away from it, from the down-to-earth contact with people. The old footman walked around and knew everybody in the neighborhood—well, our population almost makes this impossible now—but there is no reason, and it is strongly advised, that the policemen in their areas contact youth groups, recrea-

tion centers, troublesome spots, and keep in contact with the kids, and show them that you're an individual. . . .

Due to the "high crime rate" and changes in population, the police believe that they are forced to use procedures which do not easily lend themselves to nonofficial contacts with juveniles. The administration states that it is policy to encourage such contact, but there was little evidence found in observations or in interviews with patrolmen that such contacts are deliberately sought out or that they occur with any frequency.

7. PLANNING AND COORDINATION

When the police become aware of a juvenile dance or other social event which is to take place, they have a standard plan of approach.

> . . . naturally they [the notices of the events] would go on our daybook and also the Juvenile Division would be alerted to this dance coming up, and we would assign extra patrol in the area to actually be on guard against any violations that might occur, and then our plainclothes juvenile officers would also attend and cover these dances from time to time, checking on them inside, seeing any potential [trouble] that might be in the making.
> . . . the men [officers in the Patrol Division], prior to going on watch, should be made aware that there is a dance there and potentially there is trouble there and should keep this in the back of their minds; their supervisor also should, if there is a problem, send . . . what is needed. . . .

It is the responsibility of the managers of the social event to insure that ". . . for every 100 there, there will be one private patrolman" and the police will then assign extra police personnel to also look in on the dance and check for misconduct outside. The police look upon ". . . planning of these things as a method to prevent any occurrences from happening . . . prevent it before it happens."

The police believe that it is important to understand and to have some knowledge of social events.

> I would think that a background study would be needed: Where do these people go after they leave the dance? What do they usually do after they leave the dance? Does a disturbance occur at the dance?—things of this nature.

This knowledge permits logical deployment of police manpower. If the police problem at a specific social event progressively gets worse, "I think I'd try to find out exactly why this is happening; . . . juvenile gangs in opposition . . . possibly it's too much booze in the dance, or what have you. . . ." Liaison is also established by "contacting the . . . operators of the dance . . . sort of let the word get out, too, that if there is going to be trouble, that enforcement is going to be applied."

8. THE USE OF JUVENILE OFFICERS

The discussion of the juvenile officer's role in this section will not attempt to explore the full implications; mention will only be made of those duties specifically pertinent to the policing of a juvenile social affair. Juvenile officers work primarily in the preparation stages and they perform an intelligence function during the event.

> They [juvenile officers] can go to the schools . . . a lot of times they have knowledge of these people that are causing the disturbance, maybe they can go to the troublemakers and let 'em know we know they're doing it and that something is going to be done about it; or go to the schools and talk to the kids that are involved . . .

During the dance or other social event the juvenile officers will gather information and replay it to the Patrol Division.

> . . . our plainclothes officers are pretty much sent out as observation teams or intelligence or an information team, feeding back information to our Patrol Captain in whose hands or judgment it is to police, with his uniformed patrol, this [social] function.

Another special function of the juvenile officer is to follow up on juveniles who have displayed hostile attitudes towards officers during field interrogation.

> . . . where the [patrol] officer has indicated that this boy has a poor attitude . . . that FI card is assigned to a juvenile officer for a follow-up, and this follow-up entails the officer making the contact with that juvenile, preferably at home, and sitting down with the child and his parents at a time and a place where the only thing they're going to talk about is: "Son, we're here to make this a better place for you to live."

This procedure recognizes that field interrogation techniques may result in some resentment among young persons toward the police.

9. SHOW OF FORCE

The standard police response to a pending or potential juvenile problem is a show of force. The technique and its results at one event are explained, as follows:

> . . . the commanding officer decided to handle it one week; we sent so many units up there and they would cruise the parking lot where a

> lot of the trouble was starting . . . we would have officers check inside of the dance along with the Sergeant periodically; he had about eight to ten units up there just patrolling the area all evening long, and the trouble seemed to me to go down. We didn't have to take any action.

The show of force is used ". . . to prevent anything from happening, and I am certain that the great majority of the people . . . have no objection to seeing the police around when they leave . . ." Police do not view the show of force as harassment although to some officers it does have at least two disadvantages: first, such a policy "drains" police protection away from other parts of the city; second, it is possible to have "too much show," and this may be actually provocative. By and large, however, it is reasonable to conclude that the Department believes in such a tactical display of power in handling juveniles. The consensus of police opinion is that ". . . the more police officers you have on the scene, the less trouble you have, and the less action that has to be taken, regardless. . . ."

> They have fights and we get in there and try to break it up and they mill around and if the police back off then they start throwing rocks and things at the police cars that are there, so we have to keep a certain force there or else we have trouble.

10. EXTRA-LEGAL ACTIVITIES

In addition to the above enforcement techniques, the police often utilize methods of handling juvenile problems which may fall outside legally approved limits. At certain dances, usually those which have had trouble in the past, the San Diego Police Department stations a regular patrolman at the front entrance and ". . . all the boys are searched for weapons when they enter." Policewomen are also stationed there to check all girls' pocketbooks for liquor. The police believe that this procedure is necessary to minimize the potential problems. The police also ". . . break up any crowds they see in order to persuade people to either go back inside or continue on their way," for the purpose of preventing group conflict and/or illegal activities which may go unobserved if hidden among large numbers of youngsters. In addition, the police believe that the "hangers-on" who cannot get into such a dance—either because they are too young or because they have been drinking—create dangerous situations which may provoke incidents. Their operating rationale is to prevent these incidents by "stopping them in the bud."

11. BORDER INSPECTION STATION

The Border Inspection Station is located at a four-lane control entrance at a point just north of the Mexican border. Police officers are stationed at a position in the center of the traffic flow, a point from which they can visually scan people coming through. Cars containing juveniles who are not accompanied by adults are ordered to stop and the occupants are directed to a building where their age and possession of parental permission to cross the border can be verified by other police officers. If the officer's suspicions are confirmed that a juvenile is under age and that he does not have parental permission to go into Mexico, the juvenile is turned back at the border. The juvenile's name and address is taken, and the Police Department sends a form letter to the juvenile's parents informing them of the encounter.

Several members of the research staff visited the Border Inspection Station at various times. One member made the following observations about the police techniques employed at the Station:

> They [police officers] ask for a person's wallet or purse and conduct a search. They have no hesitancy, apparently, about going directly into the purse and browsing around for something which will contradict the identification which the person has given. This seems to be a liberty that I question, and I think it's probably more out of expediency than implied consent, because I'm sure that it does pose some *prima facie* question of being an illegal search. They also, with males, many times order the juveniles to empty their pockets, and then go through them and check, to prove false I.D.

Other members of the research staff made observations. One pointed to a possibly subtle form of discrimination which was being exercised against youths who appeared to be of Mexican descent. They were rarely stopped or discouraged from entering Mexico, despite their youthful appearance. If this form of discrimination is, in fact, being exercised, it means that the police are exercising less "protective control" over Mexican-American youths than over other youths.

Another practice which was noted was the tendency of officers—at least during the varied times of the observations—to discriminate against youths wearing "mod" clothes. (Much of the repartee which took place between the officers and the youths may have been in jest, but it was also obviously resented by many youths.) Girls wearing either "jump suits" or "pants suits" and boys with long hair or beards were frequent recipients of caustic comments. Girls were frequently asked, "Why are you *boys* going to Mexico?" Boys were similarly the objects of sarcasm when they were asked, "What are you trying to do, prove your age wearing a beard?" or "Boy, with that hairdo, you'll have to be careful or some sailor will pick you up!"

When questioned about the Border Station generally, the police maintain that the system serves a constructive purpose, not only in terms of stopping criminal violators, but also in preventing runaways and protecting juveniles from exposure to the immorality of the border towns. When asked whether the public supports them in this venture, ranking officers in the Department report that favorable adult response to the program has been overwhelming.

C. Conclusion

Although it has been noted that the list of functional responsibilities for the Juvenile Bureau of the Police Department is "protection" and "enforcement" oriented, the description of policies and procedures tends to indicate negative relationships with youths. By their very nature, enforcement activities on the part of the police may be inherently negative. Because such activities tend to restrict the activities or to punish the juvenile, they uniformly evoke a negative response in the youth. The data collected demonstrates, however, that so-called "protective" services also tend to evoke resentment, at least among some juveniles. The manner in which these services are performed and the mannerisms which are often used by the officer give the impression that these services also are more punitive than positive. Even these potentially positive acts on the part of the police give rise to hostility.

Philadelphia—A Case Study

A. Police Views of Juvenile Problems

The Juvenile Aid Division was established in 1933 to assist in efforts to deal with the problems of juvenile delinquency. At the time of this study the Division was comprised of approximately 189 personnel. It is under the command of an Inspector. The personnel of Juvenile Aid Division are assigned to work either out of one of the seven Patrol Divisional Headquarters in the city or to work with one of the specialized units at Juvenile Aid Division Headquarters. At Headquarters, personnel may be assigned to any of the following units: Line Squad, Morals Squad, Policewomen, Gang Control, or Patrol.

The Juvenile Aid Division has jurisdiction over all offenses which are committed by a juvenile (under 18 years of age) or those in which a juvenile is a victim. In addition, the Division has responsibility for discovering conditions in the community which might prove a moral danger or corruptive influence upon juveniles.

One of the current problems faced by the Juvenile Aid Division is the overcrowded conditions at the Philadelphia Youth Study Center. The Youth Study Center is a separate agency, but its relationship to the Police Department is permanent and real. Juveniles who are taken into custody are detained at these facilities in central Philadelphia. The juvenile population of the Center averages approximately twenty percent over its rated capacity. Consequently, the Center is unable to accept every child Juvenile Aid Division personnel wish to send there.

Despite recent emphasis on the need for police-community relations and the increased concern about juvenile delinquency, particularly the growing restlessness on the part of ghetto youth, the Juvenile Aid Division does not participate with other agencies in planning recreational activities.

In order to analyze the relationship between the police and youth, it is important to determine the role concept which Juvenile Aid Division personnel have of their work. Furthermore, it is desirable to determine the way in which the community responds to the work of the Division. In the following sections, an analysis will be made of both matters.

1. CAUSES OF DELINQUENCY

There is a consensus of opinion among personnel concerning the causes of delinquency. Two relatively new officers state:

> Citizens should start training their kids when they're young and not throw them on the streets and make a problem for us. The kids today, they haven't the slightest bit of respect for a policeman or law or authority.
>
> How can you expect someone to have respect for a policeman—a juvenile or an adult—when they have no respect for their own parents. You can't expect them to have respect for someone they don't know, which you [the policeman] are. . . . There's no respect for law. . . .

More experienced officers independently agree with this analysis. In a group interview, five officers, among whom were a Lieutenant, a Captain, and an Inspector, believed that juvenile delinquency is caused by the lack of home training and discipline. They believe that juveniles today have lost respect for "man and God." Another police captain mentions the failure of parents to exercise their proper role and to assume their entire responsibilities with regard to their children. Therefore, modern youth lack respect for themselves, their homes, their parents, and the police.

There were differing opinions about the rates of delinquency growth. The majority of officers interviewed on the subject believe that juvenile problem is increasing disproportionately. The Captain of a police district far removed from minority areas felt, however, that the crime rate has remained fairly static over the last few years and that the increase in juvenile crimes reported has been proportionate to the increase in population. A second Captain, assigned to an area populated by large numbers of minority youth, also thought the juvenile crime rate was growing in proportion to the crime rate in general.

The major problem areas associated with juvenile delinquency are listed as drinking, disorderly conduct, vandalism, and bicycle and car thefts. One group mentions the use of LSD among college students and several officers cited that it is on the decline.

2. THE FUNCTION OF THE POLICEMAN

Juvenile Aid officers believe the primary purpose is a positive one:

> . . . three words title this unit. "Juvenile Aid Division"—the middle word, "Aid" the juvenile. Strictly speaking we should *aid* them so we should have a certain amount of social consciousness.

The purpose of the Gang Control Unit is stated as follows:

> In keeping with the general philosophy as defined by the operation of the Juvenile Aid Division as a whole, the Gang Control Unit functions to render assistance and guidance to the youth of the community - as well as the investigation and prevention of acts of juvenile delinquency and crime in the specific area of organized gangs.

One individual characterized Juvenile Aid personnel as the "line squad." He feels that units within Juvenile Aid, such as Gang Control, are specialist units, but regular juvenile officers are "tantamount to the grass roots level." Another officer explains that the "Juvenile Aid Division is directed in its work with its clientele." This fact helps to understand the purpose of the Division.

3. SOCIAL WORK

One Philadelphia Police Inspector does not think that social work has a rightful position in police work: ". . . once a police officer becomes a social worker he isn't any good any more as a policeman." Correspondingly, Juvenile Aid Division officers made a distinction between their function and that performed by organizations fundamentally concerned with aspects of social work:

> Their role is to direct the activities of juveniles into behavior which is not antisocial—this is their final responsibility. Our job is to gather intelligence from any sources whatsoever, including these other organizations. Our field is law enforcement, theirs is more or less social work.

Administrative personnel within Juvenile Aid Division explained that among the optimum requirements they would like for new recruits would be, as follows:

> . . . possibly maybe a few years of college with some social background, not necessarily to be a social worker, but some social science to give them some insight and perspective into the work.

4. SOCIAL WORK AGENCIES

Police officers apparently believe, however, that social work agencies perform desirable and necessary services in respect to the gangs. The main working relationship which exists between these two types of agencies consists of the cooperative exchange of information. Yet in so doing, Juvenile Aid Division attempts to gain information in a secretive fashion when it is of such a nature as to be detrimental to the relationship between gang member and gang worker. Conversely, when gang workers are able to favorably influence the disposition of a particular youth, the Juvenile Aid Division endeavors to make this knowledge available to the youngster.

The only conflicts which reportedly exist between these organizations are individual personality clashes. However, one officer stated that too close a relationship was not advisable:

> . . . we're tied in with them to a great degree and we shouldn't be because we're practically working at opposite ends in many cases.

5. CONSTITUTIONAL RIGHTS

A logical extension of the positive purpose which Juvenile Aid Division personnel see for themselves is related to the role they interpret for the Juvenile Court. Accordingly, Juvenile Aid Division officers see the function of the Court to consist of the following:

> The purpose of that court, of course, is to assist and guide and counsel the youth, you know, about their righteous living, so to speak—this is the basic foundation—not so much to attempt to try them for their particular crime . . . as a result it's not a criminal court.

Several police officers, therefore, feel that the issue of constitutional rights, as stressed in Supreme Court decisions, is *not* a basic problem with juveniles:

> I don't think that there's any great problem as far as their constitutional right or rights are concerned. Juveniles certainly don't waive anything, in a sense, because they're being tried on a delinquency charge. . . .

A directive which was recently issued to the Police Department concerned informing adults of their legal rights. Some members of the Juvenile Aid Division staff indicate that this policy is applied to all juveniles as well. One individual explains that the original directive was not explicit about age, thus it was interpreted as being also appropriate for youth. An Inspector states that juveniles are informed of their rights when court action is imminent. In Pennsylvania, if the child is fourteen years old or over, he can be tried as an adult if the crime is serious enough. Should certification occur, then, police officers wish to be prepared. It is possible that those connected with the Juvenile Aid Division believe in the necessity of following the new guidelines more as a means of assuring conviction than as an essential right of the defendant:

> . . . it's the law, and you have to go by the law, and if you deviate from this there's a chance that a case might be thrown out on a technicality. Now, these decisions help us in this respect, in that they guide us . . . it's just like a game, practically—you abide by the rule, anything you do is constructive and it'll be accepted, there won't be any chance of anyone saying, "Well, you didn't do it the right way, so this is to be thrown out."

In their interviews, policemen indicated they are personally reluctant to accord juveniles the rights adults have won. One member of the Juvenile Aid Division commented, "Normally they have all the protection of the Constitution right now." He later added that the reasons the differences between juvenile and criminal court practice have not yet been challenged is because there's been no strong lobby against it. For instance, the American Civil Liberties Union, or the Bar Association itself, have not *demanded* that they have the same treatment as an adult. However, in his opinion it is slowly coming to that.

Whenever a youngster is brought into a District station, parents are notified prior to the arrest, and officers estimate that "approximately 95 percent or 99 percent of the time, the parents or guardians are there when the investigator arrives." According to the police, all interrogation, therefore, is made in the presence of the parent. This practice extends to the school system in Philadelphia also. Sometimes it is necessary for police to interrogate students in the school building and the following directive outlines the appropriate procedure:

> Interviews of pupils by police and court officers should take place in the presence of the principal or his representative. The interview should take place in a private room with a woman member present when girls are involved. In some cases the principal may consider it advisable to invite the parent to be present. . . .

Recently, in fact, school administration officials have recommended to the Police Department that parents should be present during any interrogation of their youngsters.

An interesting statement was made by another member of the Juvenile Aid Division:

> And I'd be surprised if anything we have in our Juvenile Court actions that is in conflict with the Constitutional rights of an adult's

will eventually be knocked out. Of course, the Constitution doesn't differentiate between adults and juveniles, no more than it does between Negroes and Whites. . . .

6. CORNER-LOUNGING[1]

Much of the contact juveniles have with policemen concerns actions precipitated by "corner-lounging." Most of this contact is with District uniformed policemen and not with officers of Juvenile Aid Division. A recent directive, read at roll call each day, informed officers not to disperse groups during the summer months, unless destructive behavior occurs. Most officers agree that juvenile behavior during or subsequent to corner-lounging is likely to erupt into acts deserving police attention. Therefore, dispersal orders are viewed as crime prevention measures.

Youths may create a disturbance if they remain on the corner. Several policemen mentioned that "nasty" remarks or obscene gestures are directed to women or young girls who must pass by groups of boys.

> Young girls, they don't even want to go to the corner drugstore because they know that somebody's going to make some nasty remark or while she's looking around at one, another one will pat her or something.
> I knew of one boy who kicked a pregnant girl in the stomach . . . this guy made a remark to a girl and this girl didn't take to the remark, so he went over and gave her a shot. . . .

Other officers have encountered "a radio on real loud, and there might be dancing around the radio or something."

Trouble may also be imminent because groups of juveniles converge for a period of time:

> They'll sit there on the corner and they'll talk and pretty soon they get bored and they say: "Let's go get into something."

One Juvenile Aid Division officer refers to the fact that adults close by often complain to the police.

> . . . several people in the neighborhood got together and stated that a group of boys were congregated in this particular area; and as a result of this congregation, it may not be initially a disorderly thing, but the longer it remains, the more disorderly this group does become.

[1] This term is used to describe the congregation of persons on a street corner. If a policeman should ask the group to disperse and they refuse, he often arrests them. Throughout the study, members of the research staff were intrigued by the dynamics of the "battle for the corner." Many of the participants—both police and youth—view the developments on the corner as part of the "grand strategy." "To lose a corner" is to suffer a moral defeat. The battle of the corner will be discussed in this and subsequent chapters.

In many cases, the contact arises because of citizen complaints about disturbances:

> That's why there aren't too many arrests made on this type of offense. Unless someone complains.

Police action apparently varies according to the individual officer concerned with the problem.

> And he arrives at the situation, and the group may be disorderly at the time and if they are, it becomes the judgment of the police officer; either he may disperse them immediately and/or take them in, depending upon the situation.

The officer bases his decision, at least partly, upon his familiarity with the group involved:

> Every situation is different, and every corner is different, and I think that each policeman, as he is out there a while, gets to know the individual corner and the individual crowd.
> You have to know your individual corner. You can have a group of fellows on one corner, which will be there every night of the week, and you don't bother them—they don't bother anybody. They sit and talk quietly. . . . When a decent hour comes, they break up and they go home. You may have the same amount in the next block or on the other side of the street, that you know, they are the troublemakers . . .

If the police officer merely orders the juveniles to disperse, one method of preventing further trouble is described as follows:

> . . . you don't let them go in the same direction . . . you get out to check them out to see if they have any weapons; then you send two this way, two that way and two another way. . . .

Despite this alternative and the discretion which may be exercised, many policemen apparently deal with these groups in a punitive manner.

A significant number of the policemen—juvenile officers included—are unsure about whether there is a specific ordinance relating to corner-lounging. The following verbatim statements taken during one group interview represent the diversity of opinion among policemen themselves.

> There is no ordinance to my knowledge, and I don't think there's any law in the city that you can't stand on the corner.
> Corner-lounging. The ordinance we have on corner-lounging is what he's referring to.
> I don't think they ever settled that.
> I . . . no, there's no ordinance on corner-lounging. . . .

Well, it's tantamount to what we do—we bring them in—that's tantamount to disorderly conduct.

Actually, it's disorderly conduct further refined to corner-lounging, or something like that.

It's a phrase here. I don't think there's a law in the country that says a person can't stand on a corner.

It's not illegal until the participants of this group on that particular corner either become disorderly as far as neighborhood goes, and then . . . we have . . . breach of the peace or disturbing the peace or what have you. . . .

Actually, in addition to merely ordering the crowd to disperse, a number of different violations are used to deal with groups of juveniles. One officer's technique is to charge juveniles with intoxication.

A: Yeh, well, see, I won't charge them with disorderly conduct.
Q: What do you charge them with?
A: Intoxication.
Q: Are they normally intoxicated?
A: They have had a drink, and one drink would indicate intoxication.
A: It doesn't say to what degree they have to be intoxicated.

It also appears that arrests of juveniles are predicated upon the "antagonistic" attitude of the juvenile:

Q: What if this guy says, "——— you, officer." Is this against the law?
A: It's creating a disturbance. Other people are sticking their heads out to see what's going on, cars are stopping to see what you're trying to do—it's disorderly conduct.

Although a few of the policemen commented that they did not have problems asking juveniles to disperse ("Well, usually they don't refuse to move."), most of the officers indicated that juveniles will often challenge these orders.

. . . you have a group of guys on the corner and you tell them, "Okay, fellows, move off the corner!" Nice tone of voice and everything. All of them will move except one—that one, that one is going to challenge you.

Some policemen feel that this type of "testing" is merely a result of unfamiliarity with the individual:

I still think the old adage of the old beat man on the corner knew everybody is very, very helpful in many, many areas; because you take a new man and put him on the street on a beat, he doesn't know the area, he doesn't know the people, and they don't know him. He'll get challenged. He'll get challenged every time. As soon as he opens his mouth to move somebody or gets into any situation whatsoever, somebody is going to be there to challenge him, because they don't know him.

Once challenged, the policemen who were interviewed believed it was best to arrest the responsible youth in an attempt to prevent further trouble:

A: Now you can ride away and leave that one there.

B: You're lost. You might just as well forget about it.

A: . . . and . . . that's right . . . you're lost; so naturally you get out of the car and you have to challenge this one, whereupon he is going to rebel, and then the next thing you know, if you get in trouble with this one, then the rest of them start coming back. And it's always the same pattern. Always the same thing over and over again.

B: And once you lost the corner, you have a hard fight getting it back again. They'll go from one corner to the other, once you've let them slide like that.

The individual labeled "A" above remarked at a later point:

Naturally *he's* locked up. He's gotta be locked up. If you don't, the next night *all* of them will say the same thing . . .

Some policemen agreed that the juveniles' response to dispersal orders "depends to a great degree on personality of the officer involved:"

A certain type of officer can go over and have an assist officer[2] on every one of his situations. It's just the way that you handled it. And that's just so basic in a police operation, the way you approach . . . people . . . I believe in 99 percent of the cases, the proper approach to a situation of this type can be handled without assist officers.

A Juvenile Aid Division officer confirmed this statement:

And what I found to be the practice more so than anything else is the fact that when Gang Control arrives on a location, it's either one or two things; it's never a question of "move," because the kids are running when you come up; if there's no fight, no breach of the peace at the time, they wait and lie down . . . every once in a while, and they sit there and it's like a 'get acquainted' type thing; I mean, there's no fear involved in this particular situation. Then the man can come up and say, "move," when the rapport is established. And I say the approach in every incident is the thing.

Another officer states that simple courtesy is all that is required.

[2] An "assist officer" is police jargon for an incident where an officer needs assistance usually because of physical resistance.

If the youngster is taken to the station, several alternatives exist. The following dialogue is revealing. (Q represents the interviewer.)

> A(1): I'd hold him, straighten him out, bring him in for investigation.
> Q: And then let him go?
> A(1): Right, generally, yeah.
> A(2): Mine stay overnight. (Laughter)
> A(3): I come in in the morning to get the "comp" [compensatory time off] time.
> Q: What do you mean? You come in and appear at the Magistrate?
> A(3): Yes.
> A(2): I don't appear up against them. I don't appear against them if they stay overnight.
> Q: And if you don't appear, then they're automatically dismissed?
> A(3): Yes.

Corner-lounging is one of the most frequent reasons for which juveniles come into contact with the police. Despite the constant attention police give to this type of activity, their admonitions are rarely effective:

> They'll meet up again, but at least it'll be a couple of hours, or maybe an hour or so before they meet back again.

Coupled with these facts, is the public-relations effect of the encounter:

> Well, I agree, it leaves a sour taste with the kids, number one. Number two, this is a public-relations thing also because disorderly conduct is only a summary offense, and a policeman must witness the offense himself in order to make an arrest; and if you don't have a reason to arrest the person, I don't think you have a reason to really tell them to move off the corner. I mean, he has a constitutional right—if he's not committing a crime or impeding safety or something. This leaves a sour taste possibly with the youth, but I mean, you're trying to satisfy the adults in the area, and they made a complaint. . . .

7. CURFEW

Another frequent reason for contact between juveniles and police officers is that of curfew checks and violations. Members of the Juvenile Aid Division support the theory of the curfew ordinance, although many are uncertain of its legal implications:

> . . . so you use everything to your best advantage if possible. . . . We have this law that has never been tested as to constitutionality or anything else, so as long as we have, we'll use it to the utmost, and we do. . . .

There is a strong consensus among the policemen interviewed that curfew ordinances prevent youth from getting into trouble. Most officers, however, realize that it is not equally effective with all youngsters.

> The curfew ordinance is a . . . deterrent factor to a certain group of youngsters. To the hard-core group, curfew really matters very little if they intend to commit some type of a crime. Curfew, in itself is a wonderful thing. . . .

In addition to the positive aspects which enforcement of curfew has for youth, many Juvenile Aid Division officers also believe it aids the parent in home discipline:

> . . . curfew is aimed at the responsibility of the parent. Curfew violation is sent to the parent. A lot of parents are unaware that the children are out after curfew.
> . . . the parents welcome it because if you have weak parental control, they can always say, "Oh no,—remember the curfew. Oh, I'd like to let you stay *but.*"

Therefore, they feel that parents generally support curfew ordinances and the rationale behind them:

> . . . most parents thank us when we pick up the kids and take them home.

The usual procedure is for uniformed officers or members of the Juvenile Aid Division to stop any youngster who appears to be under the age of seventeen and who is out after 10:30 P.M. weekdays or after midnight Friday or Saturday evenings. Juveniles are often asked to show identification, and they should provide information about their name, age, mother's and father's name, and church and school they attend. If the officer doubts the veracity of any item, he has the right to take the juvenile to the District station, whereupon his parents are notified. In addition, a form is sent to the youngsters' home advising his parents that he was violating curfew.

If the juvenile is violating curfew, but he is either accompanied by a parent or he has a note attesting to parental permission because he may be on an errand, he is considered to be on legitimate business. Juvenile officers dislike this existing loophole and feel that it is not necessary. They believe that an adult should either "do without" or go out after his own "hoagy."

Generally, the officer will not transport the child home except in certain instances. If, for example, a young girl is a long distance from home, the officer may take her there or, if it is a Juvenile Officer, he may ask a nearby District car to do so. Whenever a girl is involved, at least two policemen must be in the transport car for the protection of both parties concerned.

Usually, however, the child is taken to the station and her parents called. Certainly one of these alternatives would be utilized since the youngster would not be allowed to walk long distances alone and at night. The exception to this practice, of course, applies in cases where the teenager is near his house.

> A large percentage of the time they're on their way home when you stop them, and most of the time they're in the block where they live, so you watch them go in the house.

Violations of curfew are apparently forgiven the first time, but records are kept and if there is a repeat of the violation the juvenile and his parents may be subpoenaed for a Magistrates' Hearing:

> In other words, the first—it's like any crime, the first shot—all right—we'll give you a chance. But if it happens the second time . . .

Curfew is equally enforced in all areas of the city according to the police. Policemen did not believe that the rate of curfew violations was greater in any one area than in another.

> I think that where you have more people to control you obviously have more curfew violations.
> So naturally with the higher number of policemen per population, the higher number of patrol cars. In addition to special forces that are sent into the area to curb crime, well, you do come up with more curfew violations. . . .

According to the police, the availability of "places to go" is also a factor in curfew violations:

> . . . in your sparse neighborhoods you might have just one local store where they hang out and that store closes its doors at curfew time—where can they go? See, it's a sparse area. They go home. Where in a congested area, there's more stores that maybe remain open later and the boys go from one to the other sometimes, and it's up to the proprietor now to check their ages, too.

Action may be taken against proprietors who maintain establishments known as "juvenile hangouts" if the owner deliberately allows those under curfew age to remain after hours.

> . . . if it's his first offense he may be warned, but on subsequent offenses he definitely will be fined if we find he's harboring these juveniles at the late hours just for a mere profit of it. . . .

Juvenile officers interviewed were all in favor of the curfew ordinances. Ironically, one individual District policeman thought the curfew would lower crime rates, city-wide, if it applied to everyone.

> . . . as far as police work is concerned, we would be better off if we had a curfew for everyone at 10:30—put everyone in the house and put them to bed and clean up the toys. . . .

B. Community Attitudes of Police-Youth Relations

Several Philadelphia residents separated police-youth relations from their general discussion of community relations. Some indicated that juveniles represent the greatest problems for police while others felt that the policeman's greatest failing is in his relationship with youth. A few residents mentioned the difficulties of anticipation and over-reaction by both police and youth. They feel this has resulted from mutual fear and stereotypic attitudes. One policeman related the view from the police perspective.

> When you drive up, you're a cop . . . you represent authority. Maybe some other policeman in the same car, on the same shift last night, hit somebody. You—it's automatically assumed that you're going to hit somebody. You may be the nicest guy in the world. So you've got a hostile group of people to start out with. Now, how do you play it? So one guy puts his hands in his pocket. You gonna stop and rationalize now? Some guy's putting his hand in his pocket to scratch his leg, or is he looking for his knife?

One individual unwittingly referred to the frustrations with which police are confronted by succinctly stating that they perform a "negative role keeping them [juveniles] off the street." Many citizens believe an officer's duty is to prevent trouble by taking this action.

Most residents praised Juvenile Aid Division personnel by characterizing them as "literally, hand-picked men," men of high calibre and possessing the "proper positive demeanor." A judge describes them as being well-informed about the gang situation and "always on top of the problems," despite their limited manpower. He specifically mentions their working attitude as one which is directed toward resolving problems through the home rather than to use the recourse of the court. Another man, associated with an organization which works with gangs, feels that the quality of Juvenile Aid Division men has recently declined; yet he still feels that they are very good officers. The Gang Control Unit was also commended.

A few individuals comment upon the limitations within police work which prevent officers from dealing extensively with the juvenile problem and, in particular, with gangs. One Caucasian male, professionally involved with both youth and police, stated:

. . . they [the police] cannot cope with it . . . [the juvenile problem]. The officer is stumped. He can't deal with them. He's not going to break them up, and he's going to be always out there fighting with the situation.

Another man, experienced in working with youth gangs, says that police "are neither sympathetic with, nor do they identify with nonpolice methods of dealing with youth." Yet another person, connected with a settlement house, feels that the police cannot reach the hard-core gang members because it is outside both their province and their abilities. An ex-policewoman explains that juvenile work is oriented only toward "arrest and investigation. It is not designed to work with the child." Those persons who feel that police fail to relate well to youth mention lack of understanding as a primary reason. To one person this meant that the police were interested only in promoting the typical stereotype of the "cop"; to another it meant officers could not comprehend that a youngster's *dignity* is involved. A youth worker says that policemen "tend to look upon kids as a particular threat in the community" but that the police themselves don't understand the community. A ghetto resident thought it important for police to understand that the lack of recreational facilities has significance for youth behavior. A priest observed that officers do not understand that weapons are equalizers for teenagers against other gangs, that they have a symbolic importance to many teenagers. A few persons, however, believe that the high quality of officers is associated with their perceptive abilities. One judge feels Juvenile Aid Division officers were appreciative of, and had a remarkable understanding of, ghetto youth. Another judge remarked that they were sensitive and aware of juvenile problems.

Citizens differed in their evaluation of the effectiveness of the work of the Juvenile Aid Division. One woman, very much involved in work with the community and with the police, stated that her area reflects competent police work; it has no large juvenile problems, such as murder or armed robberies. Others who appeared also to be close to the problem disagreed. A recreation official described the Juvenile Aid Division as ineffective, due partly to their "hard" attitudes towards gang members. He believed their biggest failing was related to their limited views of preventive work. A woman who had previously worked in the Juvenile Aid Division made the following assessment:

> I didn't think that we were accomplishing too much with juveniles. I don't know that they're doing anything. The effectiveness I'm not sure of.

Several individuals relate the police-youth problems to the inadequacies in the courts and disposition facilities. One park supervisor believes that leniency in court proceedings promotes a disrespect for the law and for the police. The contrary view was also held. A Negro male likens juvenile justice to a "kangaroo court system," while an attorney states that courts often give Negro juveniles a "short shrift." Yet a judge feels that the law for juveniles has struck a good balance, i.e., it is not so strict as to permanently cripple a youngster's life, nor is it too liberal as to be impractical. On the other hand, an ex-policewoman believes the crux of the problem rested in the inadequacy of facilities to house "repeaters."

> The Youth Study Center is overcrowded . . . (It is supposed to be a place to study the problems of juveniles, but now it's only an institution to house them because there's no other place.)

There appears to be a consensus that the police *do* discriminate against juveniles and, in particular, against the Negro youth. A Philadelphia attorney states that teenagers are discriminated against, especially those who are members of ethnic minority groups. Another individual, professionally associated with youth gangs, characterizes police-youth relations as good, *except* with Negro youth. This statement was remarkably similar to one made by a recreation leader who also excepted Italian youth. Other persons described incidents in which police either did not protect or were reluctant to protect groups of juveniles having trouble with rival groups.

Reports of harassment directed towards juveniles were fairly numerous. A Philadelphia priest characterizes the police attitude towards juveniles as being "typically and constantly aggressively hostile." Many persons mention the indiscriminate searching of juveniles with varying complaints about length of time questioned, deprivation of constitutional rights, being "locked-up" routinely overnight and being dismissed the next morning, often without charges. One attorney feels that the burden of "field interrogations" falls heavily upon young Negroes. Another cited the fact that the ratio of detentions for curfew violations in the ghetto to that of the general community was one hundred to one because ghetto youth have less rights with which to protect themselves. An explanation of this apparent discrimination is given by yet another attorney who seeks to establish the basis of police action upon the fact that teenagers' habits and dress are often considered "alien," thus close surveillance is natural when suspicions are aroused.

An incident described by a settlement house employee also referred to frequent searches. She specifically mentions the case of a young girl allegedly searched in a demeaning manner. One recreation official firmly believes that the only juveniles who complained were those who consistently were in trouble, but he reluctantly describes an incident he witnessed in which a Negro boy, with a previously good reputation, was searched, humiliated and threatened with brutality until he revealed certain information to the police.

The settlement house mentioned above had begun a program, in the past, to teach juveniles the meaning of "due process." It was soon discontinued, however, because the stories of injustice and abuse were so frequent that the huge gap between reality and theory created a disheartening atmosphere for the youth involved.

Other forms of harassment are cited. A judge, in addition to others, noted that claims of verbal abuse were quite common. A man, professionally associated with gangs, stated that juveniles are afraid of the police. They are noticeably tense when approached by policemen and fear that they will become the subjects of arrest and harassment. An ex-policewoman remarked:

> And I think that all people living in this so-called jungle area are not hostile, but the police expect them to be. So they treat everybody in this area alike. . . .

Another judge commented that in court he noticed a lack of sympathy by police towards youth, although he realized that this may be a reciprocal reaction.

A Caucasian male who had studied the police in Philadelphia said:

> I have a definite suspicion that the police use the kids and especially the gangs, to build up their own arrest statistics. They also have a technique with gangs. . . . If someone is identified as a gang member, they have a tendency to sweep up the gang in this area . . . [I]n the process of getting the gang they pull in the kids they see on the street. And those kids . . . either get booked or else they'll cool it in the station house for quite a while.

A few persons are not too concerned about police harassment of juveniles. In fact, a community worker related an incident in which teenagers harassed a policeman who exercised considerable restraint by not retaliating. A federal Probation and Parole Officer spoke of the speedy service by "red cars," whether it was an instance of potential trouble or one in which juveniles needed protection. Another individual was concerned about the leniency towards youth whereby they are often allowed to gather on corners without being asked to disperse.

A great deal of the criticism leveled against police relationships with juveniles specifically concerned charges of police brutality. Several persons describe incidents they had personally witnessed, while others spoke of hearsay accounts although they believed the veracity of these accounts. An attorney mentions that many teenagers with whom he had spoken independently described the existence of a "back room" in the Police District stations where youths were physically abused. A Negro, associated with problems of police-community relations, thought that the police may deliberately provoke juveniles in order to have an excuse for manhandling them. A woman active in the civil rights movement explains that police are caught up in the current problems of large, urban, metropolitan areas and their response is brutal and ugly. It is her opinion that sizeable disturbances occur because of police brutality, and other persons reiterated this statement.

The data collected revealed an apparently deep concern about police-youth relations on the part of many persons. An ex-policewoman, familiar with Juvenile Aid Division operations, praised personnel but questioned overall effectiveness. Her specific comments about community relations attempts were as follows:

> They do have community relations officers who go out to the schools to tell children about police work. They go to meetings in the community but they have one in each district, and this is ridiculous to try to get one policeman to go out into the community to explain the problems, with the police in the community.

In her opinion "police-community relations" need a broader scope than it currently has in Philadelphia.

C. Conclusion

Urban society is rapidly changing. Although delinquency statistics reflect a general increase, this is not necessarily the product of greater criminality per se. Rather, it may suggest that such a development is "the condition of the emerging metropolitan community." Despite the reason for the developments, however, the police find themselves increasingly coming into official contact with juveniles.

The data collected in this research suggests that the Juvenile Aid Division is the most uniformly and highly respected unit in the Police Department. Generally favorable comments were encountered in various sections of the city, in contacts with both officials and citizens. Respect was expressed for the general high quality of the officers in Juvenile Aid Division and for the prevailing philosophy of the officers assigned to the Division. Generally, the only negative comments were those of the juveniles themselves.

Even in the case of the juveniles, however, their strongest resentment was expressed toward the Highway Patrol and the general duty policeman assigned to the various geographical Districts throughout the city. It is the policeman on this level whom they most frequently encounter. It is the District policeman who is almost exclusively encountered in the "battle of the corner." Generally, the juvenile encounters a Juvenile Aid Division officer only after he has been arrested or detained by the District policeman. The juveniles' routine, daily contacts are with the policeman walking the beat or the motorized officer in the sector "red" car.

Interviews with both juveniles and District policemen reveal something of the dynamics of the "battle of the corner." Both apparently see these encounters as challenges to their manhood. Neither party expresses a willingness to allow the corner to go to the other by default. In many respects, both parties view the encounters as a game, albeit a deadly serious game. Among some of the younger officers, one encounters a sense of dedication never to lose the battle of the corner. Part of the young policeman's lore is the fact that losing the battle is seen as one of the most serious "defeats" a policeman can suffer. Older officers, of course, have often tired of these encounters and unconsciously avoid "showdowns." Many of them, however, also reveal an unwillingness to lose if a showdown is unavoidable.

"The drawing of the battle lines," however, has apparently been as much the consequence of public pressure as it has been the product of the policeman's action. In numerous interviews, policemen justify their dispersal of corner-lounging groups on the basis of complaints from the public. Visitations to various neighborhoods in the city and to various District police confirms the fact that there are many public complaints about corner-lounging groups creating a disturbance or shouting insults or obscenities. Furthermore, many policemen use their selective experience to point to the fact that many groups assemble on the corner as a prelude to more serious misbehavior and delinquency.

The increase in the juvenile population and its changing character, [as well as] specialization and sophistication within the police department, have all contributed in transforming the nature of police work. But, striving for efficiency has also led to bureaucracy; police operations have become "routine"; juvenile offenders are "processed"; relations between the two have become impersonal, and the impact upon juveniles could well be characterized as "dehumanizing."

Dehumanization is evident in the most personal types of contacts—face-to-face confrontations. Use of patrol cars in an effort to increase efficiency necessitates the existence of a relationship which is inherently negative. Rarely does the motorized officer confront the juvenile except for the purpose of admonishing or arresting him. Coupled with motor patrol is the fact that shift changes occur in Philadelphia every six days. Corner-lounging, a frequent reason for police-youth contacts, is an excellent example of the implications these factors have. Juveniles gathered together every night will be confronted by the same officer six out of every 28 days. During the interim, they must adapt to three other officers' policies. Rotation of shifts disrupts any consistency in relationships which might have been formed. Furthermore, if one of the four officers involved causes negative reactions by virtue of his techniques, this may perpetuate a condition of expectancy and anticipation which may void the positive impressions which may have been engendered by another policeman. Juveniles who dislike authority are easily given to stereotypic attitudes which may support the negative beliefs they prefer to hold. Moreover, challenging reactions may give them status in the eyes of their friends.

Comments by officers reflecting on the causes of delinquency—encompassing lack of respect and home discipline—impress upon members of the research team the fact that police often have "hardened" attitudes towards juveniles. Though individual officers may be aware of conditions which spawn certain aspects of juvenile behavior, many appear incapable of incorporating this sensitivity into actual techniques. Within the past year, the "crash" recruitment program which was organized to recruit an additional 1,200 officers may have also complicated the problem of police relationships with juveniles. Greater numbers of policemen, perhaps embodying less than normal standards, increases the probability that stereotypic attitudes will be formed.

Dehumanization is also evident in the Youth Study Center which was originally conceived as a center in which to "rehabilitate" juvenile delinquents. Overcrowding has seriously restricted the Center's planned programs. Overcrowding has also reduced the proportion of the "delinquent population" which the Police Department can refer to the Center.

The Police Department, therefore, increasingly finds itself dealing with a larger juvenile-age population, a population which is apparently being less and less influenced by family control. More and more, the Police Department finds itself in the position of confronting youth rather than having the opportunity of effectively engaging it. More and more, the Police Department personnel find themselves limiting their contact with youth to enforcement situations. If he does not possess effective relationships with the community in which he serves, the policeman inevitably finds himself and his department to be the only practical and available means of social control.

Observations in the city by members of the research staff revealed that policemen in the Districts defer generally to Juvenile Aid Division officers in matters relating to juveniles. This seems to be not so much a matter of "buck-passing" on the part of District officers as it is a genuine inclination on the part of the policeman to admit that he does not personally know how to deal with the problem. He appears to welcome the intervention of a "specialist." The primary contacts between the youth and the police in Philadelphia are not with the specialists in Juvenile Aid Division, however; these relationships are with the District policeman, the officer who is generally most willing to admit his own inabilities in the matter.

[*President's Commission on Law Enforcement and Administration of Justice,* Field Surveys IV: The Police and the Community (*Washington: U.S. Government Printing Office, 1966*), Volume 1, pp. 108–118, Volume 2, pp. 137–157.]

7 The juvenile court

NOTE: After the work on the following chapter was completed, the Supreme Court on May 15, 1967, decided *In re Gault,* dealing with procedural protection in juvenile proceedings. *In re Gault* held that, in compliance with the Due Process Clause of the Fourteenth Amendment, a juvenile, confronted with proceedings which may result in commitment to an institution in which the juvenile's freedom is curtailed, has certain rights. He and his parents have a right to notice to the charges against him in advance of court hearings. They are entitled to notification of right to be represented by counsel retained by them, or, if they are unable to afford counsel, counsel will be appointed to represent the child. Also, they have a right to confrontation and sworn testimony by witnesses available for cross-examination. The findings of the President's Commission on Law Enforcement and Administration of Justice referred to in the following chapter did not reflect that decision; however, the chapter is reprinted here for two reasons. First, it presents in greater detail the discussion at pp. 78–89 of the Commission's general report, *The Challenge of Crime in a Free Society,* issued in February 1967, which was referred to by the Court in *Gault.* Second, the findings proved to be as great or greater relevance since the *Gault* decision. The *Gault* decision appears in Appendix A of the Commission's task force report, *Juvenile Delinquency and Youth Crime.*

Juvenile courts are judicial tribunals that deal in special ways with young people's cases. They exist in all jurisdictions. The cases they deal with include delinquency (conduct in violation of the criminal code and also truancy, ungovernability, and certain conduct illegal only for children), neglect, and dependency. The young people they deal with are those below a designated age, usually set between 16 and 21; their authority extends until the youth reaches his majority. They differ from adult criminal courts in a number of basic respects, reflecting the philosophy that erring children should be protected and rehabilitated rather than subjected to the harshness of the criminal system. Thus they substitute procedural informality for the adversary system, emphasize investigation of the juvenile's background in deciding upon dispositions, rely heavily on the social sciences for both diagnosis and treatment, and in general are committed to rehabilitation of the juvenile as the predominant goal of the entire process.

The juvenile court has become the primary judicial agency for dealing with juvenile criminality, the single most pressing and threatening aspect of the crime problem in the United States. One in every nine children will be referred to juvenile courts for an act of delinquency before his 18th birthday. Considering boys alone, the ratio rises to one in every six.[1] Arrests of persons under 18 for serious crimes increased 47 percent in 1965 over 1960; the increase in that age group population for the same period was 17 percent. In 1965, persons under 18 referred to juvenile court constituted 24 percent of all persons charged with forcible rape, 34 percent of all persons charged with robbery, 52 percent of all persons charged with burglary, 45 percent of all persons charged with larceny, 61 percent of all persons charged with auto theft.[2] It is apparent that responsibility for meeting the problems of crime rests more heavily on no other judicial institution. The subsequent pages of this chapter seek to offer a series of interlocking proposals addressed to the basic deficiencies in the operation of the juvenile courts as functioning agencies in the total crime prevention effort. The essence of the proposals is as follows:

> The formal sanctioning system and pronouncement of delinquency should be used only as a last resort.
>
> In place of the formal system, dispositional alternatives to adjudication must be developed for dealing with juveniles, including agencies to provide and coordinate services and procedures to achieve necessary control without unnecessary stigma. Alternatives already available, such as those related to court intake, should be more fully exploited.
>
> The range of conduct for which court intervention is authorized should be narrowed, with greater emphasis upon consensual and informal means of meeting the problems of difficult children.
>
> The cases that fall within the narrowed jurisdiction of the court and filter through the screen of prejudicial, informal disposition methods would largely involve offenders for whom more vigorous measures seem necessary. Court adjudication and disposition of those offenders should no longer be viewed solely as a diagnosis and prescription for cure, but should be frankly recognized as an authoritative court judgment expressing society's claim to protection. While rehabilitative efforts should be vigorously pursued in deference to the youth of the offenders and in keeping with a general commitment to individualized treatment of all offenders, the incapacitative, deterrent, and condemnatory aspects of the judgment should not be disguised.
>
> Accordingly, the adjudicatory hearing should be consistent with basic principles of due process. Counsel and evidentiary restrictions are among the essential elements of fundamental fairness in juvenile as well as adult criminal courts.

[1] Children's Bureau, U.S. Department of Health, Education and Welfare, Stat. ser. No. 83 (Juvenile Court Statistics, 1964) at p. 1.
[2] 1965 Federal Bureau of Investigation Uniform Crime Reports 23.

Development of the Idea of the Juvenile Court

The juvenile court emerged from the confluence of several streams of thought and practice, some of them centuries old, others relatively recent responses to changing social conditions.

The best known source of the idea of the juvenile court is summed up in the Latin phrase, *parens patriae*. From feudal days the English chancery court has exercised protective jurisdiction over all the children of the realm on behalf of the *pater patriae*, the King. While the chancery court traditionally had broad authority over the welfare of children, its jurisdiction was exercised almost exclusively on behalf of minors whose property rights were jeopardized, on the theory that it lacked the means with which to provide for impoverished, neglected minors. When the English legal system was transplanted to the United States, the chancery court's activities were extended to include protection of minors in danger of personal as well as property injury, and it is as inheritor of the chancery court's protective powers that the juvenile court in this country has most commonly been justified against constitutional attack.

The chancery court, however, dealt only with neglected and dependent children, not with children accused of criminal law violations, and the historical basis of the present-day juvenile court's delinquency jurisdiction has been a matter of some dispute. One opinion is that the institution of the juvenile court owes more to the criminal law than to chancery;[3] other writers give the common law of crimes at least part of the credit.[4] The common law had long presumed a child under 7 years incapable of felonious intent and therefore unable to be held criminally responsible, and a child between 7 and 14 years similarly incapable unless shown able to understand the consequences of his actions. It has been suggested, however, that the older adolescent now included in the juvenile court's province cannot really be considered without legal responsibility and that, while it may be historically correct to ascribe the juvenile court's delinquency jurisdiction to the criminal law, "its logical justification seems to lie in the recognition of the failure of the older criminal courts to prevent crime and in the experimentation in judicial methods and procedure."[5]

A somewhat different view of the court's origins is that "these courts have developed as part and reflection of the growth of contemporary administrative and quasi-judicial tribunals"[6] and that the *parens patriae* theory is the *ex post facto* justification offered for practices that in fact originated with

[3] Pound, *Interpretations of Legal History* (1923), pp. 134–135.
[4] Glueck and Glueck, *One Thousand Juvenile Delinquents* (1934); Lou, *Juvenile Courts in the United States* (1927).
[5] Lou, *op. cit., supra* note 4, at p. 7.
[6] Tappan, Juvenile Delinquency (1949), p. 169; Tappan, "Judicial and Administrative Approaches to Children with Problems," in *Justice for the Child* (Rosenheim ed. 1962), pp. 144, 146.

the modern juvenile court. Similarly the Children's Bureau of the Department of Health, Education, and Welfare, emphasizing the uniqueness of juvenile court procedures, has characterized them as special statutory creations rather than direct descendants of chancery.[7]

Although the 19th century movement for reform in treatment of children was a natural enough development in the humanizing of the criminal law, it may well have been accelerated and intensified by the social conditions then prevailing. Both industrialization and immigration were bringing people into cities by the thousands, with resulting overcrowding, disruption of family life, increase in vice and crime, and all the other destructive factors characteristic of rapid urbanization. Truancy and delinquency rose rapidly, and civic-minded men and women worried about the exposure of children to tobacco, alcohol, pornography, and street life in general. With the growing concern over environmental influences came the desire to rescue children and restore them to a healthful, useful life.[8] In addition, throughout the 19th century there was a rising concern about official treatment of children—the growth of what has been called the spirit of social justice.[9] The ascending social sciences, with their optimistic claims to diagnose and treat the problems underlying deviance, seemed to provide the ideal tool for implementing the dual goals of treating wayward children humanely and offsetting their deleterious surroundings. Philanthropic men and women such as the members of the Chicago Women's Club, emancipated intellectual feminists like the Hull House group, and professional penologists and reformers joined forces to achieve recognition of the greater vulnerability and salvageability of children—first in establishing separate institutions for youth and substituting noninstitutional supervision wherever feasible, then in adopting physically separate court proceedings, and finally in altering the very philosophy underlying judicial handling of children.

Thus, whatever its historical basis, the scene was set for the juvenile court's arrival by a variety of reforms that immediately preceded it. The growing trend was early evidenced in the founding of such institutions as New York City's House of Refuge (1825), in which children were to be separated from adult offenders and given corrective treatment rather than punishment. State reform and industrial schools for juveniles followed, the first in Massachusetts in 1847, all of them aimed at teaching youths discipline and an honest trade and instilling dedication to advancement through hard work. The development of probation as a substitute for confinement in criminal cases, which began in Massachusetts in 1880, reflected the growing belief in application of the social sciences, through treatment and supervision, as a means of preventing further criminality.

---

[7] U.S. Department of Health, Education and Welfare, Children's Bureau Publication No. 346, *Standards for Specialized Courts Dealing with Children* (1954), p. 55.

[8] See generally Platt, "The Child Savers: The Emergence of the Juvenile Court in Chicago, 1966," (unpublished thesis, University of California, Berkeley, California).

[9] Lou, *op. cit., supra* note 4, at p. 1.

Awareness of the brutality of incarcerating children with adult criminals led to efforts to separate them before and during trial as well. In 1861 the mayor of Chicago was authorized to appoint a commissioner to hear and decide minor charges against boys between 6 and 17 years and to place them on probation or in a reformatory, power which the judges received in 1867. In 1869 a Massachusetts statute provided for the presence in court of an agent of the State in cases where the child might be committed to the State reformatory; the agent was also charged with finding foster homes in suitable cases and paying subsequent visits to them. A law of 1870 required separate hearing of children's cases in Suffolk County (Boston) and authorized a representative of the Commonwealth to investigate cases, attend trials, and protect children's interests. The separate trial statute was extended throughout the Commonwealth in 1872, followed in 1877 by provision for separate sessions, dockets, and court records in juvenile cases. New York established separate trials, dockets, and records in 1892. Rhode Island in 1898 instituted segregation of children under 16 years awaiting trial, separate arraignments and trials, special dockets and records, and presence at juvenile proceedings of public and private agents to protect the interests of the child.

But the reformers were not yet satisfied. Judge Julian Mack, a well-known early juvenile court judge, commented years later on the juvenile court's development out of the general movement to reform the treatment of children: "What we did not have was the conception that a child that broke the law was to be dealt with by the State as a wise parent would deal with a wayward child."[10]

The juvenile court, then, was born in an aura of reform, and it spread with amazing speed. The conception of the delinquent as a "wayward child" first specifically came to life in April 1899, when the Illinois legislature passed the Juvenile Court Act, creating the first statewide court especially for children. It did not create a new court; it did include most of the features that have since come to distinguish the juvenile court. The original act and the amendments to it that shortly followed brought together under one jurisdiction cases of dependency, neglect, and delinquency—the last comprehending incorrigibles and children threatened by immoral associations as well as criminal lawbreakers. Hearings were to be informal and nonpublic, records confidential, children detained apart from adults, a probation staff appointed. In short, children were not to be treated as criminals nor dealt with by the processes used for criminals.

A new vocabulary symbolized the new order: Petition instead of complaint, summons instead of warrant, initial hearing instead of arraignment, finding of involvement instead of conviction, disposition instead of sentence. The physical surroundings were important too: they should seem less imposing than a courtroom, with the judge at a desk or table instead of

---

[10] Addams, *My Friend Julia Lathrop* (1935), p. 137.

behind a bench, fatherly and sympathetic while still authoritative and sobering. The goals were to investigate, diagnose, and prescribe treatment, not to adjudicate guilt or fix blame. The individual's background was more important than the facts of a given incident, specific conduct relevant more as symptomatic of a need for the court to bring its helping powers to bear than as prerequisite to exercise of jurisdiction. Lawyers were unnecessary—adversary tactics were out of place, for the mutual aim of all was not to contest or object but to determine the treatment plan best for the child. That plan was to be devised by the increasingly popular psychologists and psychiatrists; delinquency was thought of almost as a disease, to be diagnosed by specialists and the patient kindly but firmly dosed. Even the judicial role began to attract extralegal specialists, men and women aware of and interested in the social and scientific developments of the day, and government-supported professional personnel and services expanded and replaced the amateur volunteers.

Within a dozen years 22 states had followed the example of Illinois, and by 1925 there were juvenile courts in every State but 2. Today there is a juvenile court act in every American jurisdiction, including the District of Columbia, with approximately 2,700 courts hearing children's cases. The alacrity with which State after State followed the Illinois example, however, must be considered in the context of the developing reform movement sketched above; the Illinois act was in many respects the reflection of an idea already widespread and the consolidation of previous efforts to realize it.

Furthermore, the mere passage of a juvenile court statute does not automatically establish a tribunal of the sort the reformers contemplated. A U.S. Children's Bureau survey in 1920 found that only 16 percent of all so-called juvenile courts in fact had separate hearings for children and an officially authorized probation service and recorded social information on children brought to court.[11] A similar survey conducted by the Children's Bureau and this Commission in 1966 revealed significant gaps still existing between ideal and actual court structures, practices, and personnel. Indeed, it has been observed that "there is nothing uniform" in the operations of children's courts and that:

> in the analysis of their procedures, confusion has come from a common inclination to picture them as uniform throughout the country and to idealize them: to describe optimium [sic] practices (or, at least, procedures conceived ideal by the analyst) as though they were characteristic.[12]

In fact, more children's courts than not are staffed by judges and other personnel who spend much of their time on civil, criminal, and other

[11] Tappan, *Juvenile Delinquency* (1949), p. 173.
[12] *Id.* at p. 179.

nonjuvenile matters, and many children's courts are unlike other courts only by virtue of their separate and more private hearings. Even among those few more specialized courts for children there are great differences in method, depending both on statutes and on the views and values of those in charge.

The Juvenile Court in Operation[13]

The structure of the juvenile court and its position or status in the State's organizational pattern vary among and even within States. Relatively few are separate, independent courts. Most are part of a circuit, district, superior, county, common pleas, probate, or municipal court. In a few jurisdictions, family courts have been established to deal with both children's and domestic relations cases. Even where the jurisdiction of children's cases is in a court that is organizationally part of a larger system, however, the judge assigned to hear children's cases often operates his court quite independently.

Although there is variation among and in some instances within States in the jurisdiction of the courts hearing children's cases, jurisdiction generally includes delinquency, neglect, and dependency. Delinquency comprises cases of children alleged to have committed an offense that if committed by an adult would be a crime. It also comprises cases of children alleged to have violated specific ordinances or regulatory laws that apply only to children, such as curfew regulations, school attendance laws, restrictions on use of alcohol and tobacco; and children variously designated as beyond control, ungovernable, incorrigible, runaway, or in need of supervision—according to national juvenile court statistics, the latter two groups account for over 25 percent of the total number of delinquent children appearing before children's courts and between 25 and 30 percent of the population of State institutions for delinquent children.[14] In addition to cases of delinquent, neglected, and dependent children, children's courts may deal with other types of actions involving children: Adoption, termination of parental rights, appointment of a guardian of the person of a minor, custody, contributing to delinquency or neglect, nonsupport.

In some States major offenses such as capital crimes are excluded from the juvenile court's jurisdiction. In other States the jurisdiction of the juvenile court is concurrent with that of the criminal court in more serious offenses.

Age, objective and readily ascertainable, has traditionally served to de-

[13] This section draws heavily on a paper on the history and problems of the juvenile court prepared for the Commission by William H. Sheridan, Assistant Director of the Division of Juvenile Delinquency Service, Children's Bureau, U.S. Department of Health, Education and Welfare.

[14] Children's Bureau, U.S. Department of Health, Education and Welfare, Stat. ser. No. 83, Juvenile Court Statistics, 1964; Stat. ser. No. 85, Juvenile Court Statistics, 1965.

limit the population subject to juvenile court jurisdiction. At present the upper age jurisdiction of juvenile courts varies from 16 to 21. Eighteen is the upper limit recommended by the Children's Bureau, and it has gained acceptance in about two-thirds of the States. In the remaining one-third the age is 16, 17, or 21—different, in some, for boys and girls. In the one or two States in which it is 21, jurisdiction above 18 is concurrent with the criminal court, and in practice youths over 18 are almost invariably referred to the criminal court.

But age is inevitably arbitrary and fails to take account of individual differences in maturity, past and present conduct, and other factors relevant to choosing between juvenile and adult court handling of a given youth. About 40 States therefore provide for waiver or transfer by the juvenile court to the adult court, thus giving the juvenile court some discretion and flexibility in exercising its jurisdiction. Waiver laws vary greatly. Nearly half attach no conditions to the judge's exercise of discretion. In about a third of the States, waiver is authorized for any offense but only of a youth above a specified age, the lowest being 13. In a fifth of the States, waiver is permitted without regard to age but only for specified offenses, or with both age and offense limitations; the lowest age is 14 and the offense must usually amount to a felony. In one or two States, less stringent waiver criteria are provided when a child already under supervision or care for a previous offense is alleged to have committed an additional one.

Written criteria to guide the judge in deciding whether or not to waive are rare. Where they do exist, they are general: "not amenable to treatment in juvenile court," "not a fit subject" for juvenile court jurisdiction. Many State statutes heretofore have required no hearing or findings on the issue of waiver, a situation changed expressly in the District of Columbia, and called into question elsewhere, by the recent Supreme Court decision that a juvenile is entitled to a hearing, the assistance of counsel, access to social records, and a statement of reasons for the judge's decision to waive.[15]

The statutes establishing juvenile courts contain few if any specific procedural requirements. Many provide simply that the hearing shall be conducted in an "informal manner," a degree of generality that reflects the juvenile court proponents' desire to eliminate adversary aspects of adjudication and that was justified on the ground that more specific procedures would gradually be established through appellate decisions and formalized rules of court. In practice, however, upper court rulings have proved rare and have provided few guidelines, often instead reflecting but not resolving basic differences from States to State, and few formalized rules have developed.

Most juveniles who appear in juvenile court are sent there by the police. Extensive screening and informal adjustment by the police on the street and in the police station significantly reduce the number of apprehended juve-

[15] *Kent v. United States*, 383 U.S. 541 (1966).

niles referred to court; these practices are discussed in detail els₁
this report. Parents, social agencies, and others may also have direct
to the court.

Juvenile court statutes frequently provide that when a complai
ceived, the court shall make a preliminary inquiry to determine whether the
interests of the child or the public require court action. The inquiry may
vary from a cursory investigation to a full-fledged social study involving
contact with numerous persons and agencies in the community. It may
include a hearing at which the child, his parents, and, rarely, a lawyer
representing the child are present. In many juvenile courts, especially the
larger metropolitan ones, the preliminary screening function, known as
intake, is performed by a special division of the probation department.
Depending upon his judgment as to basis for court jurisdiction, sufficiency
of evidence, and desirability of court action, the intake officer may dismiss
the case, authorize the filing of a petition, or in many courts dispose of the
case by "informal adjustment." In many juvenile courts approximately half
the cases referred there are informally adjusted at intake—by referral to
another agency, by continuation on "informal probation," or in some other
way.[16]

The intake officer also determines whether a juvenile should be detained
pending court action. In about one-fifth of the jurisdictions the right to bail
is extended by statute to juveniles. In most jurisdictions a juvenile taken
into custody by the police has no right to bail but is to be released to his
parents or other suitable person unless no such individual can be found or
the juvenile is believed to present a serious threat of immediate danger to
himself or the community. The intake officer, having decided to authorize the
filing of a petition, may continue the detention of a juvenile already detained,
order him released, or order detention of a juvenile previously at large.

Where a petition is filed, the juvenile then appears before the judge for an
initial hearing (arraignment). If the juvenile denies involvement, there may
be, immediately or subsequently, an adjudication hearing. In most jurisdictions, as under the Standard Juvenile Court Act, there is no right to jury
trial in juvenile court.[17] In keeping with the desired informality and non-
combativeness of the court's proceedings, evidentiary rules are not strictly
adhered to, and hearsay and unsworn testimony may be received and
considered. The standard of proof varies, but it is generally lower than the
proof beyond a reasonable doubt required in the adult criminal court. In
most juvenile courts there is no prosecutor; in some the case is presented by
a police or probation officer. Appearance of a lawyer for the child, while
still the exception, is less unusual than it once was. By virtue of recent

[16] Children's Bureau, U.S. Department of Health, Education and Welfare, Stat. ser.
No. 83, Juvenile Court Statistics, 1964, Stat. ser. No. 85, Juvenile Court Statistics, 1965.
[17] Standard Juvenile Court Act, Sec. 9, 5 N.P.P.A.J. (1959), printed in *National
Probation & Parole Association, Standard Juvenile Court Act* (6th ed., 1959) (hereinafter referred to as Standard Juvenile Court Act).

legislation at least a third of the States now provide by statute for notice of right to counsel, assignment of counsel, or both; court rules reach the same result in other States. Great variation remains in practice, however, as to the time and manner of informing parents and child of the right to counsel, time and method of appointment of counsel, and extent and nature of counsel's participation in the proceedings.

In accordance with their emphasis on protecting and helping juveniles, many courts exclude from proceedings all except persons with a specific interest in them. Where newspaper reporters are admitted, they are generally requested to refrain from using names or otherwise making the juvenile publicly identifiable. Perhaps partly because of the consequent lack of public surveillance and more because of the absence of attorneys and records, juvenile court actions are rarely appealed, a circumstance that has reinforced the informality within as well as the variations among courts.

The disposition hearing is conducted separately from the adjudication proceeding in some courts. In many, however, it is held at the same time or is separate only in the minority of cases in which the allegations of the petition are at issue. In determining disposition, the court places great reliance on the social and clinical report (similar to the presentence investigation report in adult criminal court) prepared by the probation officer to whom the case has been assigned for social study (an assignment made in some courts before and in others not until after a hearing has been held on contested allegations in the petition). The social study embodies the juvenile court's emphasis on inquiring into the child's background and its attempt to apply the social and behavioral sciences to diagnosing and dealing with the problems behind his errant conduct. Social information is of prime importance—even more important, in the view of some, than the circumstances of the specific events on which the court's jurisdiction in a given case is based. That view is reflected in the fact that in many jurisdictions the social reports, in theory a guide to disposition, in practice are given to the judge before the adjudication hearing. On the question of disclosing material in the social reports to parties and their lawyers, practices again vary among courts.

Most juvenile court judges have broad discretion in disposing of cases, being empowered to dismiss the case, warn the juvenile, fine him, place him on probation, arrange for restitution, refer him to an agency or treatment facility, or commit him to an institution. The length of institutional commitment is usually indefinite and in most States cannot extend beyond the juvenile's 21st birthday. Commitment of a young child may thus amount to a relatively lengthy term; recently developed standards therefore recommend that commitment be for an indefinite period not to exceed 3 years, renewable during minority on a finding that the child's welfare or the community's protection requires further institutionalization.[18]

[18] Sheridan, U.S. Department of Health, Education and Welfare, Children's Bureau Publication No. 437, *Standards for Juvenile and Family Courts* (1966), pp. 82–83 (hereinafter cited as Standards for Juvenile and Family Courts).

There is as much variation in the structure and organization of agencies administering services and facilities for delinquent children as there is in the structure of courts, with the consequence that responsibility for a child often shifts back and forth among courts and a variety of public and private agencies, both State and local. A recent plan developed in response to that problem and already implemented in about a third of the States vests responsibility for the administration and expansion of a State's control and treatment program in a single State agency to which all children adjudged in need of care are committed.[19]

In about 10 States the juvenile court is authorized to commit juveniles directly to institutions for adult offenders. In another third of the States a child committed by the juvenile court to an institution for delinquent children may be administratively transferred to an institution for adults convicted of crime. According to a recent report, more than 500 children were so transferred in 1962.[20] Appellate decisions are in conflict on the constitutionality of the practice.

In 1963 the National Council of Juvenile Court Judges sponsored a biographical survey of judges exercising juvenile court jurisdiction, to which responses were received from 1,564 judges (estimated at 70 percent of those appreciably involved in juvenile matters).[21] Of the total number replying, 71 percent had received law degrees—95 percent for those serving jurisdictions with population over 1 million; 48 percent had received no undergraduate degree. The average age was 53 years, the average salary (for full-time judges) $12,493.15. Almost 75 percent had been elected to office, a third of them after an initial interim appointment; 62 percent had previously been elected to another public office. Of the full-time judges in the group, 72 percent spent a quarter or less of their time on juvenile matters. The most prevalent previous occupation (73.7 percent) was practicing law, for an average of 9 years. A third of the full-time judges said there were no probation officers or social workers available to their courts; 83 percent reported no regularly available psychologists or psychiatrists.

The juvenile court judge's right-hand man is the probation officer. Probation, it will be recalled, is one of the several 19th century developments that conjoined in the juvenile court movement and embodies the ideal of individualized, rehabilitative diagnosis and treatment. Probation officers serve as investigators into the juvenile's all-important social history, establish a link between the legally trained or lay judge and the social scientists who guide him, and provide a vehicle for disposition with supervision but without institutionalization. Probation, therefore, was and still is central to the juvenile court's special functions, and its limitations are inseparable from

[19] California Welfare and Institutions Code, Sec. 1000 (1961).

[20] Sheridan, U.S. Department of Health, Education and Welfare, Children's Bureau Publication No. 415, *Delinquent Children in Penal Institutions* (1964), at table 2.

[21] Center for the Behavioral Sciences, George Washington University, *Judges Look at Themselves: Profile of the Nation's Court Judges* (prepared for National Council of Juvenile Court Judges, 1965); McCune and Skoler, "Juvenile Court Judges in the United States," *Crime and Delinquency* (1965), p. 11.

the juvenile court's own shortcomings. Probation workers, trained in the social sciences and working with juveniles who have been adjudicated as well as with preadjudication court referrals, are commonly classified as corrections rather than court personnel and accordingly are considered more exhaustively in the report of the Commission's Task Force on Corrections. What follows, since it is essential for a full view of the court itself, is a brief general description of the current state of juvenile probation services.

Juvenile probation is provided for by statute in every State, and 31 States have probation services in each county—74 percent of all counties in the United States.[22] In 165 counties spread among 4 States, however, there are no juvenile probation services at all. Probation is administered by courts in 32 States, by State correctional agencies in 5, by State public welfare departments in 7, by other State agencies in 4, and by other agencies in 3. Since State and county civil service and merit systems usually apply only to administrative employees, probation officers in court-administered (judicial branch) departments generally are not under civil service regulations; of the 235 agencies surveyed by this Commission, less than half (47 percent) reported merit or civil service coverage.

Regardless of their organizational niche, juvenile court probation officers serve two major functions: making social studies of cases referred to the court and supervising juveniles placed on probation. Their duties may in addition entail intake functions such as screening cases referred to the court and determining the necessity for detention, administering the juvenile detention facility, and managing the court's probation department and court-attached diagnostic and treatment services (clinics, camps, halfway houses, community residential facilities).

The number of juveniles touched by probation activities is very large and still increasing. In one recent year 192,000 written social studies were made of children referred to court. In the same year, 189,000 were placed on probation. In 1966, at the time of the nationwide survey of corrections services conducted by this Commission, approximately 223,800 children were under probation supervision for periods varying from 3 to 36 months.

Juvenile probation services cost an estimated $75,916,000 a year. Notwithstanding the size of that figure, salaries are low and caseloads high. Median salary for probation officers among the 235 agencies in the survey sample was between $5,000 and $6,000 (ranging from $1,500 to $11,000). Caseloads among the same 235 agencies averaged between 71 and 80 supervision cases (excluding social studies, which take at least half the time of most probation officers). Only two-tenths of 2 percent of all children on probation were, at the time of the survey, in caseloads of fewer than 20 supervision cases; 10.6 percent were in caseloads of over 100.

---

[22] This and the following information are taken from the national survey of corrections conducted for the Commission by the National Council on Crime and Delinquency and printed as appendix A of the Report of the Commission's *Task Force Report: Corrections*. The data from the survey appear also in a separate pamphlet entitled *Correction in the United States* (1966).

Given those meager salaries and burdensome workloads (even apart from the unpopularity of corrections work, a situation attributable in part to the field's limited mobility), it is hardly surprising that probation departments cannot compete successfully for the best educated in the social service field. While 74 percent of the departments surveyed required a bachelor's degree, a master's degree in social work or an allied social science is a prerequisite for employment in only 4 percent. Nor is the lack of advanced education made up by inservice training programs; 52 percent of the sample departments reported no such program, and of those with one, only 21 percent meet more frequently than once a month. Despite minimal education and experience requirements, however, juvenile courts report frequent resignations and long-lived staff vacancies.

With the exception of the Youth Services Bureau, the service agency described subsequently, the recommendations made in this chapter deal chiefly with specific institutions of juvenile justice—the police and, particularly, the juvenile court—and do not directly confront underlying issues of organization and coordination among the court and community and other agencies. In fact, the court is vitally influenced by a number of such issues, some unique to its purposes and functions, others shared by many other public and private institutions.

One of the court's better known dilemmas is the multiplicity of its mandates. While its most usual image is as a benevolent redirector of straying children—a role it is expected to fulfill with a minimum of stigma and resulting disability—it is also expected to protect the community from offenders often apparently as dangerous as those with whom the adult criminal court deals.

A less obvious source of difficulty is the court's inferior position in the court hierarchy of most jurisdictions. The consequences of its low position include low regard by lawyers, judges, and social workers; great dependence on the support of local government, local organizations, and often the local electorate for funds, clients, support; and the vulnerability to criticism that accompanies dependence.

Its lack of independence further complicates the typical juvenile court's already intricate relationships with other organizations. Increasingly the juvenile court has been looked to as provider of the social services to which local government has become more and more committed. To carry out even a portion of these obligations, it must not only dilute severely its own activities, especially its judicial ones, but must also rely heavily on good will and more tangible forms of assistance from many local groups, among them police, schools, welfare agencies. That reliance increases the court's vulnerability to pressure both in a given case and as to general operating policies.

Underlying and intensifying all of those difficulties is the court's lack of resources. Procedures for finding facts, gathering and recording information, and other essential tasks are cumbersome and antiquated. The struggle to carry out service functions with inadequate staff and facilities detracts from judicial responsibilities, with the result that neither is fully performed.

These issues, while not within the scope of this material, are of significant influence on the operation of many juvenile courts, and any effort to improve the court requires that they be given careful consideration. They are more fully discussed in "The Juvenile Court as an Institution," a paper written by Robert D. Vinter for the President's Commission on Law Enforcement and Administration of Justice, and published as an appendix to *Task Force Report: Juvenile Delinquency and Youth Crime.*

An Assessment of the Juvenile Court Today

Studies conducted by the Commission, legislative inquiries in various States, and reports by informed observers compel the conclusion that the great hopes originally held for the juvenile court have not been fulfilled. It has not succeeded significantly in rehabilitating delinquent youth, in reducing or even stemming the tide of juvenile criminality, or in bringing justice and compassion to the child offender. To say that juvenile courts have failed to achieve their goals is to say no more than what is true of criminal courts in the United States. But failure is most striking when hopes are highest.

One reason for the failure of the juvenile courts has been the community's continuing unwillingness to provide the resources—the people and facilities and concern—necessary to permit them to realize their potential and prevent them from taking on some of the undesirable features typical of lower criminal courts in this country. In few jurisdictions, for example, does the juvenile court judgeship enjoy high status in the eyes of the bar, and while there are many juvenile court judges of outstanding ability and devotion, many are not. One crucial presupposition of the juvenile court philosophy—a mature and sophisticated judge, wise and well-versed in law and the science of human behavior—has proved in fact too often unattainable. A recent study of juvenile court judges reported above[23] revealed that half had not received undergraduate degrees; a fifth had received no college education at all; a fifth were not members of the bar. Almost three-quarters devote less than a quarter of their time to juvenile and family matters, and judicial hearings often are little more than attenuated interviews of 10 or 15 minutes' duration. The National Council on Crime and Delinquency states that the family court in Cook County (Chicago), Ill., averages a little over 15 minutes per hearing—about half the time the council estimates is needed for proper consideration of the issues.[24] A recent California State study concluded:

> Based upon estimates furnished by juvenile court judges, the average time spent on a juvenile court case is approximately 10 to 15

---

[23] Center for the Behavioral Sciences, *op. cit. supra* note 21; McCune and Skoler, *supra* note 21, at p. 121.

[24] NCCD, *The Cook County Family (Juvenile) Court and Arthur J. Audy Home* (1963), pp. 28–29. See Barron, *The Juvenile in Delinquent Society* (1954), chapter 15.

minutes ° ° °. An appropriate question is whether the beneficent values of the juvenile court hearing implied by the philosophy expressed in the law can be achieved in the abbreviated time which most juvenile courts devote to each case. To what extent, for example, can a judge make a significant impact on the errant child and his parents in what is almost an assembly line judicial process? A corollary question is whether the juvenile court judge can actually explore in a brief hearing the behavioral complexities presented by each case.[25]

Other resources are equally lacking. The survey of juvenile court judges reveals the scarcity of psychologists and psychiatrists—over half a century after the juvenile court movement set out to achieve the coordinated application of the behavioral and social sciences to the misbehaving child. Where clinics exist, their waiting lists usually are months long and frequently they provide no treatment but only diagnosis. And treatment, even when prescribed, is often impossible to carry out because of the unavailability of adequate individual and family casework, foster home placement, treatment in youth institutions. Despite general acceptance of the fact that many children who cannot adjust successfully in their own homes could do so in another community setting without requiring incarceration, only 99 of the 235 agencies in the sample studied by the Commission use foster homes, and only 10 operate group homes.[26]

The dispositional alternatives available even to the better endowed juvenile courts fall far short of the richness and the relevance to individual needs envisioned by the court's founders. In most places, indeed, the only alternatives are release outright, probation, and institutionalization. Probation means minimal supervision at best. A large percentage of juvenile courts have no probation services at all, and in those that do, caseloads typically are so high that counseling and supervision take the form of occasional phone calls and perfunctory visits instead of the careful, individualized service that was intended. Institutionalization too often means storage—isolation from the outside world—in an overcrowded, understaffed, high-security institution with little education, little vocational training, little counseling or job placement or other guidance upon release. Programs are subordinated to everyday control and maintenance. Children spend weeks in limbo-like detention, awaiting bed space. Professor Glueck quotes a well-informed penologist:

> There are things going on, methods of discipline being used in the
> State training schools of this country that would cause a warden of

[25] California Governor's Special Study Commission on Juvenile Justice, *A Study of the Administration of Juvenile Justice in California* (1960), part 2, at p. 16 (hereinafter cited as the California Report).

[26] NCCD, Correction in the United States (prepared by the President's Commission on Law Enforcement and Administration of Justice, 1966, printed as appendix A of the *Task Force Report: Corrections*), pp. 64–65.

Alcatraz to lose his job if he used them on his prisoners. There are practices that are a daily occurrence in some of our State training schools that are not permitted in the prisons or penitentiaries of the same States. There are many States in which this discipline is more humane, more reasonable, in the prison than it is in the State training school.[27]

But it is of great importance to emphasize that a simple infusion of resources into juvenile courts and attendant institutions would by no means fulfill the expectations that accompanied the court's birth and development. There are problems that go much deeper. The failure of the juvenile court to fulfill its rehabilitative and preventive promise stems in important measure from a grossly overoptimistic view of what is known about the phenomenon of juvenile criminality and of what even a fully equipped juvenile court could do about it. Experts in the field agree that it is extremely difficult to develop successful methods for preventing serious delinquent acts through rehabilitative programs for the child. There is no shortage of theories of the etiology of delinquency. They range from the intrapsychic to the sociological, from the genetic to the anthropological, even to theories turning upon analyses of body types and structures. Some have looked for basic, generalized explanations of all delinquency. Some have noted the enormous variety in the types of conduct officially denominated delinquency as well as in the types of juveniles found to be delinquents and have begun to suggest narrower explanations differentiating among kinds of deviant behavior. But fundamentally delinquency is behavior, and until the science of human behavior matures far beyond its present confines, an understanding of those kinds of behavior we call delinquency is not likely to be forthcoming. Study and research tend increasingly to support the view that delinquency is not so much an act of individual deviancy as a pattern of behavior produced by a multitude of pervasive societal influences well beyond the reach of the actions of any judge, probation officer, correctional counselor, or psychiatrist.

The same uncritical and unrealistic estimates of what is known and can be done that make expectation so much greater than achievement also serve to justify extensive official action and to mask the fact that much of it may do more harm than good. Official action may actually help to fix and perpetuate delinquency in the child through a process in which the individual begins to think of himself as delinquent and organizes his behavior accordingly. That process itself is further reinforced by the effect of the labeling upon the child's family, neighbors, teachers, and peers, whose reactions communicate to the child in subtle ways a kind of expectation of

---

[27] MacCormick, *The Essentials of a Training School Program, Matching Scientific Advance with Human Progress* (NCJCL Conference, May 1950), p. 15, quoted in Glueck, "Some 'Unfinished Business' in the Management of Juvenile Delinquency," 15 *Syracuse Law Review* (1964), pp. 628, 630.

delinquent conduct. The undesirable consequences of official treatment are heightened in programs that rely on institutionalizing the child. The most informed and benign institutional treatment of the child, even in well designed and staffed reformatories and training schools, thus may contain within it the seeds of its own frustration and itself may often feed the very disorder it is designed to cure.

The limitations, both in theory and in execution, of strictly rehabilitative treatment methods, combined with public anxiety over the seemingly irresistible rise in juvenile criminality, have produced a rupture between the theory and the practice of juvenile court dispositions. While statutes, judges, and commentators still talk the language of compassion, help, and treatment, it has become clear that in fact the same purposes that characterize the use of the criminal law for adult offenders—retribution, condemnation, deterrence, incapacitation—are involved in the disposition of juvenile offenders too. These are society's ultimate techniques for protection against threatening conduct; it is inevitable that they should be used against threats from the young as well as the old when other resources appear unavailing. As Professor Francis Allen has acutely observed:

> In a great many cases the juvenile court must perform functions essentially similar to those exercised by any court adjudicating cases of persons charged with dangerous and disturbing behavior. It must reassert the norms and standards of the community when confronted by seriously deviant conduct, and it must protect the security of the community by such measures as it has at its disposal, even though the available means may be unsatisfactory when viewed either from the standpoint of the community interest or of the welfare of the delinquent child.[28]

The difficulty is not that this compromise with the rehabilitative idea has occurred, but that it has not been acknowledged. Juvenile court laws and procedures that can be defended and rationalized solely on the basis of the original optimistic theories endure as if the vitality of those theories were undiluted. Thus, for example, juvenile courts retain expansive grounds of jurisdiction authorizing judicial intervention in relatively minor matters of morals and misbehavior, on the ground that subsequent delinquent conduct may be indicated, as if there were reliable ways of predicting delinquency in a given child and reliable ways of redirecting children's lives. Delinquency is adjudicated in informal proceedings that often lack safeguards fundamental for protecting the individual and for assuring reliable determinations, as if the court were a hospital clinic and its only objective were to discover the child's malady and to cure him. As observed by Mr. Justice Fortas, speaking for the Supreme Court in *Kent* v. *United States,* "there may be grounds for concern that the child receives the worst of both worlds: that he gets neither

---

[28] Allen, *The Borderland of Criminal Justice* (1964), p. 53.

the protections accorded to adults nor the solicitous care and regenerative treatment postulated for children."[29]

What emerges, then, is this: In theory the juvenile court was to be helpful and rehabilitative rather than punitive. In fact the distinction often disappears, not only because of the absence of facilities and personnel but also because of the limits of knowledge and technique. In theory the court's action was to affix no stigmatizing label. In fact a delinquent is generally viewed by employers, schools, the armed services—by society generally—as a criminal. In theory the court was to treat children guilty of criminal acts in noncriminal ways. In fact it labels truants and runaways as junior criminals.

In theory the court's operations could justifiably be informal, its findings and decisions made without observing ordinary procedural safeguards, because it would act only in the best interest of the child. In fact it frequently does nothing more nor less than deprive a child of liberty without due process of law—knowing not what else to do and needing, whether admittedly or not, to act in the community's interest even more imperatively than the child's. In theory it was to exercise its protective powers to bring an errant child back into the fold. In fact there is increasing reason to believe that its intervention reinforces the juvenile's unlawful impulses. In theory it was to concentrate on each case the best of current social science learning. In fact it has often become a vested interest in its turn, loath to cooperate with innovative programs or avail itself of forward-looking methods.

Nevertheless, study of the juvenile courts does not necessarily lead to the conclusion that the time has come to jettison the experiment and remand the disposition of children charged with crime to the criminal courts of the country. As trying as are the problems of the juvenile courts, the problems of the criminal courts, particularly those of the lower courts, which would fall heir to much of the juvenile court jurisdiction, are even graver; and the ideal of separate treatment of children is still worth pursuing. What is required is rather a revised philosophy of the juvenile court based on the recognition that in the past our reach exceeded our grasp. The spirit that animated the juvenile court movement was fed in part by a humanitarian compassion for offenders who were children. That willingness to understand and treat people who threaten public safety and security should be nurtured, not turned aside as hopeless sentimentality, both because it is civilized and because social protection itself demands constant search for alternatives to the crude and limited expedient of condemnation and punishment. But neither should it be allowed to outrun reality. The juvenile court is a court of law, charged like other agencies of criminal justice with protecting the community against threatening conduct. Rehabilitating offenders through individualized handling is one way of providing protection and, appropriately, the primary way in dealing with children. But the

[29] 383 U.S. 541, 556 (1966).

guiding consideration for a court of law that deals with threatening conduct is nonetheless protection of the community. The juvenile court, like other courts, is therefore obliged to employ all the means at hand, not excluding incapacitation, for achieving that protection. What should distinguish the juvenile from the criminal courts is greater emphasis on rehabilitation, not exclusive preoccupation with it.

We have attempted to describe in the following pages what this revised conception of the juvenile court means in practice. In its broadest outlines it means channeling the principal rehabilitative effort into community based dispositions that occur prior to assumption of jurisdiction by the court, narrowing the reach of juvenile court jurisdiction to cases of manifest danger either to the child or to the community, and infusing in the court itself procedures designed to assure fair and reliable determinations for those who reach the point of judicial action.

Pre-Judicial Dispositions

In keeping with the spirit of reform that animated the juvenile court movement, new modes were devised for handling juvenile delinquents as distinct from adult offenders. The distinctions in procedure between juvenile court hearings and trials of criminal cases are discussed in a later section.[30] This section examines procedural differences that occur in earlier stages of the juvenile justice system—from apprehension to formal hearing and disposition. Police "station adjustment"; planned diversion of alleged delinquents away from the court to the resources of schools, clinics, and other community facilities; "unofficial" handling of delinquency cases in the juvenile court—all are examples of pre-judicial handling methods that have acquired recognized status in the system of juvenile justice. These methods have been described variously as informal, extralegal, unofficial, unauthorized, or nonjudicial. In the terminology used here, pre-judicial dispositions[31] are discretionary judgments made prior to a hearing on a delinquency petition. This section considers and critically appraises the rationale for and extent of their use.

The Rationale and Function
of Pre-Judicial Handling

The pressures and policies responsible for development of pre-judicial dispositions in the juvenile system are in part the same as those that have

[30] *Procedural Justice for the Juvenile, infra.*

[31] The term pre-judicial disposition seems more precisely descriptive of the subject of this section than the other familiar terms. The practices to be discussed may well be "official" or "authorized," depending on State law, the facts of the juvenile's behavior, and the position of the person making a disposition. The use of the term "nonjudicial" could connote decisions made by agencies other than a court or without the knowledge or guidance of the judge, whereas in fact many discretionary judgments are made by court staff within explicit guidelines evolved by or with the juvenile court judge.

led to the use of alternatives to adjudication in the adult criminal process. All stages of law enforcement, for both juveniles and adults, are permeated with discretionary authority. Not every adult wrongdoer is brought to trial for his misconduct, nor is every juvenile offender put through the mill of official processing. It is impossible to determine how many potential subjects of formal legal action are eliminated from the system at an early point, but bits and pieces of information when put together portray a law enforcement and judicial system that uses, and appears to value, substantial discretion, particularly in the initial stages of handling.[32]

Arguments against discretion (and informal handling as the product of its exercise) are based largely on promotion of the rule of law. Individual liberty and dignity are said to require precise definition of standards for authoritative intervention and careful maintenance of procedural restraints. Broad powers of discretion are susceptible of abuse, and abuse of power threatens cherished values. From an administrative perspective the enlargement of discretionary power entails dangers of a different order: inconsistent law enforcement, and the resultant evils of disrespect for and distrust of legal institutions. And there is the added fear that in incompetent hands discretionary authority will degenerate into automatic (though unacknowledged) application of rules of thumb devised to further staff convenience at the price of rehabilitation, deterrence, or other stated goals of public administration. Finally, it must be recognized that informal handling appears informal only to the officials charged with execution of certain responsibilities; to those caught up in the net of the juvenile justice system, it is impressively authoritative and formal, regardless of conditions or timing of release. A position in favor of infusing discretion into the several stages of the criminal law must take these hazards into account.

The case for discretion in criminal law rests on several arguments. First, in many cases in which technically the law has been violated, application of the full criminal process is too severe, and there is a "need to mediate between generally formulated laws and the human values"[33] in particular cases. That need is the greater in view of the anguish, harm to reputation, expense, and, if there is a conviction, formal disabilities that criminal prosecution entails. And "even the most careful of legislative draftsmanship is not likely to achieve a completely unambiguous definition of criminal conduct."[34] Modern codes demonstrate that some misunderstanding can be

[32] See generally, Breitel, "Controls in Criminal Law Enforcement," 27 *University of Chicago Law Review*, 1960, pp. 427, 428; Handler and Rosenheim, "Privacy in Welfare: Public Assistance and Juvenile Justice," 31 *Law and Contemporary Probation*, 1966, p. 377. Officials commonly responsible for discretionary determinations prior to trial or hearing are police, prosecutor, grand jury (exceptional in juvenile cases), and court intake staff (applicable to delinquency, not to criminal proceeding). In addition, the judge may effectively wield discretionary authority in the pre-judicial phase of juvenile cases.

[33] Kadish, "Legal Norm and Discretion in the Police and Sentencing Processes," 75 *Harvard Law Review*, 1962, pp. 904, 911.

[34] Remington and Rosenblum, "The Criminal Law and the Legislative Process," *University of Illinois Law Review*, 1960, pp. 481, 488.

avoided through skillful legislative formulation. But a residuum of cases will remain for administrative determination, and evaluation of legislative intent will inevitably include measuring the severity of criminal process against the particular circumstances. Many factors shape the decision to screen out of the system or defer proceedings, among them the nature of the offense, the circumstances of its commission, the attitude of the victim, and the character of the accused. Concern lest criminal prosecution impose a deviant role on the accused and thus increase the probability of successive criminal acts also motivates exercise of discretion.

A second argument for discretion in administering criminal justice arises from the tendency of legislatures to overcriminalize human conduct or to reach ends other than crime prevention through a penal code.[35] The appetites and pursuits of many men bring them into technical conflict with the law, yet scarcely disturb the public order as it is commonly viewed. Criminal process is a mighty weapon to use against bingo and private poker games, extramarital sexual adventures, loitering, and numerous other forms of conduct proscribed by law. Discretionary judgment allows this hefty bludgeon frequently to remain on the shelf—available but seldom used. Possession of vast amounts of discretion may itself be undesirable, and the scope or ambiguity of legislation aimed primarily at controlling personal behavior, as distinguished from statutes aimed at protecting the life and property of others, may lead to abuse of discretion. But the existence of crimes of status and attempts to impose conformity tilt the balance toward allowing it.

A third point in favor of discretion is plainly practical. Sheer volume demands the use of screening devices in law enforcement.[36] Official agencies are undermanned, underbudgeted, and overloaded; of necessity they must select for attention the cases that appear to them most pressing. The natural tendency appears to be to concentrate on major crimes, although there are exceptions, and some choices are open to question.

The conviction that handling by the juvenile justice system is too severe—that labeling a child a delinquent harms him and may reinforce his patterns of antisocial behavior—parallels the argument for discretion to avoid the severity of the criminal law. As in dealing with accused adults, officials are influenced by type of offense, attitudes of complainants and the public, assessment of the child and his home.

Indeed, the severity argument takes on special significance in juvenile justice. The human aspect of a criminal case exerts a powerful pull when the suspect is young. If the harshness of the criminal process supports use of discretion with adults, the argument is even more persuasive when applied to young offenders. Furthermore, underlying the special handling of the young offender is the belief that he can be changed. For him, therefore, the

---

[35] Kadish, *supra* note 33, at pp. 909–911.
[36] Goldstein, "Police Discretion Not to Invoke the Criminal Process," 69 *Yale Law Journal*, 1961, pp. 543, 561, nn 30–33.

criminal process, because of its ineffectiveness as an agent of change, seems particularly inappropriate.

Similarly, the overcriminalizing or hidden welfare aspects of the criminal law support discretion even more strongly in the juvenile than in the adult context. Non-crime-prevention provisions are far more prevalent in juvenile court law than in the most antiquated of criminal codes. Delinquency is often defined not only as violation of penal law but also as departure from behavior required uniquely of juveniles—school attendance, obedience to parents, curfew, and other conduct regulations.[37] Legislative standards for intervention are dealt with subsequently.[38] Here it should be noted that the scope of State authority over juveniles emphasizes the need for discretionary judgment. Even recent statutory revisions that narrow delinquency to commission of criminal acts fail to reduce significantly the area of discretion because they have retained other vaguely stated grounds for official intervention. Neglect is a good example; it sometimes extends beyond parental irresponsibility or maltreatment to apply to a minor "whose behavior is injurious to his own welfare or that of others."[39] And two States have adopted a new category, juveniles "in need of supervision."[40] Thus the vulnerability of the young to State control is demonstrably greater than that of adults.[41]

Discretionary judgment also provides a necessary steam valve in the juvenile justice system. Just as the administration of criminal justice is strained by growing criminal populations, so too the increasing volume of juvenile offenders builds up pressure within police departments, juvenile courts, and all the other institutions with responsibility to control delinquency.[42] Neither police ranks nor the number of judges and auxiliary staff of juvenile courts has expanded at a rate commensurate with the increase in recorded delinquency. Informal determinations as to which cases demand official action are inevitable, and in the process many juveniles are diverted to nonjudicial sources of control and service.

For various reasons and to differing extents, then, every community is committed to informal handling. Yet not everyone understands or approves. The informal handling process is conducted sub rosa with insufficient public understanding of its purpose. The consequences are ignorance of how the process works and neglect of issues of fairness and effectiveness. Concern about the workings of the juvenile justice system has generally concentrated on its formal procedures. Yet in at least some communities informal procedures are quantitatively more significant than formal ones,

---

[37] Paulsen, "The Delinquency, Neglect, and Dependency Jurisdiction of the Juvenile Court," in *Justice for the Child, op. cit. supra* note 6, at pp. 44, 49–51.

[38] *Legislative Standards for Juvenile Court Intervention* infra.

[39] *Illinois Juvenile Court Act*, Secs. 702–704(b), 1966.

[40] *New York Family Court Act*, sec. 712(b), 1966.

[41] See Handler and Rosenblum, *supra* note 32.

[42] Elson and Rosenheim, "Justice for the Child," 51 *American Bar Association Journal*, 1965, p. 341.

and it is they that are the base for all other delinquency control activities. They must be reckoned with in blueprints for the future of the juvenile justice system.

The Processes of Pre-Judicial Handling

THE ISSUES FOR DECISION

Any group or individual attempting to formulate a plan of action toward an alleged delinquent must make a number of decisions: (1) identification of an act as delinquency; (2) screening for appropriate action; (3) planning and implementing service.[43]

Ascertainment of the fact of delinquency is a duty of all official agencies trying to bring a delinquent minor under their authority. The standard of proof may vary according to the stage in the law enforcement process; the facts that justify the police in taking a minor into custody will not necessarily satisfy the juvenile court as a basis for adjudication.[44] In some instances, the reasonable grounds for official action toward juveniles at various stages of delinquency control have been legislatively articulated.[45]

Identification of delinquency is also a necessary step for agencies and individuals seeking to control lawlessness through informal means. Social agencies, for example, must determine at intake whether an individual is a delinquent and, therefore, a suitable client. Since the unofficial agencies of the delinquency control system can impose sanctions by referring clients for formal action, the factfinding procedures they employ assume considerable importance. The same is true of factfinding by official agencies bent on applying informal measures; attaching the tag of delinquency without scrupulous attention to the facts raises the same kinds of questions about fairness when done unauthoritatively—usually, nonetheless, well publicized—as it does in formal action.

At the screening stage any unit of delinquency control, official or otherwise, has several options. They include outright dismissal, acceptance for service, or referral (the last an effort to direct a youngster to community services that he needs but is unfamiliar with or resists).[46] Screening deci-

---

[43] The classification is derived from that found in Kahn, "Court and Community," in *Justice for the Child, op. cit. supra* note 6, at p. 217. For a book-length statement of his approach to the treatment and control of delinquent and neglected children, see Kahn, *Planning Community Services for Children in Trouble* (1963).

[44] Cf. Remington, "The Law Relating to 'On the Street' Detention, Questioning and Frisking of Suspected Persons and Police Arrest Privileges in General," in Sowle, ed., *Police Power and Individual Freedom*, pp. 11, 18–19.

[45] See, e.g., the specification of grounds for taking juveniles into custody in *New York Family Court Act*, 1963, Secs. 721, 722.

[46] The difficulties of securing effective referrals, especially in work with delinquents, have generally been understood. Some of them are elaborated in Spercel, *Street Gang Work: Theory and Practice*, 1966, pp. 136–144.

sions depend on the evaluator's judgment of what he or his agency can offer, what is available elsewhere, and what limitations are imposed by the known priorities for service.

Both planning and carrying out service are functions performed by every unit that accepts a case. For adjudicated delinquents, the framework of service (disposition) is set by the law; with few exceptions, however, the law is silent about permissible action toward nonadjudicated delinquents.[47] Treatment programs may include those of voluntary or ad hoc associations, of public or private delinquency prevention agencies, of welfare agencies, of the newly created poverty program units, or of other institutions that have expanded beyond their originally stated functions to reach nonadjudicated delinquents.[48]

Any individual or community group that initiates work with delinquents may properly be regarded as part of the delinquency control system. To see the system in its entirety, and to identify existing alternatives to adjudication for those classified as delinquent, it is necessary to recognize the formal and informal dimensions of the system and the stages of decisionmaking common to both. An official agency may deal with nonadjudicated as well as adjudicated delinquents; it may perform unofficial functions as well as official ones, perhaps acquiring from its formal authority leverage to operate informally.

PRESENT PRACTICES

At the outset, a broad disclaimer is essential: Information on pre-judicial handling is not sufficiently reliable to offer firm generalizations, nor can an accurate description be given of particular phases of this dispositional process. Some delinquent acts apparently are adjusted so unsystematically and informally that the process is invisible. A storeowner's intervention to adjust theft, a victim's compromise of assault, a schoolteacher's mediation in an act of vandalism are instances of unrecorded informal handling. They are known to exist, but no useful generalizations can be made about their rate of occurrence or the circumstances of adjustment.

There are reasons for that ignorance. Widespread indifference to informal aspects of bureaucratic operations explains it in part, for not until recently has research in criminal law been directed beyond the stated official functions of social institutions. The current interest is the result of heightened curiosity about the latent functions of bureaucracy. In part, too, the lack of knowledge is a product of the discreet silence that cloaks ancillary activities

---

[47] But see the provisions for adjustment efforts in *New York Family Court Act,* 1963, sec. 734, and *Illinois Juvenile Court Act,* 1966, sec. 703-e. See also *Standards for Juvenile and Family Courts.*

[48] For the indication of the range of police attempts to affect the conduct of nonadjuciated delinquents, see Neis, "Juvenile Delinquents: The Police, State Courts, and Individualized Justice," 79 *Harvard Law Review,* 1966 (hereinafter cited as *Juvenile Delinquents*).

about which an organization feels uncomfortable. A school, for instance, may in fact adjust many situations involving delinquency. It has an interest in offenses occurring in or harmful to the school, and it has an interest in its pupils. For children who inspire the compassionate attention of their teachers, the school may bend its efforts to secure adjustment even of wholly extraschool offenses. But the school may feel it cannot afford publicly to acknowledge these actions of its staff for fear of creating anxiety among parents and risking criticism for allocating time to nonacademic concerns.

In addition, adjustments by individuals may well be beyond the reach of systematic research. Where a satisfactory resolution is privately reached, the personal nature of the confrontation between a suspected juvenile and his accuser is an effective shield to recording.

Within the official agencies of delinquency control, alternatives to adjudication of delinquents have tended to emerge haphazardly, as unplanned and unofficial aspects of a community's system. At least one juvenile court law acknowledges the likelihood of screening by police[49] as well as court staff, though typically the function is implicit in other duties imposed by law, and the laws of over half the States authorize screening at the point of intake.[50] But, predictably, the emphasis in juvenile court legislation is on the law enforcement and judicial process as it applies to juveniles who are officially handled—taken into custody, formally alleged to be delinquent, adjudicated, and declared to be wards of the court subject to sanctions set forth in orders of disposition. The laws do not provide affirmative guidelines for screening out of the delinquency control system or for selecting measures of restraint or rehabilitation to apply to those so channeled.

Statistical data concerning the pre-judicial handling process are even less available than data concerning the formal processes and, as is true of data collection generally, what are available are less than systematic.[51] With few exceptions, information on pre-judicial handling is restricted to the aspects officially acknowledged. While the account that follows is therefore necessarily inadequate, it bears out impressions of the magnitude and unplanned character of the process.

Police

Statistics reveal how many juvenile offenders come into official contact with the police; they do not reveal the number of unofficial contacts on the

[49] *Illinois Juvenile Court Act*, 1966, sec. 703–2(1): "A law enforcement officer *** shall *** take the minor to the nearest juvenile officer ***. The minor, *if not released*, shall be delivered without unnecessary delay to the court or to the place designated by rule or order of court for the reception of minors." (Italics added.)

[50] *Standards for Juvenile and Family Courts*, pp. 53–60; see also Sheridan, "Juvenile Court Intake," 2 *Journal of Family Law*, 1962, p. 139.

[51] Thus, for example, little or nothing is known about police decisions not to arrest or not to take juveniles into custody. See Barrett, "Police Practice and the Law—From Arrest to Release or Charge," 50 *California Law Review*, 1962, pp. 11, 25–35; Goldstein, *supra* note 36. But see Skolnick, *Justice Without Trial* (1966), for an enlightening account of police practices in two jurisdictions.

street or in the stationhouse. In cases of more than brief or casual contact, a trip to the stationhouse for questioning by the arresting officer or juvenile specialist[52] is usually required. The dispositions available to the police range from outright release, usually to the parents, to referral to the juvenile court. Court referral may mean citation, filing of a complaint, or physical removal of the child to detention awaiting formal action. Between those extremes are referral to community resources selected by the officer and station adjustment, by which is meant the juvenile's release on one or more conditions. The term station adjustment, as used here, implies an effort by the police to control and change the juvenile's behavior. Both national[53] and local[54] data indicate great variation in the use of these alternatives. Differences, expectably, are more marked among the many jurisdictions than within a jurisdiction's pattern of handling from year to year. Across the country, it is clear, discretionary action by the police in screening juvenile offenders accounts for the removal of significant numbers from the formal juvenile justice system.

It is likely, moreover, that reliance on police discretion is especially marked in some of the major urban centers.[55] In one midwestern city in 1965, for instance, 66.1 percent of all official police contacts with juveniles were adjusted, a proportion that has stayed remarkably constant in recent years.[56] In a small eastern city, however, the proportion of offenders referred to court rose between 1963 and 1965 from 56 to 70 percent, reflecting, in the words of a report, "either a more serious nature of offense or a stricter

[52] E.G., *Illinois Juvenile Court Act,* 1966, sec. 703–2.

[53] The classification used in the Uniform Crime Reports, and the percentage for each in 1965, are: handled within department and released (46.7 percent); referred to juvenile court jurisdiction (46.1 percent); referred to welfare agency (2.9 percent); referred to other police agency (2.7 percent); and referred to criminal or adult court (1.7 percent). 1965 Federal Bureau of Investigation Uniform Crime Reports 104 (table 13). Figures are national totals for reporting agencies. FBI data do not differentiate among types of intradepartmental handling; some departments, however, distinguish between referrals to juvenile court in which the juvenile is detained and referrals to court with concomitant release to parents or other adults. See note 54 *infra.*

FBI data are reported for eight categories: six groups of cities, divided according to population, and suburban and rural areas. Data reveal intradepartmental handling and release in 38.5 percent of the juvenile offense cases reported by Group I (cities over 250,000); 48.9 percent in reporting cities of Group II (100,000–250,000); 50 percent or more in all remaining city groups (50,000–100,000; 25,000–50,000; 10,000–25,000; under 10,000) and in suburban areas; and 29.6 percent in rural areas. Referral to juvenile court jurisdiction occurred in more than 50 percent of all cases only in Group I cities and in rural areas, and the percentage of referrals to welfare agencies was larger in Group I (6.1 percent) than in any other category (between 1.0 and 2.1 percent).

[54] In one large Midwestern city, for example, data show the following pattern of police disposition in 1965: Out of a total of 38,531 offenses recorded in 1965, 25,456 cases were adjusted (11, 573 released to parents and 13,882 referred to community agencies); 5,652 cases were referred to the juvenile court; and 7,426 cases were referred for detention. Chicago Police Department, Youth Division, 1965 Annual Offense/Offender Data Sheet. These data are routinely collected but not published.

[55] But see *Juvenile Delinquents,* p. 776.

[56] Chicago Police Department, Youth Division, 1965 Annual Offense/Offender Data Sheet.

attitude on the part of the police."⁵⁷ In either event, discretionary judgment to refer or to retain for police handling was exercised in a wide variety of offenses, from the serious to the minor.⁵⁸ However sharply specific communities depart from this norm, for the Nation the tendency to use pre-judicial handling is pronounced. In the past 5 years intradepartmental handling by police has been reported to occur nationally in between 45 and 50 percent of all juvenile contacts.⁵⁹ Each option, moreover, can be and often is used for almost every type of offense. Involuntary manslaughter, rape, serious assault and battery, armed robbery, burglary, and many other felonies are adjusted by the police, frequently at significantly high rates.⁶⁰

But what action do the police initiate for those screened out? National data do not provide a breakdown; referrals to court (juvenile and adult), referrals to welfare and other agencies, and interdepartmental handling or release are the usual categories of action reported. Analyses of individual departmental reports are somewhat more helpful. So too are inquiries into practices in specific localities. According to a recent law review account, hearings are scheduled in some police departments whenever station adjustment is under consideration.⁶¹ The outcome can be release with reprimand, imposition of direct sanction, referral to a social service or similar community resource, or referral to the court.⁶²

Written standards for adjustment or referral to the juvenile courts are not uncommon. The manual of the youth division of the Chicago Police Department contains such standards.⁶³ The youth officer's attention is directed to the type of offense, the juvenile's past experiences and personal background, and the attitudes of parents as well as offenders. Existence of community resources is listed as another factor. How these and similar guides⁶⁴ are used in practice, however, is less clear.

---

⁵⁷ I Stanford Research Institute, *A Description of Active Juvenile Offenders and Convicted Adult Felons in the District of Columbia*, Juvenile Offenders 44 (prepared for Office of Law Enforcement Assistance, U.S. Department of Justice, 1966).

⁵⁸ *Id.* at pp. 47, 48, tables 60, 61.

⁵⁹ The Uniform Crime Reports for 1961 through 1965 show that informal police handling of juvenile offenses during that period occurred in no less than 45 percent and no more than 50 percent of all the cases.

⁶⁰ Special data analysis of the Chicago Youth Division reports shows adjustment rates for Part I óffenses (homicide, serious assault and battery, robbery, burglary, and theft) ranging from 9.9 percent of offenders' cases adjusted (auto theft) to 93 percent (shoplifting). There were some adjusted cases in every offense category except murder: e.g., rape (9.3 percent), armed robbery (30.5 percent), attempted burglary (66.1 percent), bicycle theft (85.6 percent). Adjustment of Part II offenses was generally higher: e.g., drinking (80.6 percent), disorderly conduct (92.6 percent), simple assault (55.6 percent), trespassing (94.1 percent); but compare incorrigibles (19.5 percent). Chicago Police Department, Youth Division, 1965 Annual Offense/Offender Data Sheet.

See Stanford Research Institute, *op. cit., supra* note 57; Terry, "The Screening of Juvenile Offenders," 1966 (unpublished thesis, University of Wisconsin).

⁶¹ *Juvenile Delinquents*, pp. 779–785.

⁶² *Ibid.*

⁶³ Chicago Police Department, Youth Division, *Manual of Procedure*, 1965.

⁶⁴ *Juvenile Delinquents*, p. 778 and n. 11.

By all accounts the type of offense is important. Court or departmental policy requires some offenses be handled by the court, though this policy may not always be followed by the police. More serious offenses, if adjusted at all, seem to be adjusted relatively less often than minor ones. A past offense or the status of the juvenile as probationer or parolee makes certain juveniles ineligible for the pre-judicial process.

Data on the impact of race on policy determinations are somewhat contradictory and difficult to assess. Several commentators have asserted that race is weighed in the scale; one study supports this.[65] But other data reflect remarkably similar court referral rates for whites and Negroes.[66]

Another imponderable is demeanor—the juvenile's behavior and apparent attitude toward the police. By policy a denial of involvement requires a court referral in some jurisdictions. Some police officers seem to feel that a denial of guilt or a defiant attitude indicates an uncooperative youth, one who will not be amenable to treatment.[67] Such a youth is considered a greater risk to the community if released, and police prefer to have that judgment made by the court. A similar rationale may account for referrals of juveniles whose parents are defensive about their misbehavior or resent police intrusions.[68] Some experienced juvenile specialists, in fact, regard the parents' attitude as more significant than the child's.

When adjustment is the course of action, typically the police issue a warning or make a referral to a nonjudicial agency. One reported practice is as follows:

> In Kansas City, for example, the police administer a stringent though informal discipline program called grounding. A typical grounded youth must attend school unless a doctor's explanation is obtained for his absence. At all other times he may leave the house only if accompanied by a parent, and then not for any activity that is primarily engaged in for pleasure. He must dress conventionally and have his hair cut in a reasonable manner; and he must study at home for a minimum prescribed period each day. After this schedule is enforced for a month, lesser conditions will be imposed for the duration of the school year. A high degree of success in preventing future offenses is claimed to result from this program.[69]

In the many neighborhoods where juvenile specialists and patrolmen are acquainted with the juveniles whose cases have been adjusted at the station, closer supervision on the street may result. In any event, the police themselves see the screening mechanism, with its adjustment possibility, as a

[65] Piliavin and Briar, "Police Encounters with Juveniles," 70 *American Journal of Sociology,* 1964, p. 206. See also Goldman, *The Differential Selection of Juvenile Offenders for Court Appearance* (NCCD ed. 1963), pp. 42–44.

[66] Terry, *supra* note 60; Stanford Research Institute, *op. cit., supra* note 57, at pp. 45, 49, 50.

[67] *Juvenile Delinquents,* p. 781.

[68] *Id.* at 781.

[69] *Id.* at p. 784.

way of assisting parents in their efforts to control a problem child, of reassuring the community, and of providing a fertile ground for friendship between the youth and the police. The net result, they claim, is an "association [that] assists in reorienting the child, gives him a new set of values, helps him to break away from undesirable associates and habits, and frequently is all that is needed to stop his wayward behavior."[70]

The discretionary options that have been considered up to this point are dismissal, community referral, station adjustment, and referral to court. Another crucial determination is whether to refer to court officials for detention. In theory court officials control decisions to detain but, in processing juveniles brought to the detention home by the police, these officials appear to be influenced significantly by the prior police determination of the need for secure custody.[71] Some surveys have indicated that in a large proportion of the cases that the police bring to detention homes, an initial period of detention follows.[72] That is, relatively few of the detention referrals are released at the point of intake to the detention unit. Many, of course, are released within a 24- to 48-hour period. Moreover, some of the juveniles initially detained are not thereafter made the subjects of petitions in the juvenile court, and of those who are, many are released after adjudication to live in the community.

It appears that the police place substantial dependence on overnight detention. Overuse of detention represents not only the problem, general to the criminal justice system as a whole, of overreliance on incarceration in lieu of release on bail or recognizance, but also a particularly vexing problem in juvenile justice. Admittedly, the police face a dilemma. They are often looked to as the only public agency available 24 hours a day. By virtue of the breadth of legislative standards for intervention in the lives of children, they possess broad discretionary powers. It is hard to say how many cases of juveniles detained briefly might have been handled otherwise, had alternative resources been available. But studies have repeatedly pointed to detention rates that are high in spite of the lack of facilities throughout the country and that could be markedly reduced. More diligent search for parents or other responsible adults might in some instances have produced satisfactory alternatives. Thus the conclusion emerges that detention has sometimes been employed not so much for protection of the juvenile or the community as for its shock effect on an alleged offender.

In sum, the range of police dispositions is considerable, and the criteria for selection of disposition are seldom set forth explicitly, ordered in priority, or regularly reviewed for administrative purposes. Inservice training designed to assist police in exercising their discretionary functions is unu-

---

[70] Wilson, *Police Planning* (2d ed. 1957), 135–136, quoted in *Juvenile Delinquents*, pp. 785–786 n. 40.

[71] Freed and Wald, *Bail in the United States*, 1964, at pp. 97–98; NCCD, *The Cook County Family (Juvenile) Court and Arthur J. Audy Home*, 1963, pp. 137, 138–139. For discussion of the detention decision as an aspect of the intake function, see Sheridan, "Juvenile Court Intake," 2 *Journal of Family Law*, 1962, pp. 139, 152–153.

[72] *Ibid.* and studies cited in Freed and Wald, *op. cit., supra* note 71, at pp. 98–100.

sual; the few examples deserve further investigation, for improvement of the police discretionary process holds promise of more discriminating judgments between offenders who should be retained in the system and those who need, if anything, service rather than adjudication.

Agencies Outside the Formal Juvenile Justice System

Many kinds of organizations can play a significant role in nonjudicial handling of delinquents. Mental health agencies, social agencies, school guidance units may offer highly relevant services. Some programs have been specifically tailored for controlling and redirecting acting-out youth; street gang work is one notable example.[73] Groups that sponsor programs designed to reduce delinquency commonly reach into high-risk areas and attempt to identify, screen, and extend service to nonadjudicated delinquents. In dealing with adjudicated delinquents, their activities parallel those of the police, judge, probation, and parole officers. Yet rarely are they closely coordinated.

In a few communities quasi-official organizations have been developed to handle certain types of juvenile offenders instead of sending them through the juvenile justice system. An obvious practical advantage of such units is relief for the overburdened official agencies by diversion of cases into new channels. From a theoretical point of view the most compelling argument in favor of this development is the imperative need to find new techniques to modify the behavior of juvenile criminals and those who appear to be crime prone.

A few juvenile court jurisdictions have experimented with informal disposition and service arrangements in local communities, rural, suburban, and densely urban. These experiments range from the institutionalized use of conference committees appointed under rule of court[74] to cooperative service agreements among juvenile court, police, and social agencies.[75] A standard feature of such innovations is case selection from the categories of relatively minor offenses and troublesome noncriminal behavior. Characteristically, the cases include vandalism, petty theft, defiance of parental authority, truancy.

Arrangements of this type are now in effect in such disparate places as Essex County, N.J. (Newark); King County, Wash. (in towns on the perimeter of Seattle); Oakland County, Mich. (Pontiac and environs); and

---

[73] There is a useful analysis of these efforts in Gold and Winter, *A Selective Review of Community-Based Programs for Preventing Delinquency* (1961). Also see the variety of programs reported in Children's Bureau, U.S. Department of Health, Education and Welfare, *Research Relating to Juvenile Delinquents* (1962).

[74] See, e.g., Rubin, "Volunteers Serve in the Court," 15 *Juvenile Court Judges Journal*, 1964, p. 19; see also Elson and Rosenheim, *supra* note 42. Arguments against this approach are set forth in Woodson, "Lay Panels in Juvenile Court Proceedings," 51 *American Bar Association Journal*, 1965, p. 1141.

[75] See, e.g., Juvenile Protective Association, *Report on the Engelwood Project* (1958); New York City Youth Board, Monograph No. 2, *How They Were Reached* (1954); Silver, "Retooling for Delinquency Prevention and Rehabilitation in Juvenile Courts," 30 *Federal Proceedings* 29 (1966).

a rural county in Illinois. One motivation for experimentation seems to be dissatisfaction with police handling, whether because of lack of juvenile specialists or paucity of police (as in the rural areas) or volume of delinquents (as in the cities), or for lack of confidence in police methods. These specialized programs, moreover, have been decentralized, thus affording timely guidance close to home to help change a juvenile pattern of misconduct.

Typically these experiments have firm structural ties with the juvenile court, which sets the ambit of authority for the local group or office. Depending on the type of community program, court probation officers may supply the service or work closely with participants from local areas. Where the local plan demands that laymen not formally attached to the juvenile court decide on disposition, probation officers sometimes provide guidance.

In a number of urban areas, local comprehensive centers for social service and related types of care are being formed. These centers, which engage neighborhood residents both as staff and as advisory board members, provide previously unavailable resources to official delinquency control agencies and thereby offer new and augmented alternatives to adjudication to the hard-pressed officialdom. Wholly extrastatutory, these and similar social structures can enhance significantly the system's pre-judicial operations. Their contribution depends on financial capacity and other factors, none more significant than the expectations of police and juvenile court. Lacking a stated role in the formal system, these centers exist at the sufferance, if not encouragement, of officials in law enforcement and juvenile administration agencies.[76]

The Juvenile Court

Published data from juvenile courts clearly indicate the significance of the screening and informal disposition functions. Although there are vast variations in practice from State to State and within each State, persistent reliance on pre-judicial dispositions is a striking fact of life in the juvenile court, viewed nationally and over a span of years. Of the delinquency cases referred to courts in 1957, the year in which the present system of reporting was instituted, 52 percent were disposed of pre-judicially. Nine years later, in 1964, the latest year for which published statistics were available at this writing, the proportion was substantially the same.

A close look at the pre-judicial aspects of the juvenile court process reveals that a number of options have been identified and put into use. Some are prevalent in all courts, some in only a few. Some are unique to juvenile justice, others common in the criminal courts as well. On examination, it appears that the special status of informal dispositions in the juvenile court is a product of the intake process, itself inherited from the social work

[76] See the evaluation offered in Wheeler, Cottrell and Romasco, *Juvenile Delinquency: Its Prevention and Control* (Russell Sage Foundation, 1966), pp. 5–10, reprinted as an appendix to *Task Force Reports*.

tradition that has given the court its administrative character. Juvenile court intake, though unique among the processes of the judicial system, is taken directly from the social agency, where it is regarded as commonplace and necessary.[77]

Intake Generally

Intake is "essentially a screening process to determine whether the court should take action and if so what action or whether the matter should be referred elsewhere."[78] Intake is set apart from the screening process used in adult criminal courts by the pervasive attempt to individualize each case and the nature of the personnel administering the discretionary process. In criminal justice, at the postarrest stage, decisions to screen out are entrusted to the grand jury, the judge, or, usually, to the prosecutor. The objective is screening, as an end in itself; attempts to deliver service to those screened out are rare.

At intake in the juvenile court, screening is an important objective. But referral to, if not insistence upon, service and imposition of controls are additional goals. Thus the express function of intake is likely to be more ambitious than that of its criminal law counterpart.[79] And the function is performed chiefly by persons who are neither legally trained nor significantly restricted, in the exercise of their discretionary authority, by procedural requirements comparable to those of the criminal law.

Thus intake is a broadly conceived screening and helping process conducted within a judicial tribunal by probation officers or by the judge as *pater patriae*. The supporting cast usual in criminal dramas is missing from most juvenile courts. Neither defense attorney nor prosecutor regularly appears. Even States with recently enacted right-to-counsel provisions in their juvenile court laws have not generally experienced significant increase in the number of attorneys appearing on behalf of delinquent juveniles; New York State is a striking exception.[80] Nor does the prosecutor[81] usually participate in the pre-judicial stages of juvenile cases except as he may review petitions, routinely or on request, to ascertain their legal sufficiency. Indeed, in metropolitan courts that task often falls to a legal assistant to the judge, not to the lawyer who represents the State's interests.

[77] See generally Sheridan, "Juvenile Court Intake," 2 *Journal of Family Law,* 1962, p. 139.

[78] *Standards for Juvenile and Family Courts,* p. 46.

[79] Indeed, the very emphasis on helpfulness to the child has given rise to—or provided a useful rationalization for—extended interferences in juveniles' lives. See Tappan, "Unofficial Delinquency," 29 *Nebraska Law Review,* 1950, p. 547; *Juvenile Delinquents passim.*

[80] Skoler and Tenney, "Attorney Representation in Juvenile Court," 4 *Journal of Family Law,* 1964, pp. 77, 80–81, 96.

[81] *Standards for Juvenile and Family Courts,* p. 73, recognizes the need for "an attorney to represent the State, especially in contested cases," but does not take a position on the controversial question of what public office should supply him—district attorney's office, corporation counsel's office, police department, or other.

In the juvenile court intake process there is nothing comparable to the key role played by the prosecutor in criminal cases during bargaining for dismissal or lesser charges. Instead, the agreement—to adjust, for example, or to file for neglect or supervision rather than delinquency—is made between the probation officer and the juvenile and his parents. In some places the judge is directly engaged in the process, as when he actively participates in informal hearings that culminate in informal dispositions. In other places he is general supervisor of the staff's execution of informal adjustments and consultant on difficult cases.

Intake and Dispositional Choice

The options at intake include outright dismissal, referral to another community agency for service, informal supervision by the probation staff, detention, and filing of a petition. Selection among them turns in part on what is available, in part on the facts. Unless a *prima facie* case of jurisdiction is established, the only defensible recourses at intake are immediate dismissal or voluntary referral to a social agency or other source of assistance.[82] Giving the juvenile and his parents information and advice is, of course, not only permissible but desirable. The line should be clearly drawn, however, between facts potentially establishing jurisdiction and those that do not, no matter how urgent the underlying human needs. Juvenile courts that are alert to the signal importance of this distinction provide all probation officers, through ready access to the judge or to a legal assistant, with consultation on interpretation of the law.

The jurisdictional grounds, however, are broad, and at intake most cases are potential subjects of the juvenile justice process—if not for specific delinquent acts, then as incorrigibility or neglect. Most commonly, therefore, the major task at this point is to determine which cases to handle formally rather than whether a case for intervention exists. The choice is generally among dismissal (with or without referral to community service resources), unofficial handling by the court, and filing of petitions. Making that choice may call for exploration of the facts of the offense, the juvenile's background, and other facets of the case.

Preliminary conferences, explicitly provided by the most recently enacted statutes, supply a forum for deliberation and negotiation. Checks on conduct and consequences of these conferences have been included, to maximize their usefulness and guard against abuse. The Illinois Juvenile Court Act illustrates the new approach:

> Section 3–8. Preliminary conferences. (1) The court may authorize the probation officer to confer in a preliminary conference with any person seeking to file a petition under section 4–1, the prospec-

[82] Cf. *id.* at p. 39, urging that casework services be supplied through the court in communities where no other resources are available.

tive respondents and other interested persons concerning the advisability of filing the petition, with a view to adjusting suitable cases without the filing of a petition.

(2) In any case of a minor who is in temporary custody, the holding of preliminary conferences does not operate to prolong temporary custody beyond the period permitted by section 3–5.

(3) The probation officer may not prevent the filing of a petition by any person who wishes to file a petition under this act.

(4) This section does not authorize any probation officer to compel any person to appear at any conference, produce any papers, or visit any place.

(5) No statement made during a preliminary conference may be admitted into evidence at an adjudicatory hearing or at any proceeding against the minor under the criminal laws of this State prior to his conviction thereunder.

(6) Efforts at adjustment pursuant to rules or orders of court under this section may not extend for a period of more than 3 months.[83]

The basic choice is between adjudication and the various nonjudicial alternatives. The selection is signified by filing a petition or deciding not to do so. Children's Bureau information[84] reveals that roughly half of all delinquency cases are disposed of without petition.[85] In some courts they outnumber the cases petitioned and heard. But the kinds of dispositional choices made in the course of pre-judicial handling by court staff are similar to those rendered in formally adjudicated cases. Institutional commitment is one conspicuous exception; apparently it is used only in adjudicated cases. The same proportion of cases, both pre-judicial and judicial, is screened out without further action: 8.2 percent. Probation, used in 49 percent of the adjudicated delinquency cases, has a counterpart in so-called informal supervision, which is applied to nearly 20 percent of the pre-judicial cases. The picture changes, however, for dismissals following investigation: only 11 percent of the adjudicated cases but almost half of the pre-judicial dispositions are so handled. Informal dispositions are used in many different circumstances—for a wide range of offenses, for first offenders and repeaters, for older as well as younger delinquents, and for both boys and girls (though far less often for girls).

It is noteworthy that the proportion of pre-judicial cases in a jurisdiction varies according to its demographic characteristics. The Children's Bureau division of courts into rural, semiurban, and urban jurisdictions reveals a

[83] *Illinois Juvenile Court Act,* sec. 703–6, 1966; cf. *Standards for Juvenile and Family Courts,* pp. 59–60.

[84] Those familiar with the Children's Bureau Statistical Series reports on juvenile courts will recognize that the terminology used in the text differs from that in the reports. The change has been made to maintain a consistent vocabulary in the text.

[85] Children's Bureau, U.S. Department of Health, Education and Welfare, Stat. Ser. no. 83, *Juvenile Court Statistics,* 1964, at p. 11, table 6.

tendency of semiurban juvenile courts to rely especially on unofficial handling: 57 percent of delinquency cases in these areas, 50 and 47 percent respectively in urban and rural areas. Among the factors that may contribute to that differential use of unofficial handling are differences in composition of populations, in types of offenses committed, in police practices, and in availability of alternatives.

Some limits have been set on pre-judicial handling. Time limits have been established by statute or policy in some States. In others, complainants and child or parents have the right to have a petition filed.[86] It is sometimes said that juveniles committing certain acts, such as sex offenses, arson, and burglary, must go directly to the formal hearing stage, but that statement is apparently open to qualification.[87]

Clearly certain offenses are adjusted less often and with more difficulty than others,[88] perhaps because greater circumspection is required when dealing informally with certain types of offenses. Extenuating circumstances must be carefully documented, consultation with the judge is essential, a plan of service must be worked out and agreed to by the parents. But it is difficult to isolate the precise elements that determine whether a case will be disposed of informally or by adjudication. Even the administrative guides available to the probation staff may be silent on this aspect of case determination. In many juvenile courts that have written instructions to staff, the guidelines for pre-judicial adjustment are couched in terms of case processing—where to seek what service—rather than in terms of the crucial elements that are supposed to govern pre-judicial case selection. Again, the influence of social work tradition is partly responsible, in its emphasis on the desirability of individualizing each case.

Discretionary decisions to dismiss or otherwise adjust are, however, by no means completely *ad hoc* and idiosyncratic. In some courts supervisory systems and in-service training attempt to promote uniformity among probation officers assigned to common tasks. Further, the experience, knowledge, and self-discipline of officers with professional training aid their efforts to articulate case selection criteria and attempt consistent application in a conscious effort to promote specific goals.[89]

---

[86] E.g., *New York Family Court Act*, 1963, sec. 734(b); cf. Sheridan, "Juvenile Court Intake," 2 *Journal of Family Law*, 1962, pp. 139, 143–144.

[87] *Statistical Report, Circuit Court of Cook County, Juvenile Division, table 4, Jan. 1, 1965—Dec. 31, 1965*, shows 252 cases of burglary adjusted out of a total of 711; no breakdown on arson, rape, homicide, armed assault is available, however.

[88] Terry, *supra* note 60.

[89] This is not to suggest, however, that increased professionalization of staff would result in a high proportion of pre-judicial dispositions. On the contrary, there is evidence to suggest that the more sophisticated the juvenile court judge and staff members are about behavioral science, the greater is the tendency to channel juveniles into the stream of official processing. Wheeler, Cottrell, and Romasco, *op. cit. supra* note 76. This underscores the necessity for clear policies of commitment to nonadjudicatory tracks of handling and for continuous administrative monitoring of their implementation.

Critique and Recommendations

Evaluation of prepetition disposition of juveniles must of necessity proceed in considerable ignorance, in view of the lack of systematic, uniform information. Certain criteria can, however, be isolated, by which to measure informal handling procedures and to indicate what appear to be some of the major evils of present arrangements. The following comments, while largely speculative, are grounded on the observations and informed opinions of many experienced officials and scholars.

What should be the goals of the pre-judicial process? First, a great deal of juvenile misbehavior should be dealt with through alternatives to adjudication, in accordance with an explicit policy to divert juvenile offenders away from formal adjudication and authoritative disposition and to nonjudicial institutions for guidance and other services. Employment agencies, schools, welfare agencies, and groups with programs for acting-out youth all are examples of the resources that should be used. The preference for nonjudicial disposition should be enunciated, publicized, and consistently espoused by the several social institutions responsible for controlling and preventing delinquency.

Such a policy would avoid for many the long-lasting consequences of adjudication: curtailment of employment opportunity, quasi-criminal record, harm to personal reputation in the eyes of family and friends and public, reinforcement of antisocial tendencies. The case for using alternatives to the criminal process has been elaborated in other portions of this report.[90] The same arguments apply—perhaps even more persuasively—to the juvenile justice system. The juvenile will wear the label longer, while he is likely to outgrow the conduct that brought him the badge; one who acquires the status of a deviant in his youth faces the prospect of lifelong stigmatization. For a certain proportion of juvenile offenders the consequences appear to be cumulative. And in some cases the stigma is for behavior that does not carry the risk of formal disabilities for adults. His future is at stake and so is society's.

At the same time that marginal offenders ought to be screened out of the formal factfinding and dispositional stages of the juvenile justice system, there should be a greater emphasis on official handling of the more serious and intractable offenders. Improvements in the several stages of the predispositional process would result in more selective and discriminating judgments as to those who should be subjected to formal and authoritative surveillance in the interest of community protection.

MISUSES OF THE PRE-JUDICIAL DISPOSITION PROCESS

The rationale for pre-judicial handling rests on the greater flexibility, efficiency, and humanity it brings to a formal system operating within

[90] See chapter 1 of President's Commission on Law Enforcement and Administration of Justice, *Task Force Report.*

legislative and other definitive policies. But pre-judicial methods that seek to place the juvenile under substantial control in his pattern of living without genuine consent are not permissible. The difficult task is to discriminate between the undesirable uses of informality, benevolent as well as punitive, and the tolerable, desirable modes of guidance.

Modes of social aid and intervention occur along a spectrum from coercion to consent, with many intermediate shades lying in the range of mild control or persuasive request. The outer reaches of the spectrum are easiest to state. A friendly word of advice, which the juvenile feels free to reject, lies at one end. At the opposite end are authoritative dispositions that send the juvenile to a penal institution. Here the intervention of the State contravenes the will of the child and abridges his parents' rights if accomplished without due observance of the prescribed formalities of juvenile justice.

The punitive uses of informality are improper and dangerous. Substantial interference with parental judgment and curtailment of the juvenile's activities must be preceded by adjudication or the intervention is extralegal. The well-known practice of informal probation is vulnerable to attack on this ground; by measuring a juvenile's conduct according to conditions informally laid down by officials of the State, it constitutes an interference with choices of parents and juvenile that is legitimate, under our legal traditions, only when the basis for intervention has been established in accordance with procedural rules.

Likewise improper is referral to detention purely for purposes of deterrence, particularly where a *prima facie* case of jurisdiction does not exist. This is not to say that detention has necessarily been used punitively if the case is later dismissed without petition. Neither would pre-trial confinement of a criminal suspect be attacked solely because his case was subsequently dismissed in court. When many cases in which detention was used are later dismissed without petition, however, there is reason for inquiry, especially if there are at the same time official expressions favoring the shock value of detention.[91]

Other possibilities for misuse of discretionary judgment are less blatant than detention or informal probation. Coercive measures that are part of treatment regimens intended and believed to be beneficent also afford opportunities for misuse of discretion. At police, community agency, and court intake stages, leverage exists by virtue of the power to file a delinquency petition. Dispositional methods prescribed at any of these stages may therefore be subject to attack as forms of coercion without adjudication.

Examples of adjustment used at those points include police programs of "grounding" or performing tasks such as carwashing on Saturday for police in exchange for the release to parents; quasi-compulsory conference com-

[91] Cf. *California Report,* part 2, p. 81.

mittee dispositions directing regular visits to a counselor or production of essays on a topic selected for its wholesomeness. The line between helpful or irrelevant but harmless duties and painful or even destructive burdens is very difficult to draw. In any event, however, officials should have no further authority to refer to the court after a voluntary agreement has been worked out with the child or his parents. Once the power of referral ends, continuation in a plan of reparation or rehabilitation should rest on consent rather than authority.

QUESTIONABLE FACTORS IN PRE-JUDICIAL DISPOSITION

Controlling discretionary judgment at the point of screening requires greater knowledge about its exercise than now exists. At this point we know little more than that a multitude of factors governs discretionary judgment. One source of the difficulty in evaluating pre-judicial disposition is the vast range of pertinent considerations. If, for example, a juvenile policeman has as guide to disposition a list of six major factors,[92] all of them subject to various interpretations, who is to say his judgment is wrong, and on what grounds?

One unstated factor in decisions to retain or release may be flatly condemned—race.[93] And there are other factors, such as place of residence (in a high-crime neighborhood, for instance) or family characteristics, which may bear an indirect association with the avowedly irrelevant factor of race. It is difficult to keep these factors separate in a decision made under stress and often without knowledge of important facts.

Even more troubling is the question of the significance of a juvenile's demeanor. Is his attitude, remorseful or defiant, a sound measure of his suitability for pre-judicial handling?[94] Can the police, or anyone else for that matter, accurately detect the difference between feigned and genuine resolve to mend one's ways, or between genuine indifference to the law's commands and fear-engendered defiance? Attaching weight to attitude also implies presupposing the child's involvement, a presupposition reflected in some referral policies that mandate court referral whenever the juvenile denies commission of an offense. If the act or conduct is minor and would otherwise be disposed of by referral, the more defensible policy would seem to be the use of pre-judicial disposition.

---

[92] See, e.g., the factors listed in Chicago Police Department, Youth Division, *Manual of Procedure* (1965), as guidelines for the three possible dispositions of community adjustment, adjustment and referral, and filing a petition in juvenile court:
1. Type and seriousness of the offense.
2. The previous behavioral history of the juvenile.
3. Environmental factors including the disposition and capacity of the juvenile.
4. The attitude of the parents and "their ability to provide the necessary supervision and guidance."
5. The attitude of the complainant.
6. Community resources.
[93] See *Juvenile Delinquents*, p. 782, and references cited at nn. 23 and 24.
[94] *Ibid.*

THE IMPACT OF SCREENING ON JUVENILE BEHAVIOR AND ON BUREAUCRACY

"Lost Opportunities"

There are two bases for concern about present pre-judicial dispositions. On the one hand, serious offenders may be released in the course of the pre-judicial process when, for the sake of public safety, they should be retained and their cases adjudicated. On the other hand, juveniles who are not risks to the community but demonstrate a need for redirection may not be directed to appropriate sources of assistance either because the resources are not present or because transfer to other social institutions is not made. Both are grave indictments of the present pre-judicial dispositional system.

Statistical evidence for these assertions is scarce. Support for them abounds, however, not only in the commonsense observations of laymen well acquainted with child behavior problems within their own communities but also in an impressive accumulation of informed expert opinion. Data reveal the inadequacy of present pre-judicial screening to protect the community. Screening that leads to numerous adjustments for a juvenile within a relatively short time provokes questions about its effectiveness. While the primitiveness of the available data may preclude isolation in any given case of the facts of the offense, the legal issues, and the goals intended to be served, it is reasonable to speculate that sequential adjustments of serious offenses by the same individual reflect great pressures on the administering officials to reduce a heavy caseload. The exercise of discretion, moreover, to relieve the load of cases may be affected by nondiscretionary policies. If a police department, for example, is expected to refer to court all instances of certain crimes, and consequently feels the weight of paperwork and court appearance that this directive produces, it may be unable to assign the proportion of its efforts to the discretionary type of case that it otherwise would. In the case of discretionary judgment that is officially allowed, the officer who makes the judgment must make a record.[95] The time that is taken by justifying decisions in relatively trivial matters is lost from investigation and deliberation in more serious ones.

It seems likely that the stresses on the crucial screening institutions—police and court intake—result chiefly from insufficient staff. Screening consequently suffers from mass production. The deficiencies that inhere in using automatic processing techniques to make highly discriminating judgments are reinforced by an almost total lack of feedback. The decisions are not regularly reviewed for internal agency consistency or, perhaps more important, for the subsequent validity of the screening judgment. Operating agencies are best located to tackle such research; yet it is almost nonexistent either within them or under outside auspices.

The absence of followthrough also has ramifications with respect to juveniles referred for nonjudicial handling. Typically the official agency

[95] For an illuminating exposition of the impact of bureaucratic pressures on police practice in general, see Skolnick, *op. cit., supra* note 51.

gets in touch with a clinic, social agency, youth board, or other similar organization. But the time to explain a referral to the juvenile or a member of his family is short, and in the impersonal, populous districts of an urban area the referral case is often lost. The juvenile may not arrive at the selected place of service, or he may be refused service[96] without the referring official's finding out in time to take other steps. Even where there is a well-articulated referral system with smoothly operating procedures, sheer number of cases may substantially lessen its effectiveness. If the time lapse between apprehension and referral is a matter of days, the subsequent followup by a selected community resource may occur at a point when the juvenile and his family have surmounted their initial fear, anger, or regret and concern, and the contact is regarded as an unwelcome reminder of past unpleasantness instead of an avenue of help in time of crisis.

Bureaucratic Considerations

Several kinds of agencies may play a part in the informal dispositional process. Who should play the major or exclusive role has been the subject of debate. The police and the probation staff will have a screening function as long as the juvenile court maintains its essential structure. But there is disagreement as to whether their screening responsibilities should be reduced and their informal control efforts altogether eliminated.

With respect to the pre-judicial function of the police, it can be argued that discretionary power increases their influence over the behavior of juveniles. Deployed about the city and county, the police have frequent contacts with juveniles and stand a better chance to identify the serious crime risks than do officials more removed; it follows that they may judge more wisely which juveniles to leave alone and which to divert to nonjudicial tracks. This line of reasoning suggests that police discretion should be enlarged in cities where existing policy requires automatic court referral for many crimes and other types of misbehavior.[97]

Opponents of substantial discretionary police powers argue that informal dispositional duties divert police from primary law enforcement tasks. The authoritative mantle of the police, moreover, is said to make them appear to the public as figures of control, hence unlikely agents of help. Internal bureaucratic pressures may produce a predominantly punitive ethic. The subtle character of screening judgments calls for different personalities and preparation and for administrative checks of a sort that can be monitored more efficiently within the juvenile court.

The case for and against discretionary judgment at the intake stage turns

---

[96] See, e.g., comment in 1963 Juvenile Court, Cuyahoga County, Ohio, Annual Report 10: "Less than on [sic] half of those cases referred to local private agencies were accepted for service." See also Kahn, *Planning Community Services for Children in Trouble*, 1963, pp. 14–15, 214.

[97] See, e.g., the recommendation to that effect by the D.C. Crime Commission Report No. 659 (1966).

on similar considerations. The intake officer's distance from the neighborhood and his lack of knowledge of the child and his environs may suggest curtailing his discretionary power. But by training and through internal supervision the intake staff may be able to reach consistent decisions based on articulated policy with less difficulty than the police.

Inserting agencies outside the juvenile justice system into the channels of pre-judicial dispositions further complicates the picture. As indicated previously, the tenure of decentralized units of delinquency adjustment outside the formal system of juvenile justice depends in large measure on the tolerance of the juvenile court judge, and their functions depend on the rules and practices governing direct court referral. To be effective the work of such local units must be geared to the operations of both police and court. Active participation by youth board workers, social agencies assuming major responsibility for neighborhood work with predelinquent and delinquent youth, and other agencies—public or voluntary—would complicate the screening process and the monitoring of referrals, and enormous efforts would be required to achieve some degree of evenhandedness. Such efforts are both warranted and necessary, however, to make effective nonjudicial disposition a reality.

RECOMMENDATIONS FOR STRENGTHENING THE PRE-JUDICIAL PROCESS

In general, the following principles should guide pre-judicial dispositions:

(1) Pre-judicial dispositions should be made as early as possible in the stages of official agency contact;

(2) They should be based on stated criteria that are shared with and regularly reviewed by all delinquency control authorities within the community; and

(3) Whenever attempts are undertaken to render guidance or exert control (as distinct from screening without further action) the pre-judicial handling agency should be alert to coercive possibilities, and the dispositions it can render should be effectively restricted.

This approach seeks to accommodate the aims of the pre-judicial dispositional process to the widely differing practices that now exist. Accordingly, it is inappropriate to specify here the preferred agencies or to limit the possible forms of pre-judicial disposition. Details are less important than insuring inclusion in a given system of all the necessary basic aspects of the pre-judicial disposition process.

[*President's Commission on Law Enforcement and Administration of Justice,* Task Force Report: Juvenile Delinquency and Youth Crime (*Washington: U.S. Government Printing Office,* 1967), *pp. 1–19.*]

8 Juvenile detention

At one time, detaining an accused person was based on the fear that, if left at liberty, he would fail to appear for trial or might commit other violations. Times have changed. Pretrial release on bond or recognizance is now commonplace for adults, especially those with money or influence. Not so for children, who may be detained—no matter how inadequate the place of detention or the type of care given—by exercise of the *parens patriae* doctrine upon which juvenile courts were established.

I. Introduction

Juvenile detention is the practice of holding children of juvenile court age in secure custody for court disposition. The most common reason for its misuse and overuse is that it is allowed to function as a substitute for probation and other community services and facilities.

Unlike statutes pertaining to adults, juvenile court law permits a child to be taken into custody for his protection from situations that endanger his health and welfare. This purpose can be served by two distinctly different types of temporary care:

1. *Detention.* Temporary care of a child who has committed a delinquent act and requires secure custody, in a physically restricting facility pending court disposition or the child's return to another jurisdiction or agency. Any place for temporary care with locked outer doors, a high fence or wall, and screens, bars, detention sash, or other window obstruction designed to deter escape is a detention facility. If a substantial part of a building is used for detention as defined above, it is a detention facility no matter how flimsy the restricting features may be.[1]

2. *Shelter.* Temporary care in a physically unrestricting facility pending the child's return to his own home or placement for longer term care. Shelter care is generally used for dependent and neglected children in boarding homes, group homes, and,

[1] NCCD. *Standards and Guides for the Detention of Children and Youth.* 2nd ed., 1961.

in the larger cities, temporary care institutions; it is also used for children apprehended for delinquency whose homes are not fit for their return but who, with proper handling, are not likely to run away and therefore do not need secure custody.

Juvenile detention, properly used, serves the juvenile court exclusively; shelter care is a broader child-welfare service not only for the court but also for child and family agencies, both public and private.

A. Statutory Base

Legislative intent as to the quality of detention or shelter care to be given a child is expressed in most juvenile court laws essentially as follows:

> Each child coming within the jurisdiction of the court shall receive, preferably in his own home, the care, guidance, and control that will conduce to his welfare and the best interests of the State, and . . . when he is removed from the control of his parents the court shall secure for him care as nearly as possible equivalent to that which they should have given him.[2]

In 41 States the juvenile court law declaiming such a purpose is directly contravened by statutory exceptions—the child's age, the judge's discretion, or the lack of appropriate facilities—that allow use of jails for children.

In some States the statute specifically makes the county responsible for providing a detention home even though few counties in the State have enough children requiring detention to justify establishing a facility.

B. History

The history of detention in the United States is a history of rejection of troubled children and youth who trouble society.

Since 1899, when the first juvenile court was established in Chicago, noncriminal procedures and a detention home, separate from the adult jail, have come to be its accepted resources—at least in principle. As State after State enacted juvenile court legislation before World War I, detention homes—most of them were converted private homes—were established in our larger cities. By 1915 specially designed buildings had been constructed for the detention of children in Milwaukee, Newark, and Chicago, but most jurisdictions continued to use the jail even though on occasion an old residence was remodeled and called a detention home.[3] In some jurisdic-

---

[2] NCCD, *Standard Juvenile Court Act*, 6th ed., 1959.
[3] Florence M. Warner, *Juvenile Detention in the United States—Report of a Field Survey of the National Probation Association* (Chicago, University of Chicago Press, 1933).

tions, the workhouses, county infirmaries, and even hospitals were pressed into use. In others, notably in Massachusetts, Connecticut, and New York, boarding homes were subsidized for 24-hour-a-day operation for children 15 years of age and under, and so successfully that the jails were comparatively empty of children.

By the end of World War II, specially designed buildings had been constructed in only a few of the larger jurisdictions. Cleveland led the way with the unit concept, a departure from congregate care. Groups of children of similar age and problems were given separate sleeping and living accommodations, all units sharing central school, dining, and gymnasium facilities in the same building. Several other midwestern cities followed the Cleveland design; all these buildings, with their large dormitories and inadequate activity areas, are now outdated.

Later on other communities, almost exclusively in the Far West, constructed detention homes within a walled area resembling a large English boarding school, with trees, grass, and playing fields—thus, the name juvenile hall (which has come to mean a large detention facility that in no way resembles an English boarding school).

One of the major problems has been a confusion between child welfare and court services, reflected, for example, in detention homes that provide care, in the same or adjacent buildings, for dependent and neglected as well as delinquent children. At the turn of the century, public child welfare services had not been developed, so the juvenile court became an all-purpose child welfare agency which included, in its *parens patriae* concept, protective services, shelter care, and even financial aid. With probation and child welfare service now provided in separate agencies, the distinction between judicial and administrative responsibilities is becoming clearer.

The first standards for juvenile detention, formulated by a committee on juvenile court standards appointed by the U.S. Children's Bureau in 1921, were adopted by a 1923 conference held under the auspices of the Children's Bureau and the National Probation Association.

Ten States have developed their own standards for detention. Six of these documents are concerned with building construction; the others deal with program, personnel qualifications, or health and safety. Most of the State standards are minimal and have proved so difficult to enforce in the absence of consultation services that they have done little to offset the damaging effects of confining delinquents together.

A comprehensive refinement of detention principles was published by NCCD[4] in 1958, under the title of "Standards and Guides for the Detention of Children and Youth"; this was followed in 1960 by "Detention Practice," a description of significant programs. Statutory material appeared in NCCD's "Standard Juvenile Court Act" (sixth edition, 1959) and "Standard Family Court Act" (1959).

[4] National Council on Crime and Delinquency.

C. Some Major Advances

1. A clear definition of detention distinguishing it from shelter care has been generally accepted throughout the Nation. Only in two or three States are there an appreciable number of facilities that combine secure detention with the temporary care of dependent and neglected children. The all-purpose institution sometimes miscalled a detention home has been largely replaced by specially designed and staffed detention homes not confused by other functions. Better child welfare and probation services, group homes for the shelter care of neglected children, and group homes for the shelter care of delinquent children who do not need secure custody[5] are beginning to be recognized as necessary court resources. Detention cannot satisfactorily substitute for these.

2. A new type of architecture has been tested during the past 10 years, and well over 100 specially designed detention facilities have been built, most of them embodying NCCD basic principles of detention home design and each replacing a county jail or makeshift facility. Group units rarely exceed 15 youngsters of the same sex, except in two eastern cities and the larger western juvenile halls, where 20 is the usual size of groups.[6] Individual rooms, visual and auditory control, attractive but foolproof furnishings, and equipment designed to facilitate constructive supervision, inherent in the standards, can be found in most of the modern detention homes.

3. Redefined objectives and new staff requirements have gone beyond the care and custody function. The better detention homes now adhere to social group work standards and provide casework and clinical services, a full and varied school and activities program, and a professional diagnostic report on the child as seen in detention. Use of professional personnel has increased markedly.

4. Regional detention centers have been established in eight States.

II. Survey Findings

The average daily population of delinquent children in places of detention is more than 13,000. In 1965, the total number admitted to detention facilities was more than 409,000, or approximately two-thirds of all juveniles apprehended. . . . These youngsters were held in detention homes and jails for an estimated national average stay of 12 days at a total cost of more than

[5] Open-ended jurisdiction of the juvenile court, in all States but New York, subjects children to the classification of delinquents whether or not they have committed offenses which would be crimes if committed by adults. Hence many children in need of supervision or shelter care are placed in secure custody (detention).

[6] California's *Standards for Juvenile Halls* calls for 2 adults with each group of 20 during the day and evening shifts after school hours, and on weekends. NCCD standards set 15 as the maximum.

$53,000,000—an average cost of $130 per child. (The average length of stay of children detained in the sample counties is 18 days.)

These estimates do not include children held in police lockups; they do include children held, prior to any official court disposition, in 242 juvenile detention homes, 4 training schools, and an unknown number of county jails and jail-like facilities in 2,766[7] jurisdictions.

A. Jails and Police Lockups

The standard declares that no child should be admitted to a jail or a jail-like place of detention.

The survey found that 93 percent of the country's juvenile court jurisdictions, covering about 2,800 counties and cities comprising 44 percent of the population (a) have no place of detention other than a county jail or police lockup and (b) detain too few children to justify establishing a detention home.

If we add, to the 87,951 children of juvenile court age held in county jails . . . the number who are held in police lockups, the total number admitted to jails and jail-like facilities in the United States would exceed 100,000.

The claim that jails are never used for children is made by only Connecticut, Puerto Rico, and Vermont. Several States have successfully reduced their jailing of delinquent children by using shelter care in special boarding homes when secure custody is not essential.

Less than 20 percent of the jails in which children are held have been rated as suitable for adult Federal offenders.[8] Nine States forbid placing children in jail, but this prohibition is not always enforced. In 19 States the law permits juveniles to be jailed if they are segregated from adults, but this provision also is not always adhered to.

When children are segregated from adults, lack of supervision (even by adult prisoners) has resulted in physical and sexual aggression, suicide, and even murder by other children held in the jail.

In Arizona in January 1965, four teenage boys, jailed on suspicion of stealing beer, died of asphyxiation from a defective gas heater when they were left alone for 11 hours in a jail.

In Indiana, a 13-year-old boy, who had been in five foster homes, drove the car belonging to the last of his foster fathers to a county jail, considered one of the finest in the State, and asked the sheriff to lock him up. The boy was well segregated from adults pending a hearing for auto theft. When he had been detained for about a week, his body was found hanging from one of the bars of his cell. Next to it was a penciled note: "I don't belong anywhere."

---

[7] This figure includes 5 jurisdictions, each of which has more than 1 detention home, and a number of small jurisdictions in which no children are detained; it does not include 63 jurisdictions known to use detention homes in other counties.

[8] *Report of Attorney General's Committee on Poverty and the Administration of Criminal Justice*, p. 69.

Incidents such as these, which have occurred from time to time in all parts of the country, graphically illustrate not only the lack of proper facilities, but also the lack of child welfare and court personnel to implement the intent of juvenile court law so that when a child is removed from his home and his parents the court shall secure for him care as nearly as possible equivalent to that which they should have given him. The jailing of children is condemned not only by the law in most States and by the standard, but also by psychologists, psychiatrists, sociologists, penologists, the International Association of Chiefs of Police, the National Sheriff's Association, the U.S. Children's Bureau, and the National Council on Crime and Delinquency.[9]

Although 13 States have taken some responsibility for juvenile detention, only 9 States have taken responsibility for providing regional detention centers for counties with too few children to detain to justify constructing local facilities.

Children under 7 years of age have been held in substandard county jails for lack of shelter care in foster homes. Some of the youngsters had committed delinquent acts; some were merely dependent or neglected. On the same day that the Arizona tragedy was reported, a police chief in New Jersey took two teenage runaway larceny suspects to his own home for lack of any suitable place of detention pending hearing and commitment.

Jail detention is characterized by enforced idleness, no supervision, and rejection. It is a demoralizing experience for a youngster at a time when his belief in himself is shattered or distorted. Repeated jailing of youth has no salutary effect on the more sophisticated youngster; on the contrary, it reenforces his delinquency status with his peers and his self-identification as a criminal. Enforced idleness in a jail gives the sophisticated juvenile ample time and reason for striking back at society.

Juvenile detention is frequently misused as an immediate punishment for delinquent acts. If punishment is the court's only disposition, it ought to be administered only after all the facts are in—not as an immediate reaction to the charge.

B. Detention Homes

A detention home is defined as a secure but nonjail-like facility separate from any jail and from any public building other than a juvenile court. Of 242 such homes in the United States, 48 percent have been constructed for the purpose; the others, usually remodeled residences or other makeshift facilities, are often found to be neither fire resistant nor designed for proper supervision.

Because of their jail-like character, a few of the specially designed buildings barely come within the detention home definition. Others meet most

[9] See "Children in Jail," a careful onsite documentation, in *Parade* magazine. Nov. 17, 1963.

NCCD standards on secure but nonjail-like custody, 24-hour-a-day direct supervision, small groups, individual counseling and constructive group interaction, and observation and study for the court.[10]

Because of their generally urban location, detention homes serve over 50 percent of the population of the United States but only 7 percent of the counties. . . .

The detention homes that are satisfactorily designed or staffed are able to hold juveniles without supplementary use of the jail whatsoever; the others merely serve as an unnecessary supplement to the detention of children in jail.

Detention homes are usually administered by courts or their probation departments. A few are run by the city or county government, the welfare department, a State agency, and, in one State, by a lay board. The type of administering agency appears to have little effect on the quality of detention service rendered. NCCD surveys show that better coordination between probation and detention can usually be achieved when detention is administered under a director of court services. Regional detention appears to be most satisfactory when administered by a State agency.

1. PERSONNEL

(a) Professional Services

. . . [M]ore than half the detention homes still provide storage-type detention. A child disturbed enough to require secure custody pending court disposition must be studied—which cannot be done in a program vacuum.

(b) Number of Staff

About 7,900 persons are employed to care for an average daily population of 13,113 delinquents in detention. . . .

(c) Educational Requirements

The educational level of personnel has risen considerably in the past decade. Sixty-three percent of the facilities from which information was obtained required at least a bachelor's degree for the detention superintendents, with 16 percent requiring a graduate degree. Fifty-three percent require a bachelor's degree for staff supervisors, and 14 percent set the same educational standard for group supervisors. . . . In the larger cities it is not unusual to find college graduates in the behavioral sciences working in detention homes while completing work for a master's or doctor's degree.

[10] NCCD, *Standards and Guides for the Detention of Children and Youth.* 2nd ed., 1961.

(d) Inservice Training

Working with confined delinquent children calls for unusual staff skills. The rapid turnover of children in detention, the degree of their anxiety, and their withdrawn or explosive behavior call for the kind of staff intervention that will relieve rather than aggravate their problems. Continual inservice training of a high caliber is therefore essential; a college degree in itself, even with training in social work, by no means guarantees ability to work successfully with delinquent children.

In spite of the increased professional services noted above, only 39 percent of the counties visited claimed to have any inservice training program at all and only one-third of these had such training as frequently as once a week. . . . In many instances "training" was a euphemism for "staff meeting" at which professional training rarely, if ever, took place.

(e) Hours

In accordance with committee standards, 71 percent of the counties visited maintained a 40-hour workweek or less. Fifteen percent worked 41 to 50 hours; 14 percent worked over 50 hours weekly. Some small homes employed alternating couples who were on duty for 72 hours at a stretch.

(f) Salaries

In the survey sample, the median salary for superintendents was $7,001–$8,000; the lowest salary was in the $1,501–$2,400 range and the highest in the $17,001–$18,000 range. The median for staff supervisors was $5,001–$6,000; the lowest salary was in the $1,501–$2,400 range and the highest in the $9,001–$10,000 range. The median for group supervisors (child care workers) was $4,001–$5,000; the lowest salary reported was under $1,500 and the highest was in the $7,001–$8,000 range. . . .

(g) Appointment

In 43 percent of the counties visited, the superintendent and staff supervisors were employed through a civil service or merit system. . . . With a few notable exceptions, personnel in detention homes are not subject to political interference.

(h) Relationship to Probation

Nine detention homes use group techniques ranging from supervised group discussion to a limited form of guided group interaction. Nearly half of the detention homes conduct school programs, and 12 have special education activities including remedial reading. Six homes have programs in vocational training and three in paid work. Three use volunteers.

One of the largest detention homes with well-controlled intake found that, by improving program and supervision under a professionally united staff, it could unlock the doors of three of its buildings without losing children. This demonstration of shelter care for delinquent children awaiting court disposition was achieved in a jurisdiction which already had a low rate of detaining. It is here too, that State agents work in the detention facilities, orient youngsters committed to State institutions, and, in a growing number of cases, arrange for placement in community treatment programs in lieu of institutionalization.

In spite of these advances, detention personnel have had to struggle for a salary level and status equal to the probation officer's. This struggle sometimes has a "cold war" tone, with probation regarding detention as nothing more than a custodial operation, and detention critical of probation officers for the way they use detention and for their failure to understand adolescent youngsters in a group living situation. Even so, improvement has been noted on two fronts: (a) Directors of court services have been given responsibility for both detention and probation, so that these services are brought into a more cooperative relationship; (b) the Standing Committee on Detention of the NCCD Professional Council has been publishing detention workshop material and is now regularly issuing a "Detention Administrator's Newsletter."[11]

C. State's Role

1. STATE RESPONSIBILITY

Fourteen States have assumed responsibility for detention, in whole or in part, as follows:

> Alaska—State jurisdiction over all juvenile programs, including jails in which children are detained. Standards for juvenile detention have not yet been developed.
>
> Connecticut—State juvenile court has a State system of detention homes. Does not use jails.
>
> Delaware—State-operated detention home serves all three counties. A second facility will shortly serve the two southernmost counties.
>
> Georgia—about to establish six State-operated regional detention centers to serve juvenile courts in counties without detention homes.
>
> Massachusetts—four regional detention centers serving local juvenile courts are State-constructed and operated by the youth service board; State-inspected juvenile quarters in police lockups are used for 24- to 48-hour holding, pending release or transfer.
>
> Maryland—two State-operated regional detention and diagnos-

---

[11] See *A Practical Bibliography on Detention* (1966), available free from NCCD.

tic facilities available to all counties in the State; county jails and State training schools are also used for detention of juveniles.

Michigan—does not operate detention homes but has a part-time consultant; provides standards; reimburses counties for half the cost of care; and conducts an annual workshop on detention for judges, probation officers, and detention administrators.

New Hampshire—State training schools are used for the detention of juveniles on local court order pending disposition; jails are used only for the overnight holding of juveniles when imperative.

New York—does not operate detention homes but has a full-time consultant on detention; provides standards; reimburses counties for half the cost of care.

Puerto Rico—four State-operated detention homes with diagnostic facilities and correctional treatment programs.

Rhode Island—same as New Hampshire.

Utah—State standards for regional detention and substantial reimbursement to counties meeting these standards; subsidy does not guarantee statewide coverage.

Vermont—State training school, used on local court order, is the only place of detention for juveniles; the jail is not used.

Virginia—same as Utah.

2. REGIONAL DETENTION

Eight States have established regional detention centers, and two others have promoted regional detention by State subsidy. Vermont, New Hampshire, and Rhode Island utilize State training schools for predisposition holding (a practice which neither NCCD nor the States themselves consider satisfactory); they have, however, demonstrated the practicality of a State-operated regional facility to serve county courts.

Massachusetts, Maryland, and Delaware operate regional detention facilities as a service to county juvenile courts. Puerto Rico operates four regional detention homes (not constructed for this purpose) for district courts. Connecticut's statewide juvenile court is served by four regional detention homes; with exclusive original jurisdiction to age 16, it claims it has never had children kept in jails and police lockups since it was established more than 20 years ago.

By no means are all these regional facilities up to recognized standards of building design or staffing; not all of them have achieved statewide coverage; and all but two find it necessary to use the jail for overnight holding or because full State coverage has not yet been achieved. In Massachusetts the legal authority to establish standards and to inspect and control jails and police lockups used for the overnight and weekend detention of juveniles (pending release or transfer to regional detention homes) has resulted in the improvement of the holdover facilities.

The experience in operating a State detention service for local courts has proved that problems of transportation and intake control can be worked out. Delaware is expected to achieve full State coverage with two detention homes by 1967. Maryland, with two facilities for partial State coverage and a statutory detention period limitation of 30 days, offers a well-designed program that includes clinical observation reports to the courts prior to disposition. Training schools and jails are still used, but a new State agency for children and youth services will help to control the use of juvenile facilities.

Virginia and Utah have assumed responsibility for regional detention through State subsidy. Virginia has established juvenile court and detention districts for purposes of planning. Eight of these districts now have regional detention homes with two others on the drawing board. The State reimburses counties meeting its regional detention standards up to $50,000 for construction, two-thirds of the staff salaries, and all of the operating expenses.

Virginia provides consultation services through four full-time consultants and a supervisor in probation and detention. These services include planning assistance, approval of plans, and State leadership in staff training through workshops and special grants. As a result, the State is acquiring a system of well-designed detention homes to replace its former use of jails.

Utah's State Department of Social Welfare has a similar approach but with only a part-time consultant. The State reimburses the counties up to 40 percent of their building and operating cost if they meet specific standards established for any one of three classes of detention homes: (a) overnight holdover facilities separate from the jail, (b) detention homes for predisposition care with program but no psychiatric services, and (c) detention homes with program and clinical services. (At present the only one in this class is in Salt Lake City.[12])

The holding of children in Utah's jails received much publicity several years ago. Jail detention of children has now been reduced by three county-operated regional detention homes with regional detention services and two holdover facilities. Jails are used for detention because of lack of other facilities. Utah is the first State to promote the use of approved overnight holdover facilities instead of jails and police lockups for children requiring immediate secure custody until released or transported to a regional detention facility. Problems of transportation and communication have been worked out even though some regional detention homes are more than 150 miles away from the court.

3. CONSULTATION AND INSPECTION

Effective consultation calls for a trained person who has worked in a juvenile detention center, has studied national standards and practices, and is familiar with the better detention homes in other States. When such a

---

[12] *Minimum Standards of Care for the Detention of Children,* (Salt Lake City: Utah Department of Public Welfare, 1961).

person is hired—not easily done at the salaries paid to State personnel—he cannot accomplish much if he is responsible for other statewide functions and is available only on request.

Exemplary practices cannot be reduced to simple formula because they may depend upon other services and facilities not up to par. A jurisdiction with an excellent detention building may be poorly staffed; one with a good child-care staff may have communication problems with the probation department; one with an excellent probation department and detention facility may be overused by the police without court control. For this reason high caliber consultation and coordinating services on a State level are of utmost importance if poor routine practices are to be avoided.

Twenty States have provision for consultation services on detention care to counties, half of them by the Department of Welfare and the rest by various State agencies ranging from the board of training schools to a department of mental health. Examination of the extent of these services reveals that little consultation is actually given and that few States have staff qualified to give it. Most consultation is given on request only, although 15 States claim to have an inspection service.

4. STATE PLANNING AND COST SHARING

Although no State has a model program as yet, all nine regional facilities including those in Virginia and Utah favor State constructed and State-operated regional detention homes for counties unable to provide a satisfactory detention service.

County operating costs for detention are shared in Michigan and New York, under a plan whereby the State reimburses counties for half the cost of detention care and counties reimburse the State for half the cost of training school care. Both States employ consultants to inspect and advise, and funds can be withheld if standards are not met.

Only Virginia and Utah share in county detention construction costs.

5. NEW CONSTRUCTION

About half the detention homes are more than 20 years old. . . .

The survey found that facilities with a total capacity of more than 1,700 are now under construction. . . . In addition, construction has been authorized for a capacity of more than 2,200 and is projected (for completion by 1975) for about 3,100. If all are built, there will be, by 1975, space in detention facilities for about 7,100 more juveniles than at present.

If the availability of new facilities raises the current rate of detaining, as has always happened in the past, and if this new construction is carried out as a substitute for sufficient probation and clinical staff at the local or regional level, the buildings will be insufficient by 1975, aside from the fact that they will have become dumping grounds of questionable value.

On the other hand, if intake controls are established so that the presently high rate of detaining can be reduced, the new facilities now under construction, authorized, and projected will turn out to be unnecessary.

State planning for detention calls for strategic location of detention centers. Where there is no State control, counties tend to build detention facilities for their own needs regardless of the needs of surrounding counties. Thus, later regional planning is obstructed by a number of small facilities badly located from the point of view of State planning.

D. The Use of Detention

The child's first experience in detention influences his attitude toward society, for good or bad. The assumption that a disagreeable experience will assure his staying out of trouble has no foundation in fact. Removed from parents and community agencies which failed him, he sizes up society's intentions by the kind of substitute care, guidance, and control he receives in detention.

The use of detention differs so widely from county to county and State to State that whether a youngster will be detained is a matter of geographic accident.

1. THE STATUTES AND THE CRITERIA

One of the many reasons for variance in practice is the juvenile court statute itself. Juvenile court jurisdiction in most States is so broad that almost any child can be picked up by the police and placed in detention. The following, in abbreviated form, lists the acts or conditions included under the heading of delinquency in juvenile court laws in the United States:

> Violates any law or ordinance.
> Immoral or indecent conduct.
> Immoral conduct around schools.
> Engages in illegal occupation.
> Associates with vicious or immoral persons.
> Growing up in idleness or crime.
> Enters, visits house of ill repute.
> Patronizes, visits policy shop or gaming place.
> Patronizes place where intoxicating liquor is sold.
> Patronizes public poolroom or bucket shops.
> Wanders in the streets at night, not on lawful business (curfew).
> Wanders about railroad yards or tracks.
> Jumps train or enters car or engine without authority.
> Habitually truant from school.
> Incorrigible.
> Uses vile, obscene, or vulgar language (in public place).
> Absents self from home without consent.

Loiters, sleeps in alleys.
Refuses to obey parent, guardian.
Uses intoxicating liquors.
Deports self so as to injure self or others.
Smokes cigarettes (around public place).
In occupation or situation dangerous to self or others.
Begging or receiving alms (or in street for purpose of).[13]

Because of confusion between court and child welfare functions, many legal definitions of delinquency make no distinction between crime and child neglect; hence children are often detained when their only offense is one of the acts or conditions listed above.

Most statutes which attempt to regulate the use of detention leave the admission door legally wide open. This is particularly true when they provide for detention when the child is in physical or moral danger in his own home. In such a situation, the law should provide for shelter care, not detention.

The standard declares that no child shall be placed in any detention facility unless he is delinquent or alleged to be delinquent and there is a substantial probability that he will run away or a serious risk that he will commit a serious offense pending court disposition. Detention, the standard continues, is not to be used as punishment, or as a convenience for officials.

Most State laws emphasize that a child apprehended for delinquency should be returned to his parents where practicable, pending the court hearing. Herein lies room for conflicting interpretation unless legal criteria further limit the area for police and court judgment.

The director of detention in the country's largest metropolitan area made the following statement:

> The decision to detain should be based on demonstrated behavior, not on subjective opinion . . . To assume that a child will abscond, there should be a history of absconding. To assume that he will not appear in court, he should first be given the opportunity to appear. For a child to be considered a menace, there should be some serious malbehavior supporting the thesis. We must get away from present practices of incarcerating children because their parents or their neighborhoods are not adequate. These are cases for shelter care, not cases for detention.[14]

Another variant in the statutes is the age of juvenile court jurisdiction. In some States the court has exclusive original jurisdiction to 16, so that no child under that age may be waived to criminal court; in other States the age is 18, with concurrent jurisdiction to 21. Until recently in one State in

[13] Sol Rubin, *Crime and Juvenile Delinquency—A Rational Approach to Penal Problems*, 2nd ed., (New York: Oceana Publications, 1961), p. 49.
[14] From an unpublished letter by J. Martin Poland, director of Youth House, New York City's detention institution.

the Midwest, a child of 10 could be tried in criminal court and held in jail even though a detention home was available.

The result of the low age limit in many States is that large numbers of children under 12 years of age are detained when they are in need of shelter care and child welfare, not court services. Here again, wide differences in detention practice are noted. Jurisdictions with age limitations to 16 detain more children under 12, proportionately, than do jurisdictions where the age limit is 18.

2. DIVIDED AUTHORITY

Ultimate responsibility for detention rests with the judge but, in practice, probation and police officers often make decisions to detain for which the court takes no responsibility.

The first decision to detain or release is usually made by the police. Unlike probation services, which are technically subject to court control, police services are administered by a separate agency. Therefore, unless an authorized person is available to make a decision for the court shortly after apprehension, a child may be detained as a result of a police officer's judgment or a police agency's practice. When the source of referrals to a single juvenile court is more than a hundred police agencies, the use of detention as an initial step in the court process is far from uniform.[15] The exception occurs where court control over detention has been achieved through cooperation with the law enforcement agencies so that common practice prevails and authorization for detention, during or after court hours, rests with a court intake service.[16] Without such court intervention at the point of intake, some children are detained overnight only to be released the following morning by a probation officer after an interview with the child and the parent which could have taken place the day before had probation staff been available. In some jurisdictions children, once placed in detention by the police, remain there until released by the court at a hearing, which may not take place for a week or more.

The second point of decision is reached when a probation officer releases a child or continues the detention initiated by the police. Only in a few States does legislation require the judge to review this decision.

According to the standards, a petition should be filed for every child detained.

In 21 States, children may be detained without the filing of a petition.

---

[15] Nathan Goldman, *The Differential Selection of Juvenile Offenders for Court Appearance* (New York: NCCD, 1963), pp. 101–102.

[16] Lane County (Eugene), Oreg., Harris County (Houston), Tex., Summit County (Akron), Ohio, and New York City have developed intake controls through court rules which keep detaining rates low. Intake workers on duty or on call 16 hours or more daily, agreements with law enforcement agencies, availability of counsel, and careful court review of all admissions and length of stay are among the techniques used for controlling detention.

Police and probation officers in these jurisdictions are free to exercise what should be exclusively a court prerogative.

The third point of decision, after a petition is filed, rests with the court itself. According to the committee standard, the juvenile court is responsible for detention admissions and releases and for establishing written policies and procedures for detention. The Standard Juvenile Court Act requires that, when a child is taken into custody, both the parents and the court are to be notified immediately, and, should the child be detained, the parents must be notified in writing that they are entitled to a prompt hearing regarding release or continued detention. The act provides, furthermore, that no child shall be held in detention longer than 24 hours unless a petition has been filed, or 24 hours beyond that (excluding nonjudicial days) unless the judge signs a detaining order.

Data are not available to show the proportion of jurisdictions in which children and parents are, in fact, assured or denied these legal protections. Professional observers note that once police or probation officers detain a child, the court seldom challenges the wisdom of their decision even though it may release the youngster pending disposition of the case. Furthermore, when a child is detained and social information justifying his release is not available to the judge, chance revelation in the brief factfinding or detention hearing will usually determine his continued detention or release. Court rules make the acquisition of preliminary social data by the probation officer a mandatory requirement for the initial hearing.

3. INCONSISTENCY IN RATE OF DETAINING

The rate of detaining is the total number of children detained for delinquency divided by the total number apprehended and booked for delinquent acts. (Both figures exclude dependent children, traffic cases, and material witnesses.) Much as police statistics vary, the arrest base is generally more satisfactory for establishing a rate of detaining than is county population or court referrals for delinquency. Where arrest figures are not available, court referrals can be used, modified by estimates of the police-to-court referral rate.

NCCD's recommended rate of detaining—10 percent of juvenile arrests—is merely an indicator of the need to examine intake practices when the detaining rate rises significantly above it.

Inconsistency in the use of detention from one jurisdiction to another raises serious question about the validity of detaining in many cases. Judges and court personnel in counties with low detaining rates were questioned to find out whether released children fail to appear in court or commit other offenses while awaiting hearings. Replies consistently said "rarely," "less than with adults released on bond," etc.

In some jurisdictions all arrested children are detained routinely; in others, less than 5 percent are detained. A 30-percent rate is not uncommon. Whatever rate of detaining is customary in one jurisdiction is usually defended to the death, by the judge and the probation or law enforcement officers, against another wholly different concept defended with equal fervor in another State or in another county in the same State. No research has been designed to prove the efficacy of either practice. Since removal of a child from his home before all the facts are available is drastic action, the burden of proof rests on judges whose courts have high detaining rates, not on judges who detain sparingly.

An increasing rate of detaining often creeps up on a court after the construction of a new building without anyone aware of the change. The courts usually explain the increase by a rise in population or an increase in delinquency. They rarely compute the rate of detaining and compare it with the alleged increase in the alleged causes.

Even the recommended 10-percent rate referred to above may some day be regarded as too high. Where intake is held down, by design or by custom, the rate can drop below this figure.[17]

A midwestern county judge, who believed in making children responsible for their own behavior and parents responsible for their children pending court disposition, reduced the overcrowded population of the detention home from a previous average of 53 to an average of 36 delinquent children within 2 weeks and suffered no repercussions about lack of community protection.

Of all the children detained in a western county, approximately two-thirds were referred to the probation department after adjudication; of these, less than half were placed under official supervision. A Governor's commission suggested that most of the two-thirds originally detained could have been left at liberty to await court hearings without endangering the community. Following a juvenile court law revision which eliminated the free use of detention by the police, the statewide rate of detaining dropped from an average of 41 percent to 29 percent; in some counties there, the rate is considerably lower and is still going down.

A 1965 study of detention in New York City showed a detaining rate of less than 13 percent (computed on the total number of juvenile arrests).[18] The intake service established by the New York City Office of Probation under the New York Family Court Act reduced the volume of delinquency referrals to the court by 37 percent in 1 year and reduced the daily detention population of boys from 554 to 316.

---

[17] NCCD's annual detention inventories indicate variation in rates of detaining that are apparently unrelated to size or type of jurisdiction. In Greene County, Ohio, population 125,000, plans to establish a 20-bed detention home were postponed and efforts to control the use of the substandard county jail were doubled. The consequence: Out of 475 children referred to the court for delinquency in 1965, only 16 were detained.

[18] "Juvenile Detention in the City of New York" (a study to determine the capacity of detention facilities needed) (NCCD, 1965).

A recently conducted intensive study of all types of detention, including detention of juveniles, made the following observation:

> Out of all children detained overnight or longer, 43 percent are eventually released without ever being brought before a juvenile court judge, and half of all cases referred to juvenile courts are closed out at the intake stage before any judicial hearing.[19]

It is evident from the above, as well as from a case-by-case examination of detained children in almost any court, that the minor or first offender constitutes the largest group unwisely detained. Many youngsters who have committed more serious offenses are detained when they could have been released under the close supervision of a probation officer, without danger to the community.

Where backed up by proper probation services, such release helps parents to assume greater responsibility for the supervision of their child during a crucial period, and helps the child to assume responsibility for his own behavior pending the court hearing. Examples of effective intake procedures have been developed at the Lane County Juvenile Court in Eugene, Oregon; the Summit County Juvenile Court in Akron, Ohio; the Kent County Juvenile Court in Grand Rapids, Mich.; and the Harris County Juvenile Court in Houston, Tex. Other and somewhat different but comparatively effective intake practices adapted to the special conditions in each jurisdiction can be seen in the New York City Family Court, the juvenile court for the State of Connecticut, and a number of juvenile courts in Massachusetts recently studied by the Special Delinquency Branch of the U.S. Children's Bureau.

4. STATISTICS FOR PLANNING AND RESEARCH

Twenty-two States don't bother to keep any detention statistics at all. Of the 29 that do, most keep statistics that are so incomplete and so varying in form that they cannot be relied on for planning purposes. To accumulate statistics without using them for planning is a meaningless exercise, particularly when States do not agree on what kinds should be gathered and for what purpose. Those States that assume some responsibility for regional detention have good reason to know, specifically, how many children of what ages are detained, where, by whom, for what reasons, and for how long. Other facts regarding juvenile arrests, numbers referred to the court, staffing patterns, and costs are important for purposes of research and planning. Statistics recommended for counties and States are listed in "Standards and Guides for the Detention of Children and Youth."[20] California, Pennsylvania, Michigan, and Ohio head the list for the most complete

[19] Vera Foundation, *Bail in the United States, 1964*—a report to the National Conference on Bail and Criminal Justice, Washington, D.C.

[20] *Supra* note 10.

statistics on detention, but even these States have difficulty securing consistent data from every county jail since each keeps statistics in its own way or,
more often, not at all. Estimates have frequently been found wholly unreliable.

5. LENGTH OF STAY

Theoretically the detention stay is the length of the predisposition period,
usually 10 days to 2 weeks in a court with good probation and clinical
services—and in a court where juvenile sessions are held only twice a
month. In some courts without adequate probation services, the average
length of stay may be only 2 or 3 days at most.

The average length of detention stay may be lowered by a number of
overnight to 3-day police detentions, or it may be raised by a number of
cases waiting for psychological or psychiatric interviews. More frequently,
the reason for long average stays is the large number of children who have
been committed by the court to a State institution but cannot be sent there
because of lack of room. For this situation the counties that have high
commitment rates are usually as responsible as the State through its failure
to provide correctional treatment resources. Detention, inappropriately, is
left holding the bag.

Another reason for long detention stay is the time spent on looking for an
appropriate foster home or private institution placement for a child. Frequently, after considerable time the child either is returned to his home on
probation or is committed to a State institution for delinquents. A partial
solution to this problem is a 30-day statutory length of stay. A better solution is for the courts to demand, more clearly and forcefully than they have
in the past, the kind of probation and placement resources they need and to
encourage citizen action for appropriation of funds to obtain them.

The range of stay in the detention places in counties studied in the
survey, which included jails as well as detention homes, was from 1 day to
68 days; the average was 18 days. Nearly all the smaller county jails reported
stays of usually 1 to 3 days. Longer average stays were consistently found in
the detention homes and other facilities. These survey data raise questions
about the purposes for which detention homes are used. . . .

. . . . .

High ratios of admission to detention homes and long stays there usually
stem from the mistaken notion, held by many judges, that these facilities
are all-purpose institutions for (*a*) meeting health or mental health needs,
(*b*) punishment or treatment in lieu of a training school commitment, (*c*)
retarded children until a State institution can receive them, (*d*) pregnant
girls until they can be placed prior to delivery, (*e*) brain-injured children
involved in delinquency, (*f*) protection from irate parents who might harm
the child, (*g*) a material witness in an adult case, (*h*) giving the delinquent
"short sharp shock" treatment, (*i*) educational purposes ("He'll have to go

to school in detention"), (*j*) therapy, (*k*) "ethical and moral" training, (*l*) lodging until an appropriate foster home or institution turns up.

The problems of proper care for these children can hardly be imagined. The comings and goings of detained children fresh from encounters with the police make a place of detention inappropriate for rehabilitation. Program geared to short stays does not lend itself to long-term treatment, particularly when the treatment called for is so varied. No research has yet proved the validity of extensive or long-term detention. Hence, standards do not endorse the construction or use of detention homes for dependent and neglected children or for a variety of other purposes.

6. CONFUSED OBJECTIVES: A SUMMARY

Confusion and misuse pervade detention. It has come to be used by police and probation officers as a disposition; judges use it for punishment, protection, storage, and lack of other facilities. More than in any other phase of the correctional process, the use of detention is colored by rationalization, duplicity, and double talk, generally unchallenged because the law is either defective or not enforced, and because it is always easy to make a case for detaining on the grounds of the child's offenses or the demands of the public as interpreted by the police or the press.

Detention too often serves as storage, a means of delaying action. It protects the police, the probation officer, and the judge from criticism in the event that a released child commits another law violation while awaiting court hearing. It removes from the probation officer his obligation to help parents assume responsibility for supervising their child in his own home and to help the child assume responsibility for his own behavior in the community. In short, it serves as a substitute for the casework so urgently needed by both parent and child to begin unraveling the problem of which the delinquent act is but a symptom. What are some of the "delinquent acts" for which many children are detained? Truancy, for one; the child is detained because the school has failed to deal with the causes of his truancy. Incorrigibility, for another; often it is the parents that need help as much as the child. Or he may be a runaway, frequently with good reason for running. These youngsters and their parents need assistance, which is frequently delayed by the detaining process; sometimes, they never get it.

The child, the parent, and the public are led to believe that the youngster's detention was, in fact, his correctional treatment and that, after a lecture from the judge and possibly a postcard type of probation, he is supposed to straighten out. Little wonder that many law enforcement officers object to the leniency of the juvenile court. They reason that if they detain, at least they have played their part in punishing the child and safeguarding the community, even though the court may dismiss the case. (The statistics show 409,218 children detained but only 242,275 children placed on probation or committed to an institution.)

Many judges, realizing that prolonged detentions are unsatisfactory and bending to community pressures for prompt action, are quick to commit delinquent children to training schools already crowded with youngsters who failed to receive effective probation services in the community.[21] The result of a high commitment rate is a backlog of children in jails and detention homes awaiting transfer—and so the vicious circle continues.

If the evils of detention are to be corrected, it is necessary first to strengthen probation and other correctional treatment services; second, to develop community resources for shelter care; third, to use detention only for its proper functions.

[*President's Commission on Law Enforcement and Administration of Justice*, Task Force Report: Corrections (*Washington: U.S. Government Printing Office, 1967*), appendix A, pp. 119–129.]

---

[21] NCCD surveys show that in approximately half the commitments to State training schools, probation had not been attempted at all or had been only nominal. That is, there was no recorded attempt to work with the child and parents around the problems which resulted in his delinquency. In many instances there was failure to investigate other more appropriate placement possibilities.

9 Juvenile probation

Juvenile probation, which permits a child to remain in the community under the supervision and guidance of a probation officer, is a legal status created by a court of juvenile jurisdiction. It usually involves (*a*) a judicial finding that the behavior of the child has been such as to bring him within the purview of the court, (*b*) the imposition of conditions upon his continued freedom, and (*c*) the provision of means for helping him to meet these conditions and for determining the degree to which he meets them. Probation thus implies much more than indiscriminately giving the child "another chance." Its central thrust is to give him positive assistance in adjusting in the free community.

I. Introduction

A. Historical Development

Though juvenile probation has had its major development in the present century, its roots run back through a rather considerable history. In England, specialized procedures for dealing with youthful offenders emerged as early as 1820, when the magistrates of the Warwickshire Quarter Sessions adopted the practice of sentencing the youthful criminal to a term of imprisonment of 1 day, followed by his conditional release under the supervision of his parents or master.[1] This practice was soon thereafter further developed in Middlesex, Birmingham, and London, where probation supervision was first supplied by police officers, then by volunteer and philanthropic organizations,[2] and finally by public departments.

In the United States, juvenile probation developed as a part

---

[1] Paul W. Tappan, *Crime, Justice, and Correction* (New York: McGraw-Hill, 1960), p. 542.
[2] *Ibid.*

175

of the wave of social reform characterizing the later half of the 19th century. The new and enlarged definition of the state's responsibilities to its children produced such precursors of the future of child welfare practice as laws directed against cruelty to children, philanthropic associations for the protection and aid of the dependent and neglected child, and specialized institutions segregating the child offender from adult criminals. Probation emerged as another of the new era's means of mitigating the harshness of the criminal law and of employing the developing knowledge of the behavioral sciences on behalf of the child. Massachusetts took the first major step toward the development of a juvenile probation service. Under the act passed in 1869, an agent of the State board of charities was authorized to appear in criminal trials involving juveniles, to find them suitable homes, and to visit them periodically. These services were soon broadened and strengthened so that by 1890 probation had become a mandatory part of the court structure throughout the State.[3]

The emerging social institution, with its individualized, parental approach to the erring child, made a central contribution to the development of the concept of the juvenile court. In fact, in some States the early supporters of the juvenile court movement accepted probation legislation as its first step toward achieving the benefits that the new court was intended to provide.[4] In turn, the rapid spread of the juvenile court during the first decades of the present century seems often to have brought about the development and enrichment of probation. The two closely related and to a large degree interdependent institutions sprang from the same dedicated conviction of the educability of the young and the same positive affirmation of public responsibility for the protection of the child.

At the mid-1960's juvenile probation has become a large, major, complex social institution touching the lives of an enormous number of our children and young people. In 1964, about 686,000 delinquency, 150,000 dependency and neglect, and 442,000 traffic cases were referred to the country's juvenile courts.[5] According to rough estimates, about 11 percent of all children will be referred to the juvenile court on delinquency charges during their adolescent years, and as much as 18 percent of all boys will be so referred.[6] Juvenile probation has the main responsibility for processing and servicing most of these cases. As a service, it represents investments in future citizens. It cannot be cheaply purchased. At present, it costs an estimated $74,-750,727 a year.

[3] Margaret K. Rosenheim (ed.), *Justice for the Child* (New York: The Free Press, 1962), p. 3.
[4] *Ibid.*
[5] U.S. Department of Health, Education and Welfare, Children's Bureau, *Juvenile Court Statistics—1964* (Washington: Children's Bureau, Statistical Series No. 83, 1965), pp. 1–6.
[6] *Ibid.*, p. 1.

B. Goals and Functions

1. GOALS

The dominant purpose of the total correctional process is promotion of the welfare and security of the community. Within this overall goal, juvenile probation's specific assignment includes (*a*) preventing a repetition of the child's delinquent behavior, (*b*) preventing long-time deviate or criminal careers, and (*c*) assisting the child, through measures feasible to the probation service, to achieve his potential as a productive citizen.

Thus, the central services of probation are directed to the child found delinquent by the court and, often, to his family. However, in some jurisdictions probation departments are also assigned responsibilities in broader, delinquency-prevention programs. Though the proper boundaries of probation's services in this role are not clear and may vary from one jurisdiction to another, it seems clear that a probation department should at least assume the responsibility for assembling and reporting its special knowledge about delinquent children, their needs, and the community conditions that produce delinquency. It is also vitally necessary for the department to be an active partner in the process of community planning for meeting the needs of young people.

2. FUNCTIONS

The modern probation department performs three central—and, sometimes, several auxiliary—functions. Its central services are (*a*) juvenile court, probation department, and detention intake and screening, (*b*) social study and diagnosis, and (*c*) supervision and treatment.

(*a*) Intake and Screening

The juvenile court and the probation department are highly specialized sociological agencies. The scope of their jurisdiction and services is defined and limited by law, but their limitations are not understood by everyone in the community, and their intervention is not effective in all types of cases. Further, many of the agencies referring cases to them do not have the time or the staff with trained diagnostic skill to determine whether a specific case can best be served by the probation department. As a result, a probation staff member must engage in preliminary exploration with the child, the family, and the referring source to determine with them whether there is a legal basis for court intervention or whether the problem can be resolved better by use of the services of some other community resource.

Frequently the probation department must also decide or participate in deciding whether the child should be admitted to, continued in, or released from detention pending disposition of his case by the court. Removing the child from his home and family and holding him in a detention facility, even for a temporary period, constitute a major intervention in his life and his family's. For some children this may be necessary and helpful; for others it may be deeply damaging and may contribute powerfully to alienation from conforming society and its institutions. The problem is rendered even more tragically complex by the fact that, in many jurisdictions in the United States in the 1960's, juvenile detention is provided in facilities that degrade and brutalize, rather than rehabilitate.[7]

(b) Social Study and Diagnosis

Characteristically, the juvenile court exercises tremendous power to make authoritative decisions concerning vital aspects of the lives of children and families found to be within its jurisdiction. The delinquent child may be returned to his home and family without further intervention, he may be placed under probation supervision, or he may be removed from his family's control for a period ranging from a few weeks to several years. Such decisions, therefore, which may powerfully shape for good or evil the total future of the individuals involved, must be made only on the basis of the most careful and competent diagnostic study.

Such a study involves the awesome task of predicting human behavior. The focal concern is the probable nature of the child's response to the necessary demands of society. Will he or will he not be able to refrain from offending again if permitted to continue to reside in the free community? An even more complicated question is: What will be his adjustment under the various possible conditions of treatment—i.e., if he is returned home without further intervention, or if he is provided differing sorts of community supervision and service, or if he is confined in an institution? Only by illuminating such questions can the social study be of value to the court's dispositional decision.

If the diagnostic study is to accomplish its purpose it must include skilled analysis of the child's perceptions of and feelings about his violations, his problems, and his life situation. It must shed light on the value systems that influence his behavior. It must consider the degree of his motivation to solve the problems productive of deviate behavior, as well as his physical, intellectual, and emotional capacities to do so. It must examine the influence of members of his family and other significant persons in his life in producing and possibly solving his problems. Neighborhood and peer group determinants of his attitudes and behavior must be analyzed.

All of this information must be brought together into a meaningful picture of a complex whole composed of the personality, the problem, and the environment situation which must be dealt with. This configuration

---

[7] The frequent overuse and misuse of juvenile detention and the complications of the probation department's role in detention intake and release screening are detailed in chapter 8 *supra.*

must be considered in relation to the various possible alternative dispositions available to the court. Out of this, a constructive treatment plan must be developed.

Accomplishment of this enormously complicated task by the probation staff requires dedication, intelligence, professional understanding of the forces shaping human behavior, and highly developed skills in interviewing and in making use of the potential contributions of medicine, psychiatry, education, religion, and numerous other professional disciplines.

(c) Supervision and Treatment

Probation involves far more than giving the child "another chance." This last phrase often describes a course of action in which the child is returned unchanged to a family and community situation that produced delinquency in the first place and can be relied on to do it again. Consequently, probation has been assigned the task of contributing to the process of change, through supervision and treatment, in the situation and behavior of the offending child.

The three major elements of effective supervision and treatment are surveillance, service, and counseling. Usually, no one of these elements is effective by itself; each is a part of an interrelated whole.

(1) *Surveillance.* The officer must keep in touch with the child, his parents, his school, and other persons involved in and concerned about his adjustment. He must keep generally informed of the extent to which the probation plan is being carried out. Is the family providing adequate care and supervision? Is the child responding to parental supervision? Is he attending school, or working, or in other ways conforming to the general probation plan? Properly used, surveillance constitutes much more than a threat. It is a method of helping the child become aware of his responsibilities and the demands that life makes upon him as a member of the society. It is a resource for the individualization of such demands as they apply to his particular life situation. It constitutes a confrontation with reality, and it may be a source of support by contributing a precise understanding of that reality and the consequences of his failure to respond to it. It provides assurance that society, represented by the court and a court officer, is aware of and interested in him, is concerned that he not engage in future violative and self-defeating behavior, and is determined to assist him in avoiding such behavior.

(2) *Service.* The officer must determine the extent to which the problems confronting the child and the family may be alleviated by use of available community services. He must then muster such services in an organized way and help the child and family make use of them effectively—often an extremely complicated task when he is dealing with a family that has long been at odds with and suspicious of any agency it regards as representing the authority of society.

(3) *Counseling.* Counseling, the third aspect of the officer's task, makes it possible to perform the other two effectively. The child and family and other persons concerned must be helped to understand and face the existence of the personal or environmental problems productive of the child's delinquency. Frequently they must be helped to gain some degree of understanding of their roles in the production—and thus in the solution—of such problems. They must be encouraged and stimulated to mobilize their strengths and energies and to invest them in the problem-solving process. The performance of this function depends upon the officer's professional ability to offer them understanding, his obvious dedication to helping them find satisfaction in a socially acceptable manner, his skillful presentation to them of society's demands that they conform to its minimal expectations, and his determination to help them do so.

(d) Auxiliary Functions

In addition to the three central functions noted above—(1) intake and screening, (2) social study and diagnosis, and (3) supervision and treatment—probation departments frequently perform significant auxiliary tasks. Large departments often operate mental health clinics providing diagnostic and, sometimes, treatment services for children referred to the court. Some administer a variety of other treatment services, which may include foster home programs, forestry camps, group homes, and other residential or nonresidential treatment facilities. Others vigorously engage in community planning and community organization efforts on behalf of children and youth. Some operate delinquency prevention services for endangered youth.

Direct operation of many of the treatment and delinquency prevention programs noted above is considered by most authorities to be a proper responsibility of community agencies other than the court and the probation department. Some experienced practitioners disagree with this position, however, and they point out that, in many instances, courts organize and operate these programs through community default—that is, because no other resource has shown willingness or capacity to do it.

C. Standards for Evaluating Practice

Universally accepted standards proven by research methods to correlate with movement toward specified goals have not been developed for the field of juvenile probation. The same statement can be made of all other aspects of correction, as well as of education, public administration, political science, and most other fields concerned with human behavior. This does not mean that the quality of a probation system cannot be assessed. However, the criteria by which such assessment is made must be recognized as a sort of distillate of current "practice wisdom" rather than the product of definitive inquiry. This process has resulted in standards generally accepted among experienced practioners and eminently applicable to today's practice. Among the most useful compilations of such standards are (*a*) the one prepared by the Special Committee on Standards (President's Commission on Law Enforcement and Administration of Justice), (*b*) NCCD's "Standards and Guides for Juvenile Probation,"[8] and (*c*) The Children's Bureau's "Standards for Juvenile and Family and Courts."[9]

As noted above, juvenile probation is charged with the loftiest of goals. Like any other major social institution, its worth, in the long run, must be judged not only by its goals but also by its performance.

The assumption that probation contributes to the achievement of its defined goals depends on the validity of two prior assumptions: first, that probation actually does have the theoretical and knowledge base that would enable it to predict and influence behavior; and, second, that the manpower, the money, and the other resources necessary to its effective performance actually are or can be made available.

The survey permits only very general consideration of the degree to which probation's theoretical and knowledge base are adequate to the task at hand. However, it does make possible some fairly specific assessments of the availability of necessary manpower and other resources.

The theoretical and knowledge base upon which probation operates is still in the process of formation, is by no means universally agreed upon, and is nowhere clearly stated.

Traditionally, the theory embodied in the law and its allied functions has been that behavioral change can be coerced by deterrent punishment. Probation cannot perform so as to undermine the deterrent power of the law; however, few persons are unaware of the peril of too easy reliance on the ancient but never tested assumption that our deterrents do, in fact, usually deter. The correctional agency's clientele seems to consist largely of persons repeatedly subjected to—and unaffected by—many of society's sanctions. We can produce fear in the offender. But in so doing we also produce hate and the determination to strike back. Further, he appears generally not capable of weighing the pleasure of immediate gratification against future (and uncertain) punishment; and he is subject to peer group and other pressures stronger than those we are able to engender.

Thus, modern probation is generally dedicated to other theories of behavioral change. These depend largely on the combination of (*a*) confronting the offender with the behavioral alternatives available to him and the probable consequences of each and (*b*) helping him solve the problems of social functioning that impede his securing necessary and normal human

[8] National Council on Crime and Delinquency, "Standards and Guides for Juvenile Probation" (preliminary draft), a report of the Juvenile Court Services Committee of the Professional Council (New York: NCCD, 1965), mimeo.

[9] William H. Sheridan, *Standards for Juvenile and Family Courts,* U.S. Department of Health, Education and Welfare, Children's Bureau (Washington: U.S. Government Printing Office, 1966).

satisfactions in socially acceptable ways. Thus, it is hoped, he will internalize conventional value systems and will come to perceive such values as inherently appealing and productive of satisfaction.

In their efforts toward these ends, some practitioners seem to operate on the basis of little or no organized theoretical framework. Others are committed to any one of a variety of theoretical positions, some of which stress the dominance of one variable or another—intrapersonal, intrafamilial, subcultural, or sociocultural—in the production of deviant behavior. Many of these positions stress only the origins of such behavior and provide few action guides for influencing behavioral change.

Nonetheless, there seem to be gradually emerging a practice wisdom and a practice theory that stress the work of the officer in (a) seeking out, stimulating, and drawing into the problem-solving process the offender's motivations and his capacities to solve his problems of social functioning and (b) working with the offender and other persons and social institutions in his environment toward expansion of the opportunity structure available to him.

One of the major challenges facing scholars and practitioners is to formulate the assumptions upon which present practice is based and then to test and further refine them.

II. Survey Findings

A. Probation Coverage

Juvenile probation service is authorized by statute in each of the 50 States and the Commonwealth of Puerto Rico. The study conducted in conjunction with the preparation of this report shows that in one recent year some 192,000 written social studies were made on behalf of children referred to our courts and that some 189,000 children were placed under probation supervision. At the time of the survey, approximately 223,800 children were under such supervision. Supervision usually extends over significant periods of the child's life. Among the agencies included in the sample, the average period of supervision ranged from 3 months to 3 years, with a median of 13 months. In the sample of 250 counties, 233 had probation services.

Fundamental to any definition of desirable probation practice is the availability of paid, full-time probation service to all courts and all children needing such service.

The survey reveals that, though every State makes statutory provision for juvenile probation, in many States probation service is not uniformly available in all counties and localities. The data on this point may be summarized as follows:

1. In 31 States all counties have probation staff service.
2. A total of 2,306 counties (74 percent of all counties in the United

States) theoretically have such service. In some of these the service may be only a token.

3. In 16 States that do not have probation staff coverage in every county, at least some services are available to courts in some counties from persons other than paid, full-time probation officers. The sources of such services include volunteers (in six States), child welfare departments (in five States), and a combination of child welfare, sheriff, and other departments (in five States).

4. In 165 counties in 4 States, no juvenile probation services at all are available.

Generally, the country's more populous jurisdictions are included among the counties served by probation staff. However, in the smaller counties service may be expected to be spotty. Comments such as the following occur in the observations of the experienced practitioners gathering the survey data:

> The . . . State Department of Public Welfare does provide, upon request, probation and aftercare services to the courts and to institutions. These services are part of the child welfare program, and no differentiation is made as to specific caseloads. A general impression is that . . . there is not an acceptance of this service, and it is not used in many counties.

Many of the State agencies that are theoretically responsible for providing services are not prepared to do so. However, some child welfare departments acknowledge the provision of probation services as a major responsibility, assign capable staff to the function, and provide services of good caliber. . . . [Yet] the development of practitioners in the court setting who have specialized knowledge of the diagnosis and treatment of acting-out, behavior-problem children remains a challenge to probation practice. This task is doubly difficult when the staff is not oriented specifically to these problems. It is particularly inappropriate to expect specialists in law enforcement (sheriffs, police, etc.) to become skilled in probation diagnosis and treatment as well as in their own specialized functions. And rare is the volunteer who has the time, energy, and resources to so equip himself (though the volunteer often plays a valuable role when working upon carefully defined problems in cooperation with a trained and experienced member of the probation staff).

Whether a child subjected to the truly awesome powers of the juvenile court will be dealt with on the basis of knowledge and understanding, usually the product of a good probation social study, is determined by chance—the accident of his place of residence. The same accident determines whether the community treatment resource of probation as an alternative to incarceration will be available to him. The following observation about one State was made by a member of the survey team:

In the entire State, only two counties have probation services. The other counties have no service. A child placed on probation in these counties is presumed to be adjusting satisfactorily until he is brought back to the court with a new charge. . . . The Department of Welfare will not accept referrals of delinquent children from the courts.

B. Organization of Services

Juvenile probation services are organized in a State in one of the following ways:

1. A centralized, statewide system.

2. A centralized county or city system, the services of which are strengthened and supported by State supervision, consultation, standard setting, recruitment, assistance with inservice training and staff development, and partial State subsidy of the local department.

3. A combination of the above systems, with the more populous and prosperous jurisdictions operating their own departments and with service being provided by the State in the other areas.

Which of the three organizational plans is to be preferred is a question that has to be resolved by such factors as prevalent State administrative structures, political patterns and traditions, and population distribution. However, for many States, a well-coordinated State plan appears preferable. Such a pattern (a) has greater potential for assuring uniformity of standards and practice, including provision of service to rural areas; (b) makes certain research, statistical and fiscal control, and similar operations more feasible; (c) best enables recruitment of qualified staff and provision of centralized or regional inservice training and staff development programs; (d) permits staff assignment to regional areas in response to changing conditions; and (e) facilitates relationships to other aspects of the State correctional program.

In some States, it may be that local agencies are in a better position to respond to changing local conditions and to assure investment of local resources in the solution of essentially local problems. These benefits usually occur in a city or county relatively high in tax potential and progressive leadership; corresponding progress does not take place in adjoining jurisdictions. To assure at least acceptable performance throughout a State where probation is a local responsibility, State supervision, standard-setting, consultation, assistance in staff recruitment and inservice training, and similar services are required. The problems all too often resulting from the absence of either a centralized State probation service or adequate standard-setting for local services are illustrated by another comment emerging from one of the State studies:

In [the small State of . . .] juvenile probation . . . offers 11 different programs, with widely differing philosophies of institutional use, much variation in procedures, and no possibility of influencing the quality of probation work through any centralized training effort. Political appointment of officers is standard practice and there is no merit system offering the possibility of a career in probation.

Intrastate uniformity in achieving acceptable standards often requires that local probation be subsidized by the State. State expenditure for this purpose is an excellent investment, for it mitigates against the ever present danger of indiscriminate commitment to the State correctional program. This and similar benefits seem to have been obtained by such a program recently introduced in one State, where the conference with correctional officials held in connection with the survey produced the following observation:

> Juvenile probation has . . . seen substantial improvement in the past few years with the help of a State subsidy that provides that in order to participate the local county must add to its existing staff. A number of small counties which had never had probation services prior to this study have now created departments. Larger counties have been able to expand their services. . . . The general effect of the subsidy has been to generate considerable interest on the part of some judges where little or no interest previously existed.

1. COURT ADMINISTRATION VERSUS ADMINISTRATIVE AGENCY

County and city systems are organized mainly according to two patterns. In the prevalent one, probation services are administered by the court itself or by a combination of courts; in the other, the services are provided to the court by an administrative agency, such as a probation department established as a separate arm of local government.

The survey reveals that juvenile probation is administered as follows:

	In States
By courts	32
By State correctional agencies	5
By State departments of public welfare	7
By other State agencies	4
By other agencies or combination of agencies	3

Some authorities arguing in behalf of the first pattern, in use in most jurisdictions, hold that administration by the court is necessary and desirable since it is the court that is responsible for determining which delinquents are to remain in the community and under what circumstances they are to be permitted to do so. Proper discharge of this responsibility, they say, means that the judge must have the authority to select and control the probation officer, who functions as an extension of the court.[10]

[10] For discussion of this issue see Paul W. Keve, "Administration of Juvenile Court Services," in Rosenheim, *op. cit. supra* note 3, pp. 174–176.

Other authorities argue that the more widespread use of the first pattern may well be the result of historical accident rather than careful analysis of the advantages and disadvantages of the two plans. They point out that conditions have changed since the administration-by-the-court pattern was first established and that now many probation departments are large, complex organizations. Their administration requires a background of training and experience in, as well as an inclination toward, administration—qualifications that do not necessarily accompany judicial function. The judge should be an impartial arbiter between contending forces. His administration of an agency often party to the issues brought before him in the courtroom may thus impair—or may seem to one or the other of the parties to impair—performance of his judicial function. Further, if the court is composed of many judges, it is likely that the juvenile court judgeship assignment will rotate frequently, so that true assumption of administrative leadership may never take place.

In any event, the major administrative leadership role in the operation of probation services must be clearly recognized. The total juvenile court function is rendered almost impossible without good probation service, which cannot develop without good administration. It may be that some judges can perform both the judicial and the administrative function effectively. But, as Keve points out:

> It seems that at this point in its history, the juvenile court must face its growing administrative task and decide whether it is to relinquish its administrative duties to a separate administrative body, or accept the administrative character of the juvenile court and deliberately develop the structure and capacities of the court to a greater extent than is usually true now.[11]

(a) *Citizens Advisory Committees*

Whether administered at the State or the local level, the juvenile probation department often finds that a carefully selected citizens advisory committee or board is enormously helpful. The functions of such a committee should include: (a) Participation in the department's policymaking processes so that the thinking of major forces in the community and major sources of pertinent expertise is represented; and (b) constant interpretation to the community of the functions, problems, and needs of the department.

The committee should include representation from business and industry, organized labor, the bar, medicine (including psychiatry), the social services, education, religion, and other pertinent community forces.

2. STATE STANDARD-SETTING

In 13 of the 45 States in which some or all of the courts are served by local departments, an agency of the State government sets at least some

[11] *Ibid.*, p. 177.

standards governing probation performance. The aspects of the local departments' functions so governed are as follows:

	States
Staff qualifications only	6
Standards of practice only	2
Combination of staff qualifications, salary, etc.	5

Efforts were made during the course of the survey to discover whether, in the professional opinion of the experienced practitioners gathering survey data, the introduction of State standard-setting had resulted in the improvement of local probation service. In 9 of the 13 States, such improvement was considered to have taken place; in 2, no change could be observed; and in 2, evaluations could not be secured.

3. STATE SUBSIDY OF LOCAL PROBATION

In 19 of the 45 States offering probation on a local basis, some subsidization of the service is available from State funds. The items covered by such subsidies are as follows:

	States
Personnel	7
Personnel and other items	5
New personnel only	1
Operational costs	2
Other items	4

Complete data on the proportion of the local department's budget coming from state subsidy are not available. In six States this proportion is 50 percent or less; in one, it is more than 50 percent; and in three, the total costs of local probation services are subsidized by State funds.

In nine States professional judgments were generally to the effect that subsidy programs had resulted in the improvement of probation service. In two States no change was considered to have resulted.

4. OTHER STATE SERVICES

In 19 States a central State agency provides consultation service to local courts. Other services sometimes rendered for local departments by State agencies include statistical analysis (10 States), staff training programs (6 States), and direct probation service in some counties (2 States).

(a) *Statewide Statistics*

The pressing need for continuously available, up-to-date information about the nature and extent of juvenile delinquency, juvenile probation, and other correctional problems can be satisfied only by a State agency that assumes responsibility for the collection, analysis, interpretation, and publication of the statistical data in each of the State's local jurisdictions. This function is now performed in only 38 States, by (*a*) the correctional agency, in 13 States; (*b*) the department of public welfare, in 9 States; (*c*) an administrative office of the State's courts, in 4 States; and (*d*) some other State agency (including the department of health) in the other States.

C. Age Groups Served by Juvenile Probation

The upper age limit for eligibility for the services of juvenile probation is determined by the statute establishing the jurisdictional limits of the juvenile court. The Standard Juvenile Court Act provides that the court shall have jurisdiction over a child alleged to have committed an offense "prior to having become 18 years of age."[12] Setting the upper age limit of juvenile court jurisdiction at 18 years is endorsed by the U.S. Children's Bureau and is generally supported by most serious students of the problem; however, . . . it is far from universal practice.

Persons 16 or 17 years old are not considered, for most purposes, to be adults. In many jurisdictions they are restricted in the employment in which they may engage and are not permitted to enter into contracts, to marry, to vote, and even, in some instances, to be abroad upon the streets at night. Yet in 15 States a 17-year-old boy who violates the law is dealt with as a fully responsible adult.

D. Probation Officers

1. CRITERIA FOR EMPLOYMENT

For a long time society has protected its citizens by establishing procedures for admission of lawyers and surgeons to practice and by specifying criteria for certification of veterinarians, barbers, and architects. But only now is it beginning to determine the necessary qualifications for those to whom it assigns the duty of mending the broken lives of its children and families. Obviously, the enormously complicated task of the probation officer described above, which is essentially a matter of diagnosis and treatment of problems of social maladjustment, cannot be performed by persons about whom nothing much more can be said than that they are "men of good will."

The Committee on Standards endorsed the previously recommended personal, experimental, and educational criteria for the employment of probation officers. These suggest two sorts of qualifications. First, officers

---

[12] National Probation and Parole Association (now National Council on Crime and Delinquency). *Standard Juvenile Court Act* (1959), sec. 8. The act also provides that the court may retain jurisdiction until the child reaches his 21st birthday (sec. 10) and that it may transfer certain 16- and 17-year-old children to the adult court (sec. 13).

performing the basic probation function should possess the highest personal attributes. They should have emotional and intellectual maturity, ability in interpersonal relations, positive value systems, and dedication to the service of others. Second, they should have the training and experience that will supply the knowledge and skill necessary for their enormously complicated work. Since their tasks include diagnosis and treatment, they must have professional training in these functions. Thus, they should have a master's degree from an accredited school of social work or comparable training in one of the related social sciences.

It is impossible now, however, to find the necessary number of staff possessing this preferred educational background. The recommended standards, therefore, set forth these minimum qualifications: (*a*) a bachelor's degree in the social sciences; and (*b*) 1 year of graduate study in social work or a related social science, or 1 year of paid, full-time experience under professional supervision in a recognized social agency. Persons recruited under this provision will particularly require on-the-job training in the essentials of probation diagnosis and treatment.

No survey or research evaluation has been made of the personality attributes of probation officers serving children in the United States. However, most qualified observers agree that the personality coefficient of present juvenile probation staff is quite high. Although some positions are still held by political appointees who probably have good intentions but also have little true interest in, aptitude for, or dedication to the job, probation departments are attracting alert, capable, and dedicated individuals who possess the personal attributes vital for positively influencing the attitudes and behavior of the young.

The survey data on the educational qualifications for employment as a probation officer or chief probation officer are not encouraging. They indicate that many appointing authorities have no understanding of the necessary attributes of persons who are to be assigned the task of producing change in human behavior.

. . . [I]n 22 percent of the departments included in the survey sample, the educational qualifications for employment of probation officers are below the recommended minimum educational standard. In 74 percent of the departments, that part of the minimum standard calling for at least a bachelor's degree is maintained, but no information is available on the requirement for 1 year of graduate education or 1 year of supervised employment in a social agency. Only 4 percent of the agencies maintain the preferred educational standard of a master's degree in social work or one of the allied social sciences.

In employing chief probation officers, only 15 percent of the sample agencies apply the preferred educational standard; 63 percent meet the recommended minimum, and 22 percent fall below even that line.

There are no reliable data on the proportion of presently employed probation officers meeting the minimal recommended standards for employment. However, one survey conducted a few years ago indicated that, of some 2,000 officers responding to a U.S. Children's Bureau questionnaire on the subject, only 10 percent had graduate degrees.[13]

It thus appears that most of the country's juvenile courts employ as probation officers and chief probation officers persons who lack professional training in diagnosis and treatment. This clearly suggests the necessity for extensive use of inservice training and other staff development tools in probation departments.

2. ON-THE-JOB TRAINING

The standards call for on-the-job training opportunities for staff. In addition to an orientation program for new workers calculated to help them become acquainted with the agency's rules, procedures, and policies, the major forms of such stimuli for development are the following:

(a) A continuing inservice training program carefully designed to meet the needs of staff at various levels, including the supervisory and administrative. Larger agencies should assign full-time staff to this function; smaller agencies should be assisted by appropriate state departments in organizing training regionally.

(b) Casework supervision (teaching and consultation on diagnosis and treatment). Without this help it is extremely difficult for the untrained worker to translate into practice the teachings of the training program.

(c) Educational leave provisions for both part-time and full-time salaried leave so that particularly promising or key staff members will be helped to meet desired qualifications and improve their professional competence.

(a) Inservice Training

The survey reveals that 48 percent of the departments included in the sample have an inservice training program; 52 percent do not have one. A qualitative survey of these programs was not possible, but the data show that where such programs exist, training meetings are held weekly in 21 percent of the departments, monthly in 33 percent, quarterly in 21 percent, annually in 6 percent, and irregularly in 19 percent—figures that point to a discouraging picture of the quality of training provided. No substantial impact on the probation officers' understanding of the situations, problems, and persons he deals with can be achieved in sessions meeting less frequently than once a week.

(b) Casework Supervision

The generally approved supervisor-officer ratio is about 1:6. The survey data for juvenile probation departments permit an estimate that there are

---

[13] U.S. Children's Bureau and National Institute of Mental Health, Department of Health, Education and Welfare, *Report to the Congress on Juvenile Delinquency*, 1960, p. 42.

1,084 supervisors and 5,236 officers—an actual ratio of 1:4.8. However, the casework supervision picture is not as encouraging as the impression given by these figures. The data include the heads of small departments whose functions are essentially administration with some supervision included (a situation which is known to occur very frequently). Further, qualified observers who have studied many individual departments find all too often that the supervisor himself is untrained in the professional aspects of probation and does not even regard teaching and consultation as part of his function.

(c) *Stipends for Educational Leave*

Not all of probation's training needs can be met by inservice programs, which presume the availability of well-prepared training and supervisory personnel. Further, the continuing growth of the correctional agency and of the field in general demands that particularly promising or key personnel should be assisted toward completing their professional education so that they may make their maximum contribution to training and practice.

This graduate professional training consists of (a) education at the master's degree level in social work, which normally requires 2 years' work beyond the bachelor's degree or (b) education at the master's degree level in sociology, psychology, criminology, public administration, or correctional administration, which usually requires 1 year's work beyond the bachelor's degree.

The agencies in the survey sample report a total of 108 educational stipends. At the time of the survey (which took place during the normal university year), only 84 persons were on educational leave from these agencies.

Obviously, the correctional agencies' educational leave programs on the scale suggested by the figures above will not solve the field's educational problems. Related assistance from other sources is also very limited.

Although probably more persons enter probation from social work than from any other academic discipline, the field recruits only a small portion of social work's graduates, and the percentage will remain small unless probation sharply increases the volume of its scholarship aid. Of the 6,039 students enrolled in graduate social work schools in 1963–64, 5,135 received scholarship aid,[14] which generally is given in return for the recipient's commitment to enter practice in a particular agency or a particular field of social work endeavor. Though some correctional systems (for example, Wisconsin) offer such aid, the total number is pitifully small. The major source of educational stipends in correction is the National Institute of Mental Health. During 1963–64, 156 NIMH stipends were available in 27

[14] Milton Wittman, "An Assessment of Scholarship Aid in Correction," in Charles S. Prigmore (ed.), *Manpower and Training for Corrections* (New York: Council on Social Work Education, 1966), p. 67.

schools of social work.[15] As these are for both first- and second-year students, however, only about half that number of graduates are available to the total field of correction; an unknown but small proportion of that number will enter juvenile probation.

Other sources of training aid are similarly limited. The Federal Juvenile Delinquency and Youth Offenses Control Act of 1961, which provides funds for various training programs, spent approximately $6 million during 1962–64 on 67 grants[16]; generally, however, these supported curriculum development, workshops, short courses, institutes, and seminars—in short, training centers for purposes other than full professional training. The impact of this program on the training needs of juvenile probation does not seem to date to have been extensive.

3. METHOD OF APPOINTMENT

Formal State or county merit and civil service systems commonly apply by statute only to employees of the administrative arm of government. In the majority of States, as has been noted above, juvenile probation services are administered by the court; thus, probation becomes identified as part of the judicial branch of government. Of the 235 agencies reporting in the survey, only 47 percent had civil service or merit system coverage, while 53 percent were without such coverage.

Some persons argue that civil service and the merit system have frequently been perverted in correction and are, in effect, protecting the status quo at a time when the field has many marginal employees.[17]

The best current thinking is that some form of merit system appointment through competitive examination, without residential restrictions and with assurance against arbitrary discharge, is both possible and eminently desirable in the probation system, whether it be administered by the court or by an administrative agency. It is usually considered desirable that the judge participate, either personally or through a chief probation officer, in the appointment of staff; however, it is quite possible for him to appoint from a list of persons certified as qualified by a State or local merit system.

4. SALARIES

The probation standards call for salaries commensurate with employment in positions of high trust and responsibility. Provision should be made for regular salary increments according to merit and performance. Expenses incurred in the performance of official duties should be reimbursed. Policies comparable to those in the best private social agencies should be estab-

---

[15] *Ibid.*, p. 68.

[16] U.S. Department of Health, Education and Welfare, Office of Juvenile Delinquency and Youth Development, *Summaries of Training Projects, Juvenile Delinquency and Youth Offenses Control Act*, April 1965, p. 1.

[17] Joseph W. Eaton and Menachim Amir, "Manpower Strategy in the Correctional Field," in Prigmore, *op. cit. supra* note 14, p. 79.

lished for sick leave, annual leave, hospital and medical insurance, disability and retirement coverage, etc.

Some variation in probation salary scales according to general wage scales and the cost of living in the locality is to be expected. It should not, however, be extreme. Probation departments compete nationally, not locally, for qualified staff, and therefore ought to be in a position to do so on even terms.

The survey reveals tremendous variation in annual salary scales. In the sample . . . the salary of the chief probation officer ranged from less than $2,400 to more than $18,000 (median, $8,001–$9,000); staff supervisor salary ranged from less than $3,000 to about $11,000 (median, $7,001–$8,000); and probation officer salary ranged from under $1,500 to about $11,000 (median, $5,001–$6,000). A considerable proportion of our country's juvenile probation departments have salary schedules that make it impossible for them to compete in a national (or even a local) market for staff with the recommended minimum qualifications, to say nothing of the recommended preferred qualifications.

All agencies in the sample were asked to state what they considered to be the chief obstacle to effective juvenile probation service. "Lack of staff" was the answer by 37 percent of them. . . .

E. Intake Service

As previously noted, the juvenile court and its probation department are specialized agencies whose services are appropriate only for selected children and problems. The best utilization of probation staff time, therefore, requires an intake screening service.

The intake unit receives referrals to the court and immediately reviews available reports, undertakes initial interviews with children and parents, and clears with schools and similar sources of information. It then determines which cases require immediate referral to the court or to field staff for further social study, and which seem to fall outside the legal purview of the court, to need no further court service, or to require referral to a noncourt agency. Given the support and confidence of the judge, a capably staffed intake service can often adjust as much as 50 percent of all incoming cases without further court action. The need for specialized intake service in a large department is obvious, and it is beneficial even in a department staffed by only two or three officers.

The survey shows that approximately 50 percent of the agencies in the sample provide intake and referral services, assigning a total of 541 intake officers to this function. The remaining agencies were reportedly without intake staff.

Standards call for a social study to be made in all cases referred to the juvenile court. According to the survey, 190,000 prehearing studies were reported to have been made in the 250-county sample from which juvenile probation data were collected. This number of prehearing studies represents 61 percent of the children committed or placed on probation by the courts in these same counties. It was not possible to obtain a national estimate for the ratio of social studies to dispositions, but it can be noted that, in some of the sample counties, prehearing studies were made regularly, as a matter of court policy, in all cases, while, in other counties, none were made.

F. Caseload Size

An obvious major determinant of the quality of probation service is the size of the caseload assigned to the officer. If the social study is undertaken in circumstances permitting him to make only a cursory inquiry into the motives and feelings of the child, the nature of his family life, the family's potential to meet his needs, and the community pressures that shape his attitude and behavior, it will produce only misunderstanding at best and, at worst, actual injury to the child. If probation supervision is attempted under circumstances that make possible only superficial contact with the child and the family, it is worse than meaningless, for the child subjected to it may become convinced that the officer, who to him represents conforming society and its institutions, may readily be duped or hoodwinked, is unaware of him as an individual human being, or simply is not much interested in him.

It is obviously impossible to set forth precise standards by which the proper size of a probation caseload may be determined under all sorts of conditions. Differences will exist from time to time and from jurisdiction to jurisdiction in types of cases carried, levels of officers' skills, degrees to which supplemental services are available in the community, size of the geographic area served, and financial ability of the community to invest in good service.

The generally recognized minimal standard, developed from practical experience, calls for a caseload of not more than 50 units of work a month. One case under probation supervision is counted as one unit; a new investigation and diagnostic study counts as five units since, if properly done, it may be expected to require about five times as much time and effort as will a case under supervision in 1 month.

Thus, 1 officer can carry 50 supervision cases a month if he is not making any new investigations. Ten new investigations per month comprise a full-time job, as does any combination of investigation and supervision cases totaling 50 units in any 1 month.

This standard is minimal. A 50-unit caseload allows an average of only 3 hours a month for each supervision case. When the hours spent in traveling, court attendance, supervisory conferences, dictation, etc., are accounted for, the total time available for face-to-face confrontation with the child is probably not more than 1 hour a month. Obviously, 1 hour a month is not enough time in which to reshape defective attitudes and behavior. Some cases must be given much more time than this; consequently, other cases will get even less than the 1-hour average.

Minimal though it is, this 50-unit standard is seldom met in practice. The survey data do not permit calculation of the number of work units in the average probation caseload, but they do provide information on the number of cases under probation supervision by officers in the counties studied. The median load in these agencies falls between 71 and 80 cases under supervision. Of all children being served, 0.2 percent were in caseloads where the number of supervision cases was less than 20. On the other hand, 10.6 percent were in loads where the number of supervision cases was over 100. The highest average supervision caseload reported was 281.

In most probation departments at least half of the officer's time is spent on social studies (investigations in new cases). Therefore, the number of work units in the departments included in the survey is at least twice the number of cases under probation supervision reported above.

G. Supporting Services

1. FOSTER FAMILY CARE AND GROUP HOMES

Probation is essentially a resource for helping the child make an adjustment in his community and his home. For some children this is an unreachable goal, and, whether they cannot adjust in the home or the home cannot meet their needs, commitment to an institution is generally the disposition. But it has been demonstrated that considerable numbers of children who cannot adjust in their own homes have the capacity to adjust within the free community in other environments, of which the most frequently used is the foster family home. Another type of resource highly appropriate to the needs of many adolescents is the small, open, group home, which often offers the external controls needed by the adolescent without the emotional demands common in the foster home where he may be expected to accept adults in a substitute parent role (a particularly difficult demand on a youngster who, in the normal course of development, is in the process of achieving emotional emancipation from parental figures).

Of the 233 agencies in the sample, 42 percent used foster homes for juvenile probation cases. At the time of the survey, they reported a total of 4,967 probationers under foster home care. (Interestingly, more than half of these children were in three California counties.)

Only 10 of the agencies operated group homes. They reported a total of 332 children under group home care at the time of this survey.

2. PSYCHOLOGICAL AND PSYCHIATRIC SERVICES

Psychological and psychiatric services to the probation department are not only extremely valuable in inservice training and staff development but also vitally important to diagnosis and the continuing treatment process in the cases of some children. Of the agencies included in the sample, 12 percent report that they have no such services available to them; the remainder report the availability of at least some psychiatric or psychological resource.

The survey did not attempt to evaluate the available community clinical resources, but observations by qualified observers are almost universally to the effect that they are rarely adequate. The length of the waiting list usually makes the clinic of dubious value to the child, who cannot be helped unless he becomes involved in the treatment process at the point of crisis. Commonly, also, the clinical service builds up in the child, through diagnosis, an awareness of the need for and some expectation of treatment, and then it frustrates the entire process by failing to provide any form of continuing treatment. Frequently, even when a psychiatric resource is available, diagnostic and not treatment services are called on.

3. EXPERIMENTATION AND RESEARCH

As in other behavioral science endeavors, probation's methodology for change in human behavior and attitudes still demands much experimentation and research, some of which is now being conducted in creative departments. For example, the Los Angeles County Probation Department maintains a research division, staffed by research-trained personnel, which engages in numerous inquiries that have proved to be of great practical value to that department and to the probation field as a whole.[18] Some research has been undertaken on enriched, community-based treatment programs in both probation and parole.[19]

Other departments not having research staff engage in comparatively unstructured experimentation with new methods and techniques. For example, the following creative projects are reported by one of the agencies included in the sample:

1. Group therapy with delinquent youth and parents.

2. Short term (4 months) maximum-impact probation supervision and treatment for selected probationers.

3. Assignment of staff and provision of consultation to a protective services project.

[18] Stuart Adams, "The Value of Research in Probation," *Federal Probation*, September 1965, pp. 35–40.
[19] See for example: California State Board of Corrections, "The Treatment of Delinquents in the Community: Variations in Treatment Approaches," monograph No. 1, July 1960; "Correction in the Community: Alternative to Incarceration," monograph No. 4, June 1964.

4. A program developed in cooperation with a law school for the provision of guardian *ad litem* services to strengthen the legal protections available to children and parents.

5. In cooperation with a bar association committee, development of a handbook that outlines juvenile court procedures.

6. Carefully organized endeavors to siphon off clerical and other routine processes so as to make best use of probation staff time and skills.

Efforts such as these remain all too rare. The agencies in the sample were requested to report any imaginative or unusual rehabilitation program. Approximately 56 percent reported none in progress; 10 percent reported group counseling with children; 5 percent, group counseling with parents; and 29 percent, a miscellany of other programs including work with street gangs.

If carefully designed and executed, these programs can provide a learning experience of great potential value to the field. Actually, this potential is often not realized, for two reasons: First, many of the projects are organized without the assistance of research staff or consultation and therefore do not have built into them the means to evaluate their effectiveness. Second, many of them are repetitious or unreported.

[*President's Commission on Law Enforcement and Administration of Justice,* Task Force Report: Corrections (*Washington: U.S. Government Printing Office, 1967*), appendix A, pp. 130–141.]

10 *Juvenile institutions*

A juvenile training facility is normally part of a system separate from other State and local juvenile correctional services, which usually include, at a minimum, the courts, juvenile probation, and supervision (aftercare) of those released from the training facility. Together these services provide resources for the differential treatment required for juvenile offenders committing offenses from various levels of motivation.

I. Introduction

A. Purpose Served by Training Facilities

The role of the training school is to provide a specialized program for children who must be held to be treated. Accordingly, such facilities should normally house more hardened or unstable youngsters than should be placed, for example, under probation supervision.

The juvenile institutional program is basically a preparation and trial period for the ultimate test of returning to community life. Once return has been effected, the ultimate success of the facility's efforts is highly dependent on good aftercare services. These are needed to strengthen changes started in the institution; their value can be proved only in the normal conditions of community life.

B. Historical Development

The training school[1] originated as a State activity early in American history. So far as can be determined, the first public training institutions exclusively for juveniles were established in Massachusetts, New York, and Maine. The Lyman School for Boys opened in Westborough, Mass., in 1846. Then came the New York State Agricultural and Industrial School in 1849 and the Maine Boys Training Center in 1853. By 1870, Connecticut,

---

[1] This generic term, used throughout, includes camps and other training facilities.

Indiana, Maryland, Nevada, New Hampshire, New Jersey, Ohio, and Vermont had also set up separate juvenile training facilities; by 1900, 36 States had done so. They appear now in every State, including Alaska, which opened a youth conservation camp at Wasilla in 1960, approximately 2 years after achieving statehood.

Consistent with their historical development, training programs by and large are administered by the State.

C. *Working Philosophies*

The term "school of industry" or "reformatory" often designated the early juvenile training facilities, thus reflecting the relatively simple philosophies upon which their development was based. Their reform programs sought chiefly to teach the difference between right and wrong. Teaching methods were primarily on a precept level, tending to emphasize correct behavior, formal education, and, where possible, the teaching of a trade so that the trainee would have the skills to follow the "right."

To a large extent these elements continue to bulwark many programs, but the efficacy of the old methods has been increasingly questioned, and working philosophies now are moving in new directions, primarily for two reasons.

First, although statistics vary from school to school and can be differently interpreted, most experts agree that about half of the persons released from juvenile training facilities can be expected to be reincarcerated.[2]

Second, they agree that if treatment is to produce lasting change, it must (regardless of technique) touch upon the personal reasons for delinquency. Like most people, juveniles caught in the "wrong" usually find it more comfortable to justify themselves as "right" than to acknowledge responsibility for being wrong and seeking to change. For the delinquent this means that, from the view he has of himself, he does not act out of "evil" but out of a "good" which makes sense and can be justified. Delinquent behavior may be a satisfying experience to a youngster, especially if it meets his emotional needs. The approach, therefore, cannot be merely an appeal for a change in behavior that is offensive to the school; it must be concerned with what the behavior means to the youngster himself. Therefore, according to this view, the function of a training facility is to help a minor look honestly at his own attitudes and see to what degree they create difficulties in the sense that "as ye sow so shall ye reap." Having seen this, a minor then has a personal reference point for change that is connected with his own perception of "good"; he can arrive at personally responsible behavior because he feels this personal connection.

Evidence of the practicality of this viewpoint is found in observations

---

[2] Osborne Foundation and National Council on Crime and Delinquency, "A Report of the Juvenile Institutions Project" (preliminary draft), 1966.

common among training school youngsters themselves, who are quite capable of pointing out those in their group who are "really doing good" and those who are "just playing it cool." If the training school makes conformity the hallmark of progress, it teaches duplicity because, in so doing, it is suggesting that the real problem to be met is not "genuine change of feelings" but only change of "appearances," simply doing whatever the outer situation demands to "get by." The implications of this for further involvement in trouble are clear.

II. Survey Findings

The survey findings are organized around three factors that significantly affect the operation of juvenile training facilities—(1) the presence of working philosophies that are consistent with what makes change possible; (2) a use of juvenile institutions by the courts and related groups that allows a program focused on change to operate; and (3) the presence of personnel, physical facilities, administrative controls, and other resources tailored to the job of producing change.

A. Working Philosophy

A good working philosophy clearly relates the institution's activities to its purpose and to the problems it must meet in serving this purpose.

Such a relationship between purpose and program is clearly outlined in the operations of some facilities. As a general matter, however, the absence of a clear working philosophy that ties programs to the achievement of more responsible attitudes is a significant weakness crucial to the problem of improving services.

Lack of understanding concerning the practicality of newer philosophies is a major problem. The difficulty of securing their acceptance is clearly illustrated by developments in the issue of discipline. For some years standards have declared that "corporal punishment should not be tolerated in any form in a training school program." The misbehaving youngster should see, to the greatest degree possible, the reason for a rule and its meaning for the particular brand of difficulty he encounters on the "outs." In this way discipline can become an avenue to new behavior having the force of personal meaning. The use of force shifts the emphasis away from the youngster and onto the smooth running of the institution. For someone with antagonistic attitudes, hitching behavior to the good of something he dislikes can be expected to have little lasting effect.

Thus, apart from the issue of whether physical abuse results, use of corporal punishment can reasonably be taken as a rough statistical indicator of the degree to which treatment viewpoints are actually operating. The survey found that corporal punishment is authorized in juvenile institutions in 10 States.

Another indicator of working philosophy is found in an institution's answer to the question, "How much security?" The institution's need to develop the youngsters' self-control often collides with the public's concern over escapes. Caught between the two, the administrator may set up a system of tight management which, he rationalizes, is for the youngsters' "own good." Thus the juvenile is used to serve the institution instead of the other way around.

A solution can be achieved by public and professional education. Though public expectations toward training facilities are often unrealistic, they must be met by the administrator if he wants to hold his job. Therefore, maximum efficiency—doing the best that current knowledge will allow— cannot be reached until this blurring effect is looked at honestly. If training facilities are to change youngsters, they must be allowed to operate out of philosophies consistent with this purpose. The public needs to learn that treatment approaches which allow "breathing room" are not naive but are, on the contrary, extremely practical. Properly conceived, they are directed at getting the trainee to assume more responsibility for his life rather than assigning it later to the police.

B. *Uses Being Made of Training Schools*

In theory, training schools are specialized facilities for changing children relatively hardened in delinquency. In practice, as the survey shows, they house a nonselective population and are primarily used in ways which make the serving of their theoretical best purpose, that of "change," beside the point.

This is not to say that other purposes being served by the typical training facility are not important in themselves. Rather, the point is whether they can best be served by a training facility, and, if they cannot, the effect of this extraneousness on the facility's prime reason for existence, the basic job for which it is intended. The extent to which its ability to do this job is diminished becomes clear from the following list of its "other" expedient purposes:

> Use as a detention or holding facility for youngsters awaiting completion of other plans for placement.
> Providing basic housing for youngsters whose primary need is a foster home or residential housing.
> Housing large numbers of youngsters whose involvement in trouble is primarily situational rather than deep-seated and who could be handled more efficiently under community supervision.
> Caring for mentally retarded youngsters committed to the training school because there is no room in a mental retardation facility or because no such institution exists.

Providing care for youngsters with severe psychiatric problems who are committed to the training school because of no juvenile residential treatment program.

Use of girls' facilities to provide maternity services.

The problem of varied intake is further complicated by differences in court commitment philosophies, each of which is a working view of "the best purpose a training facility should ideally serve." In summary, the effects of the diverse elements cited contribute to training facilities wherein no one is best served and most are served in default.

Variations in use of training schools are found among the states as a whole, as well as among the counties of a single State, and further show that many reference points other than "change" are the determiners of practice. If juvenile institutions were actually working in allegiance to a common "best use," statistics which reflect practice would have some uniformity of meaning. That this is not true is revealed by some of the statistical sketches below. For example, length-of-stay statistics do not now reflect differences in time needed to effect "change." If they did, one system's length of stay could be compared with another's, as a guideline for the efficacy of a given program. Rather, the data show that length of stay reflects some extraneous factor such as "overcrowding," or a population whose primary need is "housing," or children awaiting unavailable placements, or children who, though better suited to a probation program, must be held "long enough" to avoid court or community problems.

C. Resources to Produce Change

1. CAPACITY

The survey covers 220 State-operated juvenile institutional facilities in all States, Puerto Rico, and the District of Columbia.[3] These facilities, constituting 86 percent of the juvenile training capacity in the United States, had a total capacity of 42,423 in 1965 and a total average daily population of 42,389, which was 10.7 percent more than the population reported to the Children's Bureau in 1964 by 245 State and local facilities.[4]

The overcrowding suggested by daily population figures is not uniform. In 17 jurisdictions, in programs housing total average daily populations of 7,199 children (17 percent of the total), the average daily population is more than 10 percent below each system's capacity. Conversely, in 11 States, in programs housing 9,165 children (22 percent of the total reported

[3] For the sake of convenience, the total will be designated as "52 jurisdictions."

[4] *Statistics on Public Institutions for Children: 1964,* U.S. Department of Health, Education and Welfare, Children's Bureau Statistical Series 81, 1965. The remaining 14 percent not included in the present survey consists of 83 locally operated programs located in 16 States. In 1965 these had a projected capacity of 6,634 and an average daily population of 6,024. Approximately half of these programs are in California, where they are partially State subsidized.

by all 52 jurisdictions), the average daily population is 10 percent or more above their respective systems' capacities.

In many States the capacity of State and locally run training facilities is extended through use of private facilities. In some instances these are publicly subsidized, but control of the program remains in private hands. During the survey, 31 States reported using private facilities for the placement of delinquents. An estimate of the use of private facilities was not possible in eight of these States. The 23 States submitting estimates reported they had placed 6,307 youngsters in private facilities in 1965.

Concern about the increasing numbers of delinquents being housed in training facilities is growing. Only eight States at present have no plans for new construction which would increase the capacity of their institutional programs. Construction under way in 17 States will add space for 4,164 youngsters at a cost of $41,164,000. Thirty-one States report that they have $70,090,000 of construction authorized for an additional capacity of 7,090. Projecting still further ahead, 21 States report plans for additional capacity of 6,606 by 1975 at an anticipated cost of $66,060,000.

Thus, new construction, under way or authorized, will increase the present capacity (42,423 in State-run facilities) by 27 percent. By 1975, planned new construction will have increased present capacity by slightly over 42 percent.

2. PROGRAM

(a) *Diversification*

In contrast to the diversified program "balance" recommended by the standard, juvenile training facilities in most States present limited diversity of programs. Six of the larger jurisdictions now have nine or more facilities, but 8 States have only one facility serving juveniles and 14 States have only two facilities—a boys' school and a girls' school, a pattern that characterized State juvenile institutional systems for many years. . . .

In States which have expanded their facilities further, the most numerous separate new programs are small camps for boys and reception centers. . . . The camp is one of the fastest growing developments in the institutional field; 49 camps have been established in 20 States, with Illinois alone operating 10 of them. Ten States now have a total of 14 separate reception programs.

The rapid growth of camp programs has been attributed to low cost of operation, often half that of a training school in the same State, and to a good success rate, which in turn has been attributed to size and selection of population. Many of the camps have a capacity of 50 or less; standards call for capacities of 40 to 50.

(b) *Average Stay*

The length of stay for children committed to State training facilities ranges from 4 to 24 months; the median length of stay is 9 months. The number of children at the extremes of the range is relatively small. . . . Five State systems, housing 3 percent of the total, report an average length of stay of 6 months or less; eight State systems, housing 8 percent of the total, report average lengths of stay of more than 12 months. The remainder of the State systems—three-fourths of the total, housing nine-tenths of the institutional population—have an average length of stay of 6 months to a year.

Reception centers which serve primarily placement diagnostic purposes and do not include a treatment program for segments of their population report a surprisingly uniform average length of stay, ranging from 28 to 45 days.

(c) Actual Availability of Service

Services that look the same "on paper" are revealed by the survey to differ widely in quality. For example, 96 percent of the facilities contacted report the provision of medical services, and 94 percent report that dental services are provided. In fact, however, examination of operating practice in each jurisdiction shows major differences in the quality of these services. Where medical and dental services represent an especially expensive drain on hard-pressed budgets, as is true in many programs, the decision that treatment is "needed" may be reached less quickly than where services are routinely available and "paid for." Thus quality differences are born.

Similar differences between what is available "on paper" and what is available "in fact" are to be found among other services offered by training facilities. . . . The survey data indicate that nearly all programs (95 percent) provide recreational services; 88 percent educational programs; 86 percent casework, and 79 percent counseling services; and 75 percent psychological, and 71 percent psychiatric services. The question of concern, however, is not their provision "on paper" but their adequacy for the problems being faced. From this viewpoint, with the possible exception of education, improvement of all types of services seems badly needed. Support for this view is based on the existing ratios of treatment personnel to training school population. . . .

(d) Costs

Regardless of the adequacy of services, the cost of care in a training facility is high. The 52 jurisdictions report a total operating cost of $144,-596,618 to care for an average daily population of 42,389 youngsters. This means an average per capita operating expenditure of $3,411. The national average, however, conceals considerable variation in costs among the States. Forty-two jurisdictions operate training facility systems without a separate reception and diagnostic center, at an average per capita cost ranging from $871 to $7,890. Within this group, 6 States operate juvenile institutional systems for average per capita costs falling below $1,600 per year; 8 report average costs between $1,600 and $3,000; 13 report costs between $3,000 and $4,500; and 13 report average annual per capita costs above $4,500.

The inclusion of a reception and diagnostic center as part of a diversified juvenile institutional system helps to individualize institutional placements. Ten jurisdictions have set up programs consistent with the idea of specialized facilities, and another 10 are on the verge of doing so. This trend makes especially significant the costs experienced in States with separate reception programs. Among the 10 that operate such systems, per capita costs range from $1,757 to $5,723. Average per capita cost is less than $2,000 in three of these States; from $2,000 to $2,500 in two States; from $3,900 to $4,500 in three States; and $4,877 and $5,723 in the two remaining States.

3. STAFF

The impact of a program upon children is largely determined by adequacy of staff, both quantitatively and qualitatively.

In 1965, State-run juvenile facilities employed 21,247 staff in programs housing an average daily population of 42,389 trainees.

(a) Treatment Personnel

Of the total number employed, 1,154 were treatment personnel—psychiatrists, psychologists, and social caseworkers.

The standard calls for a minimum of 1 full-time psychiatrist for 150 children. On the basis of the average daily population of 42,389 in 1965, the number of psychiatrists required is 282.

The survey data show that the equivalent of 46 psychiatrists served the 220 State-operated facilities. More than half of them are found in only 5 States, with 1 State having the equivalent psychiatric time of 10 out of the total of 46 psychiatrists. Each of 37 States has less than the equivalent of 1 full-time psychiatrist available to its juvenile institution population. Only 4 States have enough psychiatric service available to satisfy the required 1:150 ratio.

To meet the requirements nationally, juvenile institutions need a total of 236 more psychiatrists than they now have.

The standard calls for a minimum of 1 full-time psychologist for 150 children. On the basis of the average daily population, the number of psychologists required is 282.

The survey data show that the equivalent of 182 psychologists work in the State-run juvenile facilities. However, as with psychiatrists, psychologists are found to be unequally distributed among the States: 106 (almost 60 percent of the total) are found in 9 States. Each of 21 States had the equivalent of not more than 1 psychologist. Only 12 States come up to the standard ratio.

To meet the requirements nationally, juvenile institution systems need a total of 100 more psychologists than they now have.

The standard declares that under ordinary conditions, a full-time caseworker in a juvenile institution should be assigned not more than 30 children. On the basis of the average daily population, the number of caseworkers required is 1,413.

The survey data show, in the 220 institutions, a total of 926 caseworkers, or 66 percent of the number required. To meet the requirements nationally, juvenile institution systems need a total of 487 more caseworkers than they now have.

Because the lack or absence of clinical personnel in many programs made comprehensive assessment uncertain, the survey established a general treatment potential index by stating the number of psychiatrists, psychologists, and caseworkers found in a system, combined in one category called professional personnel, in proportion to the number of trainees in the system. Since no single ratio was available as a national standard for such an index, the existing standards applicable to psychiatrists (1:150), psychologists (1:150), and caseworkers (1:30) were combined, making a total of 7 professional personnel per 150 trainees, or a ratio of 1:21.43 as a guideline.

. . . [T]he range of indexes for 50 States[5] is from 1:30 to 1:522. The average index is 1:64; the median is 1:33. In all, 14 State systems have treatment ratios better than the 1:21 suggested. Among the 38 jurisdictions with ratios poorer than this guideline, 22 have ratios of 1:42.9 (double the suggested guideline) or more.

(b) Teachers

The standard calls for a teacher-pupil ratio not exceeding 1:15.

Standards bearing on teacher ratios in training facilities are difficult to apply to survey data. Where public school systems assume a portion of the training system's academic burden, their teachers were not counted as institutional employees for purposes of the survey.

There were 2,495 teachers in the 220 institutions, an overall teacher-pupil ratio of 1:17. . . . In 24 States, the teacher-pupil ratio is better than the 1:15 standard cited, and in 36 States it is better than 1:20. Moreover, in the remaining States several jurisdictions have ratios that are high because of the reasons cited above.

The general picture given by the survey data is consistent with experienced observation: The established standard for training facilities is met to a far greater degree in teaching than it is in the casework or psychological counseling function. The reason is probably that, in many facilities, academic teaching has been the traditional mainstay of programming; also, the teaching role is better understood, and training for teachers is well established. In those facilities where there aren't enough teachers, the problem is

---

[5] Two State systems have no treatment staff at all.

more likely to be budget than an insufficient supply of trained teachers. Even where salaries are competitive the training school is handicapped in recruiting the good teacher because its working conditions are usually less attractive than the public school's.

(c) Chaplains

Standards call for chaplains on each staff in a number sufficient to serve the major religious faiths represented in the institution. A fair application of this standard to statistics is difficult; no clear criteria exist whereby adequate chaplaincy service may be determined. Here, probably more than in any other aspect of institutional program, a standard on adequate number should be viewed as an emerging guideline to be modified according to specific operating conditions. Review of survey data makes possible a valuable commonsense appraisal of the overall level of chaplaincy services. It shows a clear general need for more chaplains in most systems.

The 220 State institutions are served by 158 chaplains. Further, 32 State systems have less than the equivalent of 1 chaplain per facility; of these, 18 have less than half-time services per facility, and 12 have no chaplaincy service staffing at all. The overall chaplain-trainee ratio is 1:268. The ratios in 40 jurisdictions having chaplains range from 1:23 to 1:258. In 26 State systems the ratio is above 1:150—which is particularly significant in light of the standard of 150 recommended for institution capacity.

(d) Merit System Coverage

Standards call for placing all training school personnel under a merit or civil service system.

While the majority of State training facility staffs are covered under a merit system, the superintendents still remain outside such protection in 30 States. . . . With only two exceptions, States covering professional staff under a merit plan also cover supervisory and cottage staff in this manner.

(e) Salaries

In general, salaries in merit-covered systems are higher than in nonmerit systems for comparable positions. . . .

(f) Workweek

Prevailing practice in juvenile institutional facilities is approaching the recommended standard of a 40-hour workweek. In 16 States the workweek is more than 40 hours, and in 7 of these States, it is more than 50 hours.

(g) Educational Qualifications

The standard calls for the superintendent to have completed graduate training in the behavioral sciences or related fields of child development.

The survey found substantial variation among systems on educational requirements for the position. . . . Twelve jurisdictions require the superintendent to have a graduate degree; 28 require a college background; 10 have no formally established educational requirements—but this does not necessarily mean that trained persons are not sought. A number of systems recruit by trying to get the best person possible without formulating the requirements.

The standard calls for the caseworker to have graduated from an accredited school of social work.

Only three jurisdictions have failed to establish requirements for this position. Thirty-six require a college background; 11 require, in addition, a graduate degree.

The cottage staff in charge of the living unit, where most of the minor's time is spent, is the backbone of the training facility program. The key to effectiveness for this classification is ability to relate to children, emotional maturity, and flexibility in adapting to new situations.

No standard for this position has been offered. The traditional standard has been a high school education. Particularly in more sophisticated systems, graduation from college would be the preferred qualification.[6]

Under present salary schedules for the cottage staff position, college graduates, or even persons having not more than a high school education (as required in 25 States) are virtually unattainable. Salaries are so low that establishing educational requirements is beside the point; . . . 25 States set no requirement for the position. One State reports that some of its cottage staff are on public welfare.

4. HOUSING

Much of the Nation's training facility plant is old but being improved. In many States patched-onto use of the first old reform school is still evident, but sharp increases in the population of these facilities have produced, along with problems, some benefits, including mainly the development of smaller living units.

(a) Facility Size

The standard recommending that a juvenile institution be limited to 150 children is based on experience which shows that the smaller the facility the more likely it is to enhance the impact of program. "The treatment atmosphere tends to break down in institutions where the population rises above [150]" because of "such therapeutic dangers as rigidity and formality necessary to help a large organization function."[7]

Despite the advantages cited for the smaller institution, the trend has been

[6] *Institutions Serving Delinquent Children—Guides and Goals,* U.S. Department of Health, Education and Welfare, Children's Bureau publication No. 360, rev. 1962, p. 52.
[7] American Psychiatric Association, *Training Schools for Delinquent Children,* p. 19.

in the other direction. The great bulk of juvenile institutional population is now housed in facilities considerably larger than the prescribed standard. The principal concession to the standard is an occasional attempt to break down large institutions into several small administrative units in the hope that each will take on the climate of a small separate entity.

(b) Living-Unit Size

Standards generally call for the living unit to have a maximum capacity of 20 where groupings are homogeneous; the size for a heterogeneous group, or a group of severely disturbed children, should be from 12 to 16.[8] Girls should have private rooms.

Standards pertaining to size should not be applied arbitrarily; their spirit is more important than the letter. The existence of many excellent living-unit programs in living units that do not meet the accepted size standard shows that ingenuity of staffing, effective group techniques, and sincerity of effort are important, and that the lack of understanding implied by mechanical application of the standard probably guarantees a poor program.

This is merely a cautionary note; it does not impair the validity of the standard. Large living units require compensating staff and program efforts to produce results equivalent to those expected and more easily achieved in the small unit. The degree to which massness can be compensated for is limited.

The importance of the standard calling for a maximum capacity of 20 is just beginning to be realized. Of the 1,344 living units in State-run juvenile institutions only 24 percent have a capacity of 20 or less. In 68 percent of them, the capacity is from 21 to 50; in 8 percent, it is 50 or more.

In general, living-unit size is related to period of construction. Typically, the smaller units are relatively new. About 34 percent of all living units are 10 years of age or less; 16 percent are 50 years old or more.

While the standard is not met by most living units, its importance is increasingly being recognized. Survey data on living units under construction, authorized and projected, show that, in all 3 categories, over 90 percent of the units will have a capacity of 30 or less. A capacity of 20 or less is found in 55 percent of present construction, 63 percent of authorized construction, and 45 percent of projected construction. . . .

(c) Location

The institution should be separated from a metropolitan area by a buffer zone, but not of so great dimensions that the institution is virtually inaccessible. Isolation aggravates problems of staff recruitment and housing and reduces use of services offered by related agencies. Training schools have often been established in an isolated section of the State by a legislature

[8] *Ibid.*

concerned largely with bolstering the surrounding community's economy. The lack of foresight in the decision is brought home forcefully a few years later when the institution's location is shown to make its program expensive to operate and difficult to staff.

Reasonable access to a university allows for use of its faculty in staff development, research, consultation, and recruitment.

Of the 29 jurisdictions reporting bad location of 1 or more facilities, 46 percent cite it as a reason for difficulty in recruiting professional staff; 15 percent cite it as a deterrent to visits by parents.

5. ADMINISTRATIVE RESOURCES

Administration of a program consistent with the purpose of change is affected by issues of (*a*) the source of direction, (*b*) custody and release, (*c*) inspection and subsidy, and (*d*) quality of research and information.

(*a*) *Centralized Direction*

Some control over the types and numbers of children going to a given facility is necessary for development of an individualized program. Selection of the facility in which a youngster is to be placed, particularly in States having diversified programs, should preferably rest with the parent agency, if one has been established. (Direction of activities important to program within the institution—for example, the academic school service—should rest chiefly with the institutional administrator.)

The survey data show that the direction of training facility programs is increasingly being centralized to produce better coordination with related agencies and more specialized use of facilities. Centralization is resulting in common use of a parent agency to administer institutional programs. In only three States do juvenile institutions now completely administer their own programs as agencies. In 46 jurisdictions the institutions work under some type of parent agency, which, in 21 States, has only correctional responsibilities. Other common administrative arrangements place juvenile facility operation under a State department of public welfare (in 14 States) and under a State board of institutions (in 6 States).

(*b*) *Custody and Release*

The standard declares that legal custody of a child committed to an institution should be vested in the parent agency rather than the institution.

Consistent with the trend toward centralized direction, more control is being vested in the parent agency, which assumes legal custody upon commitment in 31 jurisdictions. Legal custody during commitment is vested in the institution in 13 States and in the court in 3 States.

Similarly, administrative control of release is the more common pattern. In 31 States the release decision is made either within the facility or by its controlling parent agency. In 9 States the decision is made by a parole board. In 10 States the court is involved to a varying degree in the release decision: in 5 of these States the court grants all releases; in 1 or 2 others it has the power to control release only in certain types of cases; and in the remainder it shares responsibility for the release with the institution.

(c) Inspection and Subsidy

The standard calls for the parent State agency to have inspection and subsidy authority over local delinquency treatment programs.

The survey data show that, of the 16 States that have locally run facilities, 4 set standards on personnel qualifications in local institutions and 2 of the 4 set standards on program content and details of new construction. Seven of these 16 States also subsidize the local programs to some degree. Subsidy forms include partial assumption of operating costs, various formulas for subsidizing construction, and the provision of consultation and training services.

(d) Research and Information

Programs, like people, must know what they are doing to do it well. To do an institutional job well calls for statistics and research that can help solve day-to-day program-management problems and provide a guideline for evaluating the parolees' degree of success in staying out of trouble. The information gathered for these purposes is also a resource for better public understanding of institutional problems. The standard recommends that the central parent agency be responsible for research, consultation, and collection of statistics concerning juvenile populations and programs.

Thirty-eight of the 52 jurisdictions have a central source for the collection and dissemination of statistics, . . . which evince, unfortunately, no agreement on the purposes for which they have been gathered. Much of the data collected has no reference to problems of operational importance. Few States have information on subsequent adjustment of juvenile parolees.

6. NEW PROGRAMS

The press of mounting delinquency problems in recent years has stimulated the development of numerous kinds of programs significant to the juvenile institutional field. Three of the most significant of these new types are described briefly below:

(a) Community-Based Treatment Services

As the name implies, these services include various methods of handling juveniles in a community setting as alternatives to commitment or for reducing the number of commitments. They are of special interest because of their relative economy compared with institutional commitment and because of the advantages of treatment in a setting as normal or "close to home" as possible.

The principal vehicles include intensified and selective probation and parole caseloads offering special counseling and community help plus "in and out" and trial furloughs; group homes and agency-operated residential treatment programs; "day care" in specialized institutional programs that return youngsters home at night and on weekends; regional detention centers with diagnostic service intended to reduce "dumping" into institutions; special "closed" local facilities with intensive counseling; and family involvement.

(b) Group Treatment

Group treatment techniques offer essentially the advantage of economy over one-to-one counseling relationships, plus treatment advantages gained from insights on behavior through viewpoints pressed from several sources. In the institutional setting they have included families of the trainees. Their common goal is acceptance of responsibility rather than satisfaction with shallow conformity.

(c) Diversification

Development in this direction is represented by the growth of small camp programs, halfway houses, group-treatment centers, reception and screening centers, vocational training centers, and special short-term programs.

[*President's Commission on Law Enforcement and Administration of Justice*, Task Force Report: Corrections (*Washington: U.S. Government Printing Office, 1967*), appendix A, pp. 141–149.]

11 *Juvenile aftercare*

Juvenile aftercare is defined as the release of a child from an institution at the time when he can best benefit from release and from life in the community under the supervision of a counselor. Use of the term "aftercare" rather than "parole," though not yet fully accepted even within the field of juvenile correction, has been encouraged by persons interested in social service in order to separate juvenile programs from the legalistic language and concepts of adult parole. The concept of aftercare has wider acceptance than the term, but the survey of aftercare programs in the United States today reveals wide variations in structure and program content.

I. Introduction

Aftercare service for juveniles first appeared in the United States in the early 19th century, but it has become an integral part of correctional rehabilitation for the young offender only in the past decade. In most States, aftercare is the least developed aspect of correction; in the opinion of many observers, it is less adequate than its counterpart, adult parole.

Aftercare originated in New York and Pennsylvania, where houses of refuge indentured child inmates to work in private homes for several years. The child's daily regimen rarely included anything but work. Total responsibility for the child was vested in the family that undertook to feed and clothe him, and it was the family that determined when he had earned his freedom. This form of postinstitutional treatment persisted for over half a century.

A. The Rationale of Aftercare

When the behavior of a juvenile becomes sufficiently anti-social to warrant confining him in an institution, a complex array of correctional services is set in motion. Part of it deals with the planning and operation of a program that will help him when he leaves the institution.

213

In the United States, children and youth from 8 to 21 years of age are committed to juvenile training schools. On any one day, the total population of these schools is about 42,000. Because of the wide range of age and experience, differing placement plans are essential. Pre-adolescent children need programs different in content and philosophy from those needed by young adults, who may have been in the labor force before confinement. To meet such varied needs, aftercare programs must be flexible and creative, rather than routine and superficial as they are in parts of this country today.

The rationale for aftercare is simple. Each juvenile must have a carefully planned, expertly executed, and highly individualized program if he is to return to life outside the institution and play a constructive role there. Successful reentry into society is often made difficult both by the effects of institutional life on a juvenile and by the attitudes of the community to which he returns. The aftercare plan for him must take both these factors into account.

Institutionalization does different things to different children. Some become more antisocial and more sophisticated in delinquency than they were when they entered the training school. Others become dependent on the institution and must learn how to break the ties gradually.

Community settings also differ widely. Some juveniles go back to the very conditions in which their previous delinquency was rooted. Most must face the possibility of the stigma attached to confinement in a correctional institution.

Aftercare is traditionally described as the last point on the juvenile correctional continuum. Yet, because it is in some respects the last opportunity to achieve the correctional objective, planning for aftercare must be an integral part of institutional programs. Indeed, it should begin immediately after commitment to an institution.

A good aftercare plan uses many resources inside and outside the institution. Since implementation of the plan takes place within the community, the aftercare counselor should use a variety of community resources to make the juvenile's reentry meaningful and productive. He should be working with all details of the case related to the ward's community even during the period of confinement in the State institution, forestry camp, or other setting attached to the training school.

It has taken this Nation a long time to recognize the importance of aftercare services for young people leaving correctional institutions, forestry camps, or halfway houses. Few well-developed aftercare programs were in existence 15 years ago. Some States have not yet initiated organizationally sound programs. On the other hand, a few have developed programs which stand out as models for those emerging elsewhere.

II. Survey Findings

A. An Overview of Aftercare Today

The major items in this survey include data from the 40 State-operated special aftercare programs,[1] but not from programs administered by city and county correctional systems, private institutions, and noncorrectional services of child and public welfare departments, since full information could not be obtained from them.

The 40 States reported a total of about 48,000 youth under aftercare supervision. Estimates for the other States, based on a projection of that figure, indicate that about 59,000 are under aftercare supervision in the United States. The number of juveniles in State programs ranges from 110 to 13,000.

Any study of aftercare today at the national level is plagued by inadequate statistics coming from the 50 States and Puerto Rico. As long as this situation persists, attempting a thorough study of juvenile aftercare can be described only as an exercise in futility. The gaps in vital information are so great that the reliability and validity of the few national statistics that can be gathered must be viewed with extreme caution. Efforts are being made to change this condition, but extensive organizational programing for statewide data collection is needed.

State operating costs range from $7,000 to over $4 million a year. Together the States are spending about $18 million a year. Average per capita cost is $320 a year.

This expenditure is small in comparison with the cost of State-operated juvenile institutions, which spend over $144 million a year to care for an average daily population of slightly over 42,000 at an average per capita cost of about $3,400 a year.

The fact that aftercare costs less than one-tenth as much as institutional care is nothing to be proud of. As reported by the 40 States, its relative cheapness reflects the inadequacy of the programs at least as much as it demonstrates inherent economy. It is not uncommon for 250 adolescents to be assigned to a program staffed by only 2 or 3 aftercare counselors located at the State capital or training school, which may be hundreds of miles from the communities where the juveniles are supposedly under supervision. Aside from the excessiveness of the supervisors' caseloads, sheer distance reduces the effectiveness of the program.

Thus, aftercare programs should not be judged solely by their relative economy of operation. Rather, the question should be asked: How much should be spent to make aftercare truly effective? For it should be remem-

[1] States which do not operate centralized juvenile aftercare programs are Alabama, Arkansas, Kansas, Maryland, Mississippi, New Mexico, North Carolina, North Dakota, Pennsylvania, and Virginia.

bered that effective aftercare is one of the best methods of preventing recidivism.

B. Organizational Arrangements

According to the standard, responsibility for aftercare should be vested in a State agency which is administratively responsible for institutional and related services for delinquent children.

. . . [T]he organizational arrangements through which juvenile aftercare services are administered vary widely among the States. In contrast to other programs for juveniles, such as public education, which is always administered by a State educational agency, juvenile aftercare has no clear organizational pattern. Administration may be the responsibility of, for example, a lay board, an adult correction program, a public welfare agency, a youth authority, or the training school itself.[2]

The issue of administration is further complicated by the survey finding that in only 34 States does the State department which administers the State juvenile institutions also provide aftercare services for juveniles released from these institutions. For example, in five States local probation departments are given responsibility for aftercare even though they have no official relationships to the agency administering the training schools. Patterns of local jurisdiction have developed for various reasons. In some States, there was no State agency which could provide supervision at the local level, and therefore a local social service agency was asked to perform this function. In other States, State officials preferred to give jurisdiction to local agencies because they believed the youth would receive better care from local agencies than from centralized, State-operated programs. In their opinion, local programs helped avoid duplication of services at the State level.

According to the standard, the law under which a juvenile enters a State training school should provide that the agency granted legal custody should have the right to determine when he shall leave the institution.

The opportunity for legal and jurisdictional disputes is always present. In nine States, the problem is complicated by the fact that the committing judge becomes involved in the decision to release a juvenile for aftercare services. If he is thus involved in the release decision, he must be thoroughly aware of the child's behavior and growth at the training school as well as of the factors in his home community; actually, in the nine States where this procedure is followed, he rarely has this information. In five of the nine States, the committing judge must approve all releases; in the others, he must approve only certain ones. A training school staff that has worked daily with a ward may find its aftercare plan disapproved by a

[2] William E. Amos and Raymond L. Manella. *Readings in the Administration of Institutions for Delinquent Youth* (Springfield, Ill.: Charles C. Thomas, 1965), p. 185ff.

judge unfamiliar with all the circumstances of his case. Where the State provides aftercare services, it should be unnecessary for the committing judge to approve aftercare plans for children released from State institutions.

C. Length of Commitment

According to the standard, the law under which a juvenile enters a State training school should provide that the child remain there for an indefinite period of not more than 3 years and of no specified minimum before being released on aftercare.

The survey found that specific minimums are authorized by law in three States: In one, the specified minimum is 12 months; in another, it is 18 months; in the third, it varies. And in many other States, the survey found, specific minimum length of stay in the training school has been established informally—without legal authorization of any kind but firmly established nonetheless—by superintendents, classification committees, and other groups or individuals.

D. Statewide Reporting

According to the standard, an adequate statistical reporting system should be maintained, with data on parole and aftercare uniformly and automatically reported to a central correctional statistical agency in the State.

The survey found that more than two-fifths of the States fail to meet this standard. A few States have excellent reporting systems, but the great majority have no reliable procedure, not even for simple data. A little more than half the States have a central statistical unit responsible for statistical information on the State juvenile aftercare operation. . . .

E. Juvenile Paroling Authorities

According to the standard, the authority to approve placement should be vested in the parent State agency. The decision on the readiness of the youngster for placement should be based on the considered opinion of the appropriate training school staff committee.

According to the data gathered in the survey, the authority to release juveniles from State training schools rests with a wide variety of persons, groups, or agencies. . . .

In most cases, these authorities are composed of members appointed by the Governor. Only seven States in the Nation have aftercare boards on which the members serve full time. Over half the States that have aftercare boards do not pay the members—State officials or lay citizens—for this service. In eight States aftercare board chairmen are paid, and in seven the board members receive salaries ranging from $6,000 to $18,000 a year, most frequently at the lower figure. Most board members are unpaid, are not trained for the board's special responsibilities, and are politically appointed.

Use of a central board, a relatively new event in juvenile correction, has been debated extensively. Those favoring it say the board can make sounder decisions than any other kind of releasing authority. Those questioning its usefulness say that board members are, in effect, assuming staff functions and cannot possibly know the details of the cases well enough from reading reports or hearing short presentations to make proper decisions. They believe further that competent staff in the training school or other facilities within the parent agency is better equipped than any outside group to make realistic decisions based on a thorough awareness of the details of a case.

The trend in the mid-1950's was toward the establishment of juvenile aftercare boards. This trend has ended. A large group of juvenile correctional administrators is now urging establishment of a pattern in which the training school (or other facility such as a forestry camp or halfway house) would make release recommendations to the parent agency, which in turn would authorize release.

F. Length of Aftercare Period

The survey found that approximately 59,000 young people—about 47,000 boys and 12,000 girls—received aftercare services during the most recently reported annual period, 1964–65. The boy-girl ratio, slightly less than 4 to 1, is the same as other findings in most other statistical reports on delinquency comparisons by sex.

The average length of stay under aftercare supervision varies.[3] Of the States reporting, 12 keep their juveniles in active aftercare supervision programs for an average of less than 1 year; 25 give aftercare supervision for an average of 1 year or more.

The State reports show a trend toward keeping girls under aftercare supervision longer than boys. The explanation may lie in our society's attitude that the young female requires protection for a longer period than the young male. Girls are kept longer in institutional settings than boys are, and staff working with the delinquent girl feel she needs more intense and prolonged services than the delinquent boy does. Of 14 States reporting on length of aftercare supervision, 10 show an average substantially longer for girls than for boys; 4 report an average period longer for boys.

G. Personnel

Standards have been developed for appointment of juvenile aftercare staff, educational requirements, and salaries.

---

[3] Thirteen States did not report average length of stay on aftercare.

The standard on the first of these matters states that all aftercare person-nel, as well as supporting personnel, should be appointed through a civil service or merit system from a register established through rating of examinations opened to qualified candidates without consideration as to residence. Much of the correctional field has been plagued by its close association with politics at the State and local levels. The courts, institu-tions, and parole programs in a number of States have been affected by political considerations that have influenced staffing and program opera-tions.

Of the 40 States reporting personnel data for the survey,[4] 23 have civil service or merit system coverage for the director of juvenile aftercare services, 26 have such coverage for the district supervisor, and 29 have it for the aftercare worker.

The standard for minimum educational requirements states that the juve-nile aftercare worker should have a bachelor's degree with a major in the social or behavioral sciences, plus 1 year of graduate study in social work or a related field, or 1 year of paid full-time casework experience in correction.

Of the 40 States, 34 report that they have such a requirement. The survey found, however, that not all juvenile aftercare directors actually enforce this requirement when they hire aftercare workers. The fact of the matter is that many aftercare workers have less than a college education. The minimum standard is approved in principle but not observed in practice.

Another standard calls for payment of adequate salaries commensurate with the qualifications, high trust, and responsibility required for aftercare work.

. . . [T]his standard is seldom met. . . . The reported annual salary ranges of $4,000 to $18,000 have little meaning. The median is $8,000–$9,000 for a director, $7,000–$8,000 for a district supervisor, and $5,000–$6,000 for an aftercare counselor. The opportunity for a counselor to earn more than $6,000 a year is extremely limited in most States. One State reports that it pays male counselors more than female counselors for presumably the same work. Even if the counselor does advance to a supervisory level, he can rarely earn more than $9,000 a year.

H. Caseload and Work Assignments

The standard calls for the juvenile aftercare counselor to have a maxi-mum workload of 50 active supervision cases, with one prerelease investiga-tion being considered as equal to three cases under active supervision. (Although no standard has been formulated on the matter, good practice calls for assignment of every child in a training school, or in some other facility of the parent agency, to an aftercare counselor, who should work

---

[4] No data on personnel were reported by Alabama, Arkansas, Illinois, Kansas, Mary-land, New Mexico, North Carolina, North Dakota, Pennsylvania, and Virginia.

with the parents and others in the interest of planning for the child's release.)

. . . Average caseloads range from 30 to 125 supervision cases, with the median in the 61–70 range. Since these caseloads are not weighted for the number of investigations made or for the number of children worked with by the aftercare counselors in the institutions, the actual caseload size is substantially larger than is indicated in the supervision caseload.

Caseload geography complicates the operation of a statewide juvenile aftercare service for wards released from a State training school or some other facility within the parent agency. In many States a vast distance must be covered by each member of the small aftercare staff. Thus his contacts are usually crisis oriented; that is, the counselor sees the child only when an emergency arises. In many states, supervision generally consists of a monthly report written by the juvenile himself and mailed to the State office. Wards released to rural areas rarely, sometimes never, see the aftercare worker. Youths from urban areas are likely to receive more active supervision than those from small towns. Unless several regional offices are set up in the State, released wards whose homes are distant from the central office are neglected. Courtesy supervision is occasionally requested of local welfare, court, or voluntary personnel, but these services are spotty and irregular. In short: supportive, sustained, and positive implementation of an aftercare plan is, more often than not, rare.

The total staff complement in the reporting States is as follows: district supervisors, 133; district assistance supervisors, 76; aftercare counselors, 1,033.

The range in number of State juvenile aftercare workers is from 2 to 273 per State, and the number of counselors for the entire country is exceedingly small. Isolation of the training school, vast distances to travel, diversified and excessive caseloads, and low salaries serve to complicate and frequently frustrate the work of aftercare staff.

As previously indicated, caution must be used in stating personnel totals. In many States the juvenile aftercare counselor works for a probation or welfare or similar agency and carries a caseload for that agency in addition to his aftercare assignment.

I. Staff Development

According to the standard, a staff development program should be provided, with staff assigned specifically to the training function.

The findings in this survey reveal a great lack of inservice training programs. Aside from the 11 States that have no statewide aftercare services at all, 8 of the 40 that do have such services have no inservice training program. . . . No information is available on the type, format, instructional quality, faculty, curriculum, or other important details of the training programs—information necessary for evaluating their quality. . . .

According to the standard, an agency training program should include educational leaves with pay for graduate training.

. . . Stipends are provided in not more than 13 States; the other 28 States with special State-operated aftercare programs have no educational enrichment programs outside the agency for their staff personnel.

J. Diversified Aftercare Services

The standards call for the [provision] of diversified aftercare services and facilities for children returning to the community from the institution or other correctional facility.

The survey found that services to released juveniles range from superficial supervision, consisting of nothing more than the juvenile's written monthly reports, to highly sophisticated aftercare innovations that meet the standards of good practice.

The survey asked the question: "Does the aftercare program also operate foster homes, group homes, and halfway houses?" Of the 40 States with statewide programs, 12 answered yes, including 2 that reported they did not pay for foster care but did use free home placements, and 3 that qualified their positive reply by stating that local child welfare departments found and supervised foster homes for aftercare placements. Individual foster homes are used more frequently than group foster homes. Four State-operated programs reported the use of halfway houses for aftercare.

Three types of imaginative or unusual rehabilitation programs were reported more frequently than others. They are best described as efforts at the use of groups in treatment, family centered services, and youth employment programs specifically designed for the released ward. Some of these programs were described as experimental and new. They occur only where the State-operated program is well established and has an adequate budget.

[*President's Commission on Law Enforcement and Administration of Justice*, Task Force Report: Corrections (*Washington: U.S. Government Printing Office, 1967*), appendix A, pp. 141–154.]

12 New approaches to treatment and prevention of delinquency

In recent years a number of experimental community programs have been set up in various parts of the country, differing substantially in content and structure but all offering greater supervision and guidance than the traditional probation and parole programs. The new programs take many forms, ranging from the more familiar foster homes and group homes, "guided group interaction" programs, and intensive community treatment. As such, they offer a set of alternatives between regular probation supervision and incarceration, providing more guidance than probation services commonly offer without the various disruptive effects of total confinement. They also greatly enrich the alternatives available in parole supervision. The advent of these programs in the postwar decades and their recent growth in numbers and prominence are perhaps the most promising developments in corrections today.

These programs are by and large less costly, often far less costly, than incarceration in an institution. Evaluation has indicated that they are usually at least as effective in reducing recidivism and in some cases significantly more so. They therefore represent an important means for coping with the mounting volume of offenders that will be pouring into corrections in the next decade. Although population forecasts indicate that the number of adult criminals who will be incarcerated in the next 10 years will increase only slightly, the projections for juveniles on the basis of present trends are alarming. . . . [I]t is estimated that by 1975 the number of juveniles who would be confined would increase by 70 percent; whereas in 1965, there were about 44,000 juveniles in State and Federal correctional institutions, by 1975 this number would reach about 74,000. Such an increase would place a burden on the correctional system that increased community programing could go far to alleviate.

Guided Group Interaction Programs

Underlying one of the newer programs for treating the young delinquent in the community is the premise that juvenile delinquency is commonly a group experience and that therefore efforts to change delinquent behavior should focus primarily on a group like that within which the individual operates. A number of group counseling methods have been employed, but the method called guided group interaction has been used most extensively in those programs which involved a research component.

The general strategy of guided group interaction calls for involving the offenders in frequent, prolonged, and intensive discussions of the behavior of individuals in the group and the motivations underlying it. Concentrating on participants' current experiences and problems, the approach attempts to develop a group "culture" that encourages those involved to assume responsibility for helping and controlling each other. The theory is that the offender-participants will be more responsive to the influence of their fellow offenders, their peers, than to the admonitions of staff, and less likely to succeed in hoodwinking and manipulating each other.

As the culture develops and the group begins to act responsibly, the group leader, a staff member, seeks to encourage a broader sharing of power between the offenders and the staff. At first, group decisions will be limited to routine matters, such as the schedule of the day, but over time they may extend to disciplinary measures against a group member or even to decisions concerning readiness for release from the program.

Highfields

The Highfields project in New Jersey was the pioneer effort in guided group interaction.[1] Initiated in 1950, it has been duplicated in communities and also in institutions and used with both juveniles and adults. Highfields limits its population to 20 boys aged 16 and 17, who are assigned directly to it from the juvenile court. Boys with former commitments to correctional schools are not accepted, nor are deeply disturbed or mentally retarded youths. The goal is to effect rehabilitation within 3 to 4 months, about half the average period of incarceration in the State training school.

The youths are housed in the old Lindbergh mansion. They work during the day at a mental institution immediately adjacent to their residence. In the evening they participate in the group counseling sessions. On Saturdays, they clean up the residence. Saturday afternoon is free, and Sunday is reserved for receiving visitors and going to religious services. Formal rules are few.

Early efforts to evaluate the effects of the project on recidivism, as compared with those of the State reformatory, are still the subject of

---

[1] See Lloyd W. McCorkle, Albert Elias, and F. Lovell Bixby, *The Highfields Story: An Experimental Treatment Project for Youthful Offenders* (New York: Henry Holt & Co., 1958). See also Paul Keve, *Imaginative Programming in Probation and Parole* (Minneapolis: University of Minnesota Press, 1967), pp. 137–173, and J. Robert Weber, "A Report of the Juvenile Institutions Project" (unpublished report to the Osborne Association and the National Council on Crime and Delinquency, Sept. 1966), pp. 123–126, 223–230.

academic dispute. However, it is clear that Highfields was at least as effective as the reformatory, perhaps more effective, and that it accomplished its results in a much shorter period of time at greatly reduced monthly costs.

Pinehills and Other Developments

Important variations on the Highfields project developed at Essexfields, also in New Jersey, and at Pinehills in Provo, Utah. As at Highfields, program content at Essexfields and Pinehills centered around gainful employment in the community, school, and daily group meetings. The most significant difference was that, in the Essexfields and Pinehills experiments, the offenders continued to live at home.

The regimen at both Essexfields and Pinehills was rigorous. At Pinehills, for example, all boys were employed by the city. They put in a full day's work on the city streets, on the golf course, in the cemetery, wherever they were needed. They were paid 50 cents an hour. During the late afternoon, after the day's work was finished, all boys returned to the program headquarters where they met in daily group sessions. About 7 P.M. they were free to return home. They were also free on Sundays.[2]

In the daily group sessions all group members, not just adult staff, were responsible for defining problems and finding solutions to them. By making the program operations to some extent the work of all involved, both offenders and staff, it was possible to make a better estimate of just how much responsibility for his own life a given offender could take.

The fact that these guided group interaction programs are located in the community means that the problems with which the group' struggles are those that confront them daily in contacts with their families, friends, teachers, and employers. This is one great strength of a community program over an institutional program. The artificiality of institutional life is avoided, and concentration can be placed upon the issues with which every offender eventually has to deal.

The Pinehills experiment was one of the first to set up an experimental design by which to assess the effectiveness of the project. Offenders assigned to the program were compared with two control groups: one group which was placed on probation, and another which was committed to a training school. The initial design was such that all three groups could be drawn randomly from a common population of persistent offenders living in the same county. Although there was some difficulty in exactly maintaining the research design, the data appear significant. The results, as measured in terms of recidivism, are shown in table 1.

---

[2] For further discussion of Pinehills and Essexfields, see LaMar T. Empey, *Alternatives to Incarceration*. Office of Juvenile Delinquency and Youth Development Studies in Delinquency (Washington: U.S. Government Printing Office, 1967), pp. 37–40.

Other variations of guided group interaction projects have been developed in the Parkland project in Louisville, Ky., in the GUIDE (Girls Unit for Intensive Daytime Education) program in Richmond, Calif., and in another girls' program in San Mateo, Calif. All three of these projects entail the daily gathering of the group in a center for participation in a combination of educational activities, craft projects, center development and beautification, and group and individual counseling. The Parkland project took its name from its location in two portable classrooms on the grounds of the

Table 1—Effectiveness of Three Programs for Juvenile Delinquents, Utah, 1964, as Measured by Percentages of Releasees Not Arrested Within 6 Months of Release.

Program	Percentage of releasees not arrested within 6 months	
	All boys assigned to program	All boys completing program
Pinehills (experimental)_____	73	84
Probation (controls)____ _____	73	77
State school (controls)_____	42	42

SOURCE: Adapted from LaMar T. Empey, "Alternatives to Incarceration," Office of Juvenile Delinquency and Youth Development Studies in Delinquency (Washington: U.S. Government Printing Office, 1967), pp. 38–39.

Parkland Junior High School. In addition to morning classes in the school, the program entails afternoon work in and about the Louisville Zoo and terminates with group counseling sessions and dinner.

Contributions of Guided Group Programs

These projects, like Highfields, represent an authentic departure from traditional community programs for delinquents. The Highfields type of program is unique in that the group process itself shapes the culture and social system of the total program. The key element seems to be the amount of decision-making authority permitted the group, which has considerably more authority to decide than in traditional group therapy programs. J. Robert Weber, who made a study of promising programs for delinquents, said of the Highfields type of program:

> If one asks a youth in most conventional institutions, "How do you get out?" one invariably hears some version of, "Be good. Do what you are told. Behave yourself." If one asks a youth in a group treatment program, "How do you get out?" one hears, "I have to help myself with my problems," or "When my group thinks I have been

helped." This implies a basic difference in the social system of the organization, including staff roles and functions.[3]

In the large institution, Weber concluded, the youth perceives getting out in terms of the problem of meeting the institutional need for conformity. In the group treatment program the youth sees getting out in terms of his solution to his own problems, or how that is perceived by other youths in the group.

Foster Homes and Group Homes

Foster-home placement has long been one of the most commonly used alternatives to institutionalization for juvenile probationers. The National Survey of Corrections reported that 42 percent of the 233 probation departments surveyed utilized this resource. A sizable proportion of juvenile aftercare programs also make foster placements a routine part of their work.

The utilization of foster homes or group homes in lieu of institutional confinement has several obvious advantages, provided the offender does not require the controls of an institution. Such placements keep the offender in the community where he must eventually work out his future. They carry less stigma and less sense of criminal identity, and they are far less expensive than incarceration.

Weber reported in 1966:

> Discussions with State administrators would seem to indicate that foster care is in an eclipse. Reception center staffs report disillusionment with foster care for delinquents. Yet a look at actual placement practices of the State agencies and local courts indicates an unabated use of foster care.[4]

The opinions encountered by Weber may be a reflection of the long and controversial history of foster-home placement for delinquents. The decision to sever family ties, even temporarily, is a hard one to make for the youth who might otherwise be placed on probation at home. And more difficult juveniles who might be sent to institutions are often beyond the capacity of the usual foster home to manage. It is obvious, however, that many delinquent youngsters come from badly deteriorated family situations and that such conditions are significant, perhaps critical, factors in generating delinquent behavior. When the delinquency-inducing impact of a slum neighborhood is added to a destructive family setting, placement of the delinquent away from home becomes increasingly necessary.

A number of States have begun to develop group homes as a variant to traditional foster-home care for youths who need a somewhat more institu-

[3] Weber, *op. cit.*, pp. 225–226.
[4] Weber, *op. cit.*, p. 173.

tional setting or cannot adjust to family life. The Youth Commission of Minnesota, for example, reported using seven group homes under arrangements with the home operator or with an intermediate agency. A nominal retaining fee was paid for each bed licensed; and, when a youth actually was placed in the home, the rate of pay was increased.[5]

The Wisconsin Division of Corrections in 1966 was operating an even more ambitious program. Thirty-three homes for boys or girls were in use under a payment plan similar to that employed in Minnesota. With four to eight adolescents in each home, the total population handled was equivalent to that of at least one institution, but operating costs were one-third to one-fourth less.[6]

In both States the adolescents placed in group homes were those who had been received on court commitment as candidates for institutional placement. In Wisconsin, approximately one-fourth of the group had been released from institutions for placement in a foster home. Other jurisdictions are experimenting with the group-home technique. Michigan, for example, reported a plan to use larger homes operated by State employees for parolees from their institutions.[7]

There is some doubt about the wisdom of committing offenders to State agencies for placement in foster homes or group homes, when this function could as readily be performed by the courts through associated probation and welfare services. It is far less expensive for a local court to commit a youth to the State, even though that commitment entails some additional stigmatization, than to undertake the development and operation of local resources of the same kind. This problem derives from the fragmented administrative structure of American corrections, and could be overcome by a carefully planned program of subsidies from State to local governments. Such a plan was developed in California in 1965. Under its terms subsidies are given to those county probation departments which are successful in reducing commitments to State institutions by the development of improved community-based programs.

.   .   .   .   .

Intensive Community Treatment

Perhaps the best known of the country's efforts at controlled experimentation in the correctional field is the California Youth Authority's Community Treatment Project, now in its sixth year. Operating within a rigorous evaluative design, it offers an excellent illustration of the profitable partnership which can develop when carefully designed program innovations are combined with sound research.

[5] *Ibid.*, p. 176.
[6] *Ibid.*
[7] *Ibid.*, p. 179. Cf. Keve, *op. cit.*, pp. 250–251.

The subjects of the project consist of boys and girls committed to the Youth Authority from two adjacent counties, Sacramento and San Joaquin. While under study in a reception center, each new group is subjected to a screening process which excludes some 25 percent of the boys and 5 to 10 percent of the girls because of the serious nature of their offenses, the presence of mental abnormality, or strenuous community objections to their direct release. The remaining youngsters are then either assigned randomly to the community project—in which case they form part of the experimental group—or are channeled routinely into an institution and eventually paroled.

An interview by a member of the research staff provides the basis for classification of the offender subgroups. This categorization is made in terms of the maturity of the youth, as reflected in his relationships with others, in the manner in which he perceives the world, and in the way he goes about gaining satisfaction of his needs. A variety of standardized tests seeks to measure the extent of his identification with delinquent values as well as his general personality characteristics.

The program provided for the experimental group offers singly or in combination most of the techniques of treatment and control which are in use in corrections today: individual counseling, group counseling, group therapy, family therapy, involvement in various other group activities, and school tutoring services by a certificated teacher with long experience in working with delinquents. The goal is to develop a treatment plan which is tailored to the needs of each type of offender. The resulting plan is then implemented at a level of high intensity, made possible by the availability of carefully selected and experienced staff on a ratio of 1 staff member for each 12 youths.

A program center serves as the hub of activity; it houses the staff and provides a recreation area, classrooms, and a musicroom. A limited outdoor sports activities area also is available. In the late afternoon and some evenings, the center resembles a small settlement house operation as the wards come in after school for counseling, tutoring, and recreational activity.

An unusual and controversial feature of the experiment is the frequent use of short-term detention at the agency's reception center to assure compliance with program requirements and to "set limits" on the behavior of the participants. The detention may vary from a few hours to a few days.

Results have been measured in several ways. A repetition of the psychological test battery seeks to determine what movement has occurred in the socialization of the individual offender. The responses of the various categories of youth have revealed greater success with some than with others, and may eventually provide a more reliable indicator of who should be institutionalized. Finally, the "failure rate," as measured by the proportion who are later institutionalized because they have committed additional offenses, is carefully compared with similar information on members of the control group who have been institutionalized and then returned to the community under regular parole supervision.

The latest report of the project activity available to the Commission revealed that checks of parolees, at the end of 15 months of parole exposure, showed that 28 percent of the experimental group had been subject to revocation of parole, as compared to 52 percent of the control group which was afforded regular institution and parole handling.[8]

After several years of pilot work, the California Youth Authority decided in 1964 to extend the community treatment format to the Watts area of Los Angeles and to a neighborhood in west Oakland. Both are high-delinquency areas; both are heavily Negro in population. Essentially duplications of the original experiment, the two new program units do not have a research component. Instead of random assignment of the subject, the youths committed from a given area are screened by project staff for direct release from the reception center.

In the absence of a control group, the success of the program has been measured by comparing the failure rate of the youth assigned to it with equivalent statewide rates for youths of the same middle to older adolescent age range. At the end of 15 months of parole exposure, 39 percent of project wards had been subject to parole revocation as compared to a statewide revocation rate of 48 percent for youths of the same age bracket.

The Los Angeles and Oakland adaptations of the original demonstration were initiated, in part, to alleviate acute population pressures in the institutions. With caseloads of 15 youths per officer, the $150 per month cost per boy is three to four times as much as that of regular parole. But it is less than half the average monthly cost of institutionalizing an offender. These experiments are now handling a group that is larger than the capacity of one of the new institutions that the Youth Authority is building. Thus they obviate the investment of $6 to $8 million.[9]

Reception-Center Parole and Short-Term Treatment Programs

Diagnostic parole is a program whereby all commitments from the juvenile court are referred to a reception center where they can be screened for eligibility for parole, either immediately or after a short period of treatment. This program has reached significant proportions in an increasing number of States.

While most State systems have long had some informal arrangements for returning a few cases to the community at an early date, more organized procedures developed almost simultaneously in New York, Washington,

[8] Communication from Keith Griffiths, chief, Division of Research, California Youth Authority, December 1966.
[9] The development of the Community Treatment Project is reported in "Community Treatment Reports" issued by the Division of Research, California Youth Authority, Sacramento, Nos. 1–7, 1962–1966.

Kentucky, and California in the early 1960's. These programs were conceived in part as a response to acute population pressures in overcrowded institutions. The seemingly successful results have led to a substantial increase in the volume of cases diverted from the training school to short, intensive treatment programs followed by parole in the community.

In New York the screening is undertaken by special aftercare staff while the youngsters are in New York City's Youth House awaiting delivery to the State school system. The youths selected to return to the community are those who are thought to be amenable to conventional casework procedures. Those selected are placed in an intensive casework program. The apparent success of the original unit in New York City has led to an expansion of the program and to the practice of returning still other youngsters to the community after the intake studies carried on in the State schools.

Washington, another State with a central reception center for juvenile offenders, is also screening those committed. A significant percentage of cases are assigned to immediate placement in foster homes or other community-based programs, including four halfway houses.

The California Youth Authority apparently is making the greatest use of the reception center release procedure. Currently some 20 percent of the boys and 35 percent of the girls processed are being released to regular parole or to foster-home placement at the termination of reception period. This is typically a month long, but in some instances release may be postponed for another 30 to 90 days.[10]

The California Youth Authority's Marshall Program represents an interesting variation in the practices discussed above. The program was initiated 3 years ago as a device for easing population pressures in the institutions. It provides for the selection of cases by the clinical staff and the project director for a 3-month intensive treatment program at the reception center at Norwalk.

Based on "therapeutic community" concepts, the project involves the youths in a half-day work program in institution operation and maintenance, some specialized education classes, and daily group counseling. Active participation is rewarded by progressively longer and more frequent home furloughs. Parents provide the transportation, and furloughs are scheduled so that parents can participate in group counseling activities as they return their sons to the center. Parental involvement is seen as a significant program component.

While the performance of the project graduates has not been subjected to comparison with a control group, agency research staff have sought to match the subjects with youths possessed of the same characteristics who have been processed through the regular institution programs. With 15 months of parole exposure time, 44 percent of the Marshall youths, as

[10] Data provided by the California Youth Authority.

against 47 percent of the matched group, were subject to parole revocation. Moreover, the relatively short program period of 3 months, as compared against the average stay of 8 to 9 months in the State schools, means a significant saving of public funds.[11]

The success of reception center parole has been encouraging. Other States will undoubtedly develop reception centers that feature sophisticated screening techniques and intensive treatment for those offenders who are deemed most susceptible. To date, parole from reception centers has been confined to the juvenile field. However, there is no inherent reason why this approach should not be taken with adults, and hopefully it will be so used in the near future.

.   .   .   .   .

[*President's Commission on Law Enforcement and Administration of Justice,* Task Force Report: Corrections (*Washington: U.S. Government Printing Office, 1967*), pp. 38–44.]

A National Program of Youth Development and Delinquency Prevention: General Strategies

From the web of interconnected factors which shape youthful behavior, two major themes appear again and again to guide national efforts to prevent delinquency. They are: (a) The need to involve young people with greater meaning, respect, and responsibility in those affairs of society which affect them, and (b) the need for our institutions to produce better education, strengthen family life, improve opportunities for employment, and make the activities of law enforcement and individual and social services more relevant and more accessible to those who need them most.

It becomes apparent that the multifaceted problem of delinquency will not be prevented through small or simple programs. What we need is a comprehensive effort to make changes in the system which produces juvenile delinquency and other forms of antisocial behavior. If this suggests that delivering the fruits of the Great Society to all with equal opportunity is indispensable for the reduction of delinquency, then let us accept that fact.

One cannot isolate the treatment and prevention of a social problem which has its roots in the conditions and other problems of society. Thus, a variety of programs are important to the prevention of delinquency.

The increasing urbanization and the disproportionate share of crime and delinquency in crowded innercity areas where delinquency exists side by side with problems of poverty, inferior education, poor housing, bad health, and high unemployment, suggests that the Nation's effort to eliminate poverty, rebuild the slums, and achieve maximum employment are all

[11] *Ibid.*

crucial as a base for efforts to decrease crime. The heavier crime rate among minority groups crowded into the innercities and facing the deprivations of these areas, emphasizes the importance of efforts to wipe out discrimination. While we are not content to make general recommendations about sweeping reforms in the living conditions of our society—we believe such reforms are not only essential to the prevention of crime and delinquency, but can be justified in their own right—neither can we, in good conscience, recommend only narrower programs of enforcement, control, and reform which focus on those who are already treading delinquent paths. It would be foolhardy to tout such a program as truly preventive.

In actuality, what is required is more than a program of delinquency prevention, for such a program parades under a banner with a negative slogan. America's goal for its youth should extend beyond stopping antisocial activities, and its programs for youth should not require the justification of predicted delinquency.

> We, therefore, recommend a national youth development program, which subsumes the goal of delinquency prevention, and aims to fulfill the maximum potential of young people for productive participation in society and for lives of self-actualization. Such an effort will seek increased commitment on the part of youth to a society which they can perceive as responsive, relevant, and just; a society in which meaningful opportunities are available to them; a society in which they have a significant share and stake.

Such a proposal returns us to the dilemma of scope with which we began. How can a national youth development program maintain the broad vision mandated by necessity and implied in its title, while remaining practical, feasible, and goal-directed?

Such a program must reflect our insights into the personalities and subculture of youth. It must set some priorities so that its strategies for intervention are directed at the areas most likely to have impact on the most vulnerable youth. It must be flexible enough to encompass divergent strategies. In relatively affluent and stable areas, for example, approaches to individual psychological factors may be more important, though such approaches would be insufficient where social disorganization abounds.

Problems of individuals and their interpersonal relationships must be addressed, to be sure, but a national effort must hold promise to affect large numbers of potentially delinquent youth; it cannot be dependent upon a case-by-case approach, particularly when our ability to detect those cases needing preventive services is so underdeveloped. And to focus upon individuals and groups alone can lead one down a never-ending path of offering prevention services to person after person, while an increasing number of potential delinquents is propelled by society into the waiting line.

Since the individual's aspirations, directions, and achievements are profoundly influenced by the choices provided by the institutions in his community, major emphasis on institutional changes is probably the best and most lasting way of preventing large numbers of youth from entering delinquent careers. The latter part of this discussion contains recommendations for changes in a number of institutions which play a significant role in the lives of young people.

To introduce our description of some of the significant institutions, we suggest four major strategies for organizing youth development efforts to insure that they reach the groups most vulnerable to delinquency and the institutions most relevant to its prevention.

Focus on Geographical Areas High or Potentially High in Rates of Delinquency and Social Pathology

In many census tracts of innercity slum areas, huge proportions—up to 70 percent or more—of all youth find themselves in trouble with the law at some point in their adolescence.[12] Given this fact, we can assume that, in such areas, all youth are vulnerable, and prevention efforts based on such probabilities should provide improved services and opportunities across the board to all youth. Although all who live in America interact more frequently than ever with agents of government and social service, such interaction is especially frequent among the poor. The poor are dependent to a greater extent than any other group upon the agents of society. When one considers the amount of time and influence the schools, the State employment systems, the welfare programs, public housing, courts, and police take in the lives of the slum dweller, it becomes clear that efforts should be directed at upgrading the ability of these key institutions to provide the qualitative environment which diminishes the possibilities of crime and delinquency.

The institutions in these areas should receive the bulk of attention from preventive efforts, and their services should be planned, operated, and delivered in a comprehensive and integrated manner so that they are increasingly accessible, relevant, and qualitative agents in the lives of young people. And if we are to launch a truly preventive effort, we cannot concentrate solely on those areas where delinquency already abounds. We know something about the signs which indicate that a neighborhood which has enjoyed relative freedom from delinquency is likely to see an increase in delinquency rates tomorrow. Increasing internal mobility and in-and-out migration, downward shifts in the level of employment skills, increasing rates of unemployment, dropouts, etc.—these should provide warnings that

---

[12] Various studies on file in the Office of Juvenile Delinquency and Youth Development, Welfare Administration, U.S. Department of Health, Education and Welfare, attest to this fact.

preventive measures are necessary which focus on halting the deterioration of living conditions and the quality of basic services and opportunities.

Emphasis on the Involvement of Youth

The involvement of youth should constitute a central strategy in the Nation's effort to develop the potential of its young people and to prevent antisocial behavior. Common to each of the institutions examined below is the need to recognize the phenomenon of youth culture and provide new and significant ways for youth to be involved with dignity, with meaning, and with impact. The schools, the welfare agencies, the youth-serving and recreational agencies, employment programs and business, all hold within them opportunities for greater youth participation at many levels.

We are talking about recognition of the expressed desires, needs and hopes of youth, and more inclusion of their opinions in the relevant decisions of the broader society. We are not talking about ineffective efforts of the past, such as the symbolic involvement of one or two young people on adult committees, youth councils which are largely debating societies, without power to do anything significant; or student councils tightly censored and controlled by school administrations, so that they deal only with matters peripheral to the central concerns of the school and student body.

These and similar programs have largely been for the cream of the youth crop. Real leaders who are not perceived as such because they have not followed conventional routes; those who have participated in antisocial or delinquent activities, are seen to lack the capacity to contribute anything meaningful. Future programs cannot be aimed only at the development of youth leadership; special efforts are needed to insure the inclusion of those who have traditionally been denied participation. Our experience has shown that once youth are really accepted as legitimate partners in community affairs they are more likely to participate and give support to the key systems of the community; denied, they may respond with hostility and alienation.[13]

The Federal Government has an opportunity to develop increased commitment of youth to productiveness, achievement, and responsible citizenship. It can lead its Federal agencies and local communities concerned with employment, the arts, education, economic opportunity, the family, and other areas, in a search for new understandings of youth in society, and new ways of involving them in program and policy. It can provide opportunities for young people to interact in new and challenging ways with their elders, including those who make and enforce the laws and those who administer the services, as well as adult residents of the communities where they live. It can broaden opportunities for different ethnic, class, and geographical

[13] See June Shmelzer, "Youth Involvement: A Position Paper," Office of Juvenile Delinquency and Youth Development, unpublished, November 1966.

segments of the youth culture to cross lines and interact with each other in new ways. It can encourage the development of improved new ways of work with primary peer groups, as a most important point of intervention into the youth culture. It can help service systems and educational systems develop new career opportunities within them for the young. And it can help to make a place, not only as recipients of service, but as providers and designers of service, for all kinds of youth, including the poor, the underachieving, the beat, the minorities, and the delinquent—for these are the youth most easily locked out.

Special Programs for Individuals and Groups Identified as Needing Help

Delinquency occurs in all kinds of communities. While government may put extra effort into areas where delinquency is preponderant, it cannot write off the trouble-prone youth of other communities.

In such communities, where the broad measures suggested for slum areas do not seem warranted to prevent the conditions which breed delinquency, specialized efforts might be targeted at vulnerable youth. But how do we determine which youth require special efforts and what forms these efforts should take?

Individual delinquency prediction devices have been subject to considerable question; no device yet developed can ensure that a youngster will not be incorrectly identified as a potential delinquent—with whatever consequences attend that label. In any event, intensive case-by-case analysis seems to be an unwieldy basis for a national effort.

While we need to refine our procedures for distinguishing among different forms of delinquency and different types of delinquents, we know enough now about which danger signals require our attention.

Some studies indicate that school failure—academic and behavior—is a reliable early warning sign, regardless of class and geography.[14] Certain types of encounter with the police lead more frequently than others to continued and intensified delinquent acts. Older youths who are out of school and unemployed have greater potential for delinquent involvement than others. Young people who have been through some part of the correctional system and have returned to the free society with the record and associations of institutionalization have a significant rate of recidivism. And certain signs of disengagement and alienation may be precursors to delinquency.

None of these actuarial measures is reliable enough to warrant clear

[14] See, for example, Kenneth Polk, "Those Who Fail," Lane County Youth Project, Lane County, Oreg., mimeo, 1965. Also Walter Schafer and Kenneth Polk, "Schools and Delinquency," paper prepared for the President's Commission on Law Enforcement and Administration of Justice.

prediction of delinquency, and they should not be used that way. Rather, they can be tools in the identification of youth needing service. Some youth so identified need psychological help such as counseling and clinical services; others may require different kinds of special services such as bonding assistance, remedial reading, employment services, or group-centered programs.

An advantage to the use of such informal devices for selecting individuals and groups in need of special help is that, in most instances, they can be discerned by existing community agencies without intensive analysis of families and cases.

The assurance of special help to youngsters who need it, without predicting the form of deviance—delinquency—being prevented, seems appropriate for many in low, as well as high, delinquency rate areas.

Special Attention to the Points of Entry into the Adjudication and Correctional System

The organizing principles for delinquency prevention stated above call for three different, but interrelated approaches: the first deals with sweeping changes in the basic institutions which serve the most severely troubled sections of our country; the second suggests a national emphasis on the involvement of youth; and the third requires preventive services to young individuals and groups identified by community agencies as needing help. All of these efforts are aimed at affecting the juvenile's behavior before it has brought him into significant contact with the police and courts. A fourth major strategy to prevent delinquency should be developed at the point where these efforts encounter the domain of the official agencies. Frequently, it is at this point that the escalation begins and a process intended to protect society, or help the individual, boomerangs so that the youth is increasingly a captive of his definition and treatment as a delinquent.

A variety of factors, addressed more completely elsewhere, attests to the need for alternatives to our current means of pronouncing youths delinquent and initiating them into the court and corrections system.

It seems clear that the institution of official processes is at least as likely to have no effect—and often a negative effect—upon the prospect for continued delinquency as it is to retard such prospects. Consequently, we are led to believe that a considerable amount of delinquency can be prevented by more judicious practices at the point where the community faces decisions about invoking official processes: simple exclusion of certain types of behavior from the delinquent category; clearer separation of dependency and neglect issues from antisocial behavior issues; modifications in police decisionmaking and additional resources for police referral; community-based alternatives to judicial handling; a new range of dispositional alternatives for the court. These and other approaches hold promise for the prevention of delinquency through keeping young people out of a system which has the potential for unwittingly fulfilling the prophecy which attends the delinquent label.

We believe that a considerable amount of prevention effort should be directed at that point where the responsibility for working with young people moves from the hands of his family and the community socializing institutions to the police, the court, and the correctional system.

To summarize on general approach we recommend a national policy and program which fosters youth development as well as delinquency prevention. We suggest articulating our efforts with the increasingly recognizable phenomenon of a youth subculture; making basic changes in important institutions and upgrading the services for all in high delinquency areas, utilizing community agencies to identify individuals and groups for the receipt of special services and altering the entry points into the juvenile justice system.

We suggest that young people themselves be involved in the formulation of these national policies and programs, and that clear provision be made for the inclusion, at all levels, of young people at the bottom of the ladders of social status, conformity, opportunity, commitment, and economic capacity.

Youth development efforts require the active involvement and participation of many Federal departments which would undergird and infuse programs of delinquency control and prevention, education, employment, poverty reduction, recreation, health, and other aspects of society which affect and are affected by youth.

[*From Virginia Burns and Leonard Stern, "The Prevention of Juvenile Delinquency," in* Task Force Report: Juvenile Delinquency and Youth Crime, *President's Commission on Law Enforcement and Administration of Justice (Washington: U.S. Government Printing Office, 1967), appendix S, pp. 361–364.*]

NC